Services and Uneven Development

Services and Uneven Development

J. N. MARSHALL

in collaboration with

P. Wood, P. W. Daniels, A. McKinnon, J. Bachtler,
P. Damesick, N. Thrift, A. Gillespie,
A. Green, and A. Leyshon

with commentaries by

W. Beyers, P. Wood, M. Bannon, and J. Lewis

OXFORD UNIVERSITY PRESS
1988

Oxford University Press, Walton Street, Oxford OX2 6DP

Oxford New York Toronto
Delhi Bombay Calcutta Madras Karachi
Petaling Jaya Singapore Hong Kong Tokyo
Nairobi Dar es Salaam Cape Town
Melbourne Auckland

and associated companies in
Beirut Berlin Ibadan Nicosia

Oxford is a trade mark of Oxford University Press

Published in the United States
by Oxford University Press, New York

British Library Cataloguing in Publication data
Marshall, J. N. (John Neill), 1953–
Services and uneven development.
1. Great Britain. Service industries.
Location
I. Title   II. Wood, P.
338.6'042

ISBN 0–19–823285–3

Library of Congress Cataloging in Publication Data
Marshall, J. N.
Services and uneven development.
1. Service industries—Great Britain.   I. Title.
HD9982.5.M37   1988   338.4'7'000941   88–5297
ISBN 0–19–823285–3

Filmset in Northern Ireland at The Universities Press (Belfast) Ltd.

Printed and bound in
Great Britain by Biddles Ltd
Guildford and Kings Lynn

Preface

This book is the outcome of the Producer Services Working Party (PSWP), a limited-life working party established in 1984 by the Institute of British Geographers (IBG) and funded by the IBG and the Economic and Social Research Council (grant number D00250014). The PSWP set out to produce a state of the art review of research on producer services, examine secondary source evidence on their location and role, conduct a short research investigation into selected aspects of producer services, and to outline priorities for further research.

The members of the working party were:

John Bachtler	Centre for the Study of Public Policy, University of Strathclyde
Peter Damesick	Department of Geography, Birkbeck College, University of London/ Coopers and Lybrand
Peter Daniels (Chairman)	Department of Geography, University of Liverpool
John Dawson (part)	Business Studies, University of Stirling
Jo Foord (part)	Centre for Urban and Regional Development Studies, University of Newcastle upon Tyne
Andy Gillespie	Centre for Urban and Regional Development Studies, University of Newcastle upon Tyne
Neill Marshall (rapporteur)	Department of Geography, University of Birmingham
Allan McKinnon	Department of Business Organisation, Heriot-Watt University
Peter Wood	Department of Geography, University College London

Others invited to present evidence to the enquiry were:

Richard Barras	Technical Change Centre, London
Andrew Coulson	Institute for Local Government Studies, University of Birmingham
John Goddard	Department of Geography, University of Newcastle upon Tyne

Graham Gudgin	Northern Ireland Economic Research Centre
Frank Kirwan	Scottish Development Agency
Richard Harrison	Department of Business Studies, Queen's University, Belfast
Judith Marquand	Manpower Services Commission
Robert Miall	Department of Industry
Ian Miles	Science Policy Research Unit, University of Sussex
Steve Smith	Faculty of Technology, Open University
Nigel Thrift	Department of Geography, University of Bristol
Alfred Thwaites	Centre for Urban and Regional Development Studies, University of Newcastle upon Tyne

A theme paper providing a framework for the working party's deliberations was produced by Neill Marshall, Peter Damesick, and Peter Wood. Building on this material a series of case studies were conducted:

Andy Gillespie and Anne Green—The Location of Producer Service Employment (Sections 4.3, 4.5–4.7)
Neill Marshall and John Bachtler—Financial Services (Section 5.4)
Peter Daniels, Nigel Thrift, and Andrew Leyshon—The International Context for Producer Services (Section 5.1)
Alan McKinnon—Physical Distribution (Section 5.3)
John Bachtler—Policy Towards Services (Chapter 7)
Peter Wood—Non Production Employees in Manufacturing (Section 5.2)
Neill Marshall—Business Service Offices (Section 5.5)

William Baker acted as research assistant.

This book was compiled from the case study material and the deliberations of the PSWP by Neill Marshall, with the assistance of Peter Wood, Peter Daniels, Alan McKinnon, and John Bachtler. It is our intention that the research reported here should encourage further study of service activities. To that end a conference presenting some of the results of the PSWP was convened jointly by the Urban and Industrial Activity and Area Development Study Groups of the IBG in Liverpool in September 1986. We have asked

Bill Beyers, Jim Lewis, Michael Bannon, who were invited as discussants and Peter Wood to expand upon the comments they made at the conference. These contributions highlight the relevance of our deliberations to other parts of the developed world. They show that the approach of the PSWP can be applied elsewhere as the basis for a more comparative approach than that adopted here, and indicate the current areas of academic debate with regard to producer services.

Tim Grogan supplied the art work and Lynn Ford typed the manuscript.

Contents

List of Tables

List of Figures

Acknowledgements

The author and the publisher would like to thank the following for their permission to use copyright material:

Publishers

Gower Publishing Group for Table 5.23.
Longman Group UK Limited for Table 5.25.
Pion Limited for Tables 2.2 and 4.2 and Figure 2.1.
J. Wiley and Sons Limited for Table 5.16.

Organizations

Institute of Manpower Studies for Table 5.23.
Commission of the European Communities for Figure 3.3 and Table 5.16.
Bank of England for Figure 5.1.

1

The Growing Interest in Services

There is a growing interest in service activities in most developed countries (Illeris (ed.), 1986; Bannon and Ward (ed.), 1985; Bailly and Maillat, 1986; Noyelle and Stanback, 1984). In Europe this is in large part because services have been the main source of job creation since the oil crisis of 1973 (OECD, 1984). More generally though, it is believed that services are playing an important facilitative role in the take-up and development of new information technology (Howells and Green, 1985). Despite this interest and much rewriting of the research agenda there has been little substantial research into the dynamics of service location. The way in which the growing prominence of service activities in our economies will effect uneven development is not clearly understood. Nor are we sure about the economic prospects of problem regions in a service-dominated economy.

This study contributes to a fuller understanding of the role of services, and producer services in particular, in uneven development. It is largely based on original research carried out in the UK, but it presents a general framework for understanding service location. The study also reviews the international literature on producer services and presents research priorities which should guide the further study of service activities.

1.1. THE IMPORTANCE OF SERVICE ACTIVITIES

Services are the dominant form of economic activity in many local and regional economies in the UK. They constitute well over half of gross domestic product (GDP) measured in current prices in every region and in the South East account for more than 70% of GDP. Though difficult to measure precisely, private services account for about one third of GDP in most regions and at least as large a share of GDP as manufacturing in most cases.[1] In employment terms, services are even more important because service occupations are

---

[1] Services are defined here as groups 6–9 of the 1980 Standard Industrial Classification and this excludes utilities and construction.

also found within other sectors of the economy and not just in service industries. A conservative estimate, including non-production activities in manufacturing with service industry employment, suggests that services account for about two-thirds of employment in most regions and for about three-quarters of employment in the South East.

In terms of the growth of economic activity it is an expansion in service output (measured in constant prices) which accounted for most of the regional growth of GDP after 1974.[2] Between 1974 and 1983 manufacturing output (which declined in all regions except East Anglia) contracted by almost 15% in the UK as a whole and by well in excess of 25% in Wales, Northern Ireland and the West Midlands. Nevertheless, most regions registered a growth in GDP between 1974 and 1983. Financial and business services, education and other services, which includes both private and local authority activities, recorded the largest growth in output, with the former, for example, growing by as much as 86% in the South West region.

Service industries have also been the main source of job creation during the 1970s and 1980s. Total employment declined between 1971 and 1981 in all regions apart from East Anglia, the South West, and the East Midlands, largely as a consequence of a contraction in manufacturing jobs. In contrast, service industry employment grew by 1.8 million jobs nationally, some 474,000 of these (the largest share) being recorded in the the South East region. The fastest rates of growth were recorded in the adjacent regions of East Anglia, the South West, and the East Midlands. After the mid-1970s public service employment stopped growing, and since the end of the 1970s private services have been the sole significant source of employment creation in most regions.

Of course the 1970s and 1980s have been a period of mild and then more severe recession which has particulary affected manufacturing. Also these figures say nothing about the respective roles of individual sectors in the economy. Nevertheless, there is some evidence for the view that services have made a significant contribution to many local economies during the last decade and a half, and this has fuelled academic and political interest in the role of services as a source of job creation and economic growth.

1.2.   IS MANUFACTURING THE BASIC SECTOR?

Notwithstanding this evidence there has been a preoccupation with manufacturing industry in studies of uneven development. This

---

[2] GDP has been converted to constant prices using the implicit deflator contained in the constant price series for service sector output in the Blue Book.

reflects in some instances a crude export base view of economic growth in which manufacturing is regarded as basic because of its major contribution to exports, and services are regarded as dependent, servicing local industry or consumer demand. A development of this argument emphasizes the strong backward linkages of manufacturing industry into local economies. In addition it is often claimed that concentration on manufacturing in studies of economic growth is justified because manufacturing has greater scope for improvement, being more likely than services to achieve economies of scale. The apparently low levels of productivity growth in some services further reinforces the view that services are less productive than manufacturing. More generally, a manufacturing-centred view of economic development is implicit in the economics of location literature which concentrates uncritically on production industries, assuming by default that service activity is led by and responds to changes in manufacturing.

It is not surprising in this context that one of the most popular explanations for changes in industrial location in the UK during the 1960s and 1970s concentrates on the role of large manufacturing firms (Massey and Meegan, 1982). Uneven development is argued to be a consequence of the reorganization of such firms in the face of declining demand for their production and competitive pressure, both of which encourage improvements in labour productivity. Automation and technological change are believed to make the production process more capital-intensive and reduce the demand for production workers, while within a general decline in manufacturing employment an increased share of managerial, technical, and support staff reflects the increasing tertiarization of production and the growing division of labour in large enterprises.

Locational changes reflect this growing dualism in the workforce. Manufacturing investment has moved either to areas where scarce skilled white collar workers are available (e.g. Greater South East) or to areas of low wages and high unemployment, where a semi-skilled, often female workforce can be recruited to carry out largely routine production activities in branch plants (e.g. rural or small town locations especially in northern and western Britain). Both of these trends thus favour areas outside the main conurbations and so job loss in these areas is related to selective employment creation elsewhere.

Such a brief description inevitably caricatures both previous work and what has been happening in the UK economy. For example, it neglects the role of primary and extractive industries such as oil and coal-mining in some areas, and the growth of innovative new firms particularly in less urbanized parts of southern and eastern Britain.

However, more importantly it also tends to simplify the major structural changes at work in the UK. It is no longer possible validly to assume that the economic characteristics (e.g. high levels of labour productivity) of a sector of economic activity are the product of that activity alone. The roles of services and production industries in the economy are becoming increasingly interdependent. It is not simply that there is a growing 'tertiarization' of the production labour force, though this is apparent, but also that the traditional relationship between manufacturing and services, in which manufacturing 'demands' and services 'supply' inputs to production, no longer holds true for important parts of the two sectors.

In some industries, such as the manufacture of data processing equipment, the division between production and services is difficult to draw. Here not only are service inputs (software) necessary to make the product work but they also have a critical influence on the success of the product in the market-place. Other manufacturing industries (e.g. newspaper production) have witnessed a de-materialization of production in which the service component (e.g. advertising) has become a major source of income and where the product has come into competition with other service media, such as television and radio. Production and service companies have increasingly come into competition as both have penetrated each other's traditional markets by acquisition and diversification. At the same time service activities, most notably transport, distribution, and financial services, are becoming increasingly capital-intensive, like goods-processing industries.

The contraction of manufacturing has also clearly demonstrated that not all service industries depend for their markets on manufacturing, nor simply on final demand. Other parts of the service sector and exports are also significant markets. In fact slightly more of the output of producer services goes to services than to manufacturing, and during the last decade a growing indirectness of supply of final consumer demand has been an important stimulus to intermediate services.

In such circumstances the traditional divisions between manufacturing and services no longer make much sense. As the example of the manufacture of data processing equipment implies there are circumstances in which services lead manufacturing investment. In high-technology sectors such as health care, telecommunications, and electronics, research and development work is fundamental to business success. In industries such as motor-car manufacture, consumers are becoming increasingly sophisticated, and as a consequence the design, styling, and marketing functions are becoming more important. In industry generally, more flexible and integrated systems of production require a reliable physical distribution network to minimize any disruption to production. Finally, it is also legitimate to allege that the lending policies of the financial institutions impose important constraints on production.

1.3. THE MONITORING OF CHANGES IN SERVICE ACTIVITY

While it is possible to describe the interdependence of services and other sectors, it is difficult to be more specific. The preoccupation with manufacturing in studies of industrial location stems in part from the difficulties involved in monitoring service activities. There are problems at the national level where key data sources are flawed by technical problems. Thus, the unreliability of the indices of output change at constant prices and more especially of the input–output data for the service sector are evidence of a more general bias in data quality against service activities.

At a local scale these difficulties are enhanced by the aggregation of employment data which makes it difficult to distinguish between very different service activities. Some data sources such as input–output tables are simply not available at even a regional scale for most of the UK, while the value of others, such as the Census of Population, is limited by the major changes that have occurred in the way the data are classified and the declining quality of the national statistical data base.

The heterogeneous nature of service activities and the fact that many services are offered by firms outside the service sector make them difficult to capture in conventional industry-based classifications. There has also been a variable approach to defining services in the academic literature so that contrasting views of the role and characteristics of services are reinforced by differing definitions of the subject of investigation.

1.4. THE ROLE OF PRODUCER SERVICES IN THE SPACE ECONOMY

Notwithstanding these difficulties of measurement and classification it is clear that the most distinctive feature of the location of services in the UK is their spatial concentration close to the capital city, a concentration which has been maintained despite the recent decentralization of employment from London to the Greater South East and the growth of services outside the conurbations of northern and western Britain.

To understand this spatial concentration and changing location of services it is essential first to distinguish between private and public services. While public services are relatively evenly distributed over space, and in fact, if anything, are over-represented relative to total employment in parts of Wales, Scotland, and Northern Ireland, many private services are heavily concentrated both relatively and absolutely in the Greater South East. Private services satisfying business or intermediate demand, that is producer services, are the main contributors to the spatial concentration in private service employment and for that reason they are the primary focus of this analysis. These services supply expertise which enhances the value of other sectors' output at various stages in the production process. They are traded within companies, on the open market, and through their contribution to the competitiveness of other sectors. Their demand and supply need not be geographically coincident, and by contributing to the supply capacity of local industry, they may influence uneven development more generally.

Producer services cannot, of course, be examined in isolation from other forms of economic activity or from trends in the national economy. Their links with manufacturing, the public sector, and other business and consumer services are integral to their economic role, and suggest that a thorough appreciation of their market relationships is required for a proper understanding of their function and location. It follows that a study of spatial differentiation in producer services should be based on a clear conceptualization of the nature of wider structural changes at work in the UK economy.

Unfortunately there are a number of competing models of structural changes and differing perspectives on the role of services in them. For example, one group of perspectives associated with notions such as 'post-industrial' development or a growing 'information society' takes a positive view of the role of producer services in the economy (Bell, 1974; Stonier, 1983). The recent decline of manufacturing employment and output can be seen as merely reinforcing a long-term shift towards service activity, the latter being sustained by the growing importance of knowledge, skills, and information (i.e. services) in the production process. Much of this work takes an essentially progressive view of service activity and has a relatively benign attitude towards the impact of technology on services. Developments in information techology are sometimes seen as improving the quality of work by enhancing job tasks and encouraging home working, as well as encouraging the growth of service activity by enhancing the final demand for service commodities.

In contrast, for some, the growing share of services in employment in the developed world is associated with the internationalization of capital and a shift of production activities to the New Industrializing Countries. The expansion of research-related services is seen as largely a defence-related phenomenon. Specifically in a UK context, de-industrialization is seen to be acting as a constraint on service growth (Cambridge Economic Policy Review, 1982). The growth of services is viewed largely as a product of their slow growth in labour productivity relative to other activities. Information technology could have an important bearing here because, by routinizing and automating service tasks, it could lead to the 'collapse' of service employment growth.

Whatever view is taken of the nature of structural changes in the UK economy, it is clear that the development of producer service activities is not unidimensional or necessarily solely beneficial. Elements of both a 'post-industrial' and a 'de-industrialization' perspective can be identified in the UK. In locational terms, notions associated with a 'post-industrial' perspective seem most obvious in the Greater South East. London's role as a 'world city' and the internationalization of its financial and business service activities, the concentration of corporate control functions and associated producer services including research and development activities, the growth of services to cater for international business and tourism, the development of recreational and leisure services based on the higher incomes generated by the region's other service functions; these are all prominent features of the evolving specialization of the South East's economy and employment structure, contrasting with its declining role as a base for volume consumer goods manufacture.

The negative aspects of structural change, 'de-industrialization', are more evident in northern and western areas of the UK. Here the recent decline of production employment has been most pronounced (outside London itself) and there have not been offsetting gains in producer service industries and higher-order corporate functions. Service employment growth in these areas has relied heavily upon the public sector and private consumer services; the latter, however, have been affected by the impact of industrial decline and rising unemployment, while the former operates within a stringent public expenditure regime.

This division between 'post-industrial' and 'de-industrialized' parts of the UK as opposite faces of the same coin is obviously a very over-simplified representation of the relationships between structural change, the development of services and spatial differentiation. It nevertheless represents a useful starting point from which to present a more detailed and searching set of questions concerning the dynamics of producer service activities in the UK.

1.5.   PRODUCER SERVICES IN A DEPRESSED MANUFACTURING ECONOMY

Continued growth in producer service output and employment, coinciding with an absolute decline in production jobs and, for a time, output raises new questions (reviewed in Chapter 3) about the role of producer services and manufacturing in economic growth in the UK. To what extent is the growth of producer service activity dependent on the performance of the manufacturing sector, and to what extent can such services develop independently? What considerations influence the organization of support services provided by firms within production industries themselves, and what changes have occurred in recent years in this process of internalization? How far has the recent growth in producer service industries resulted from a transfer of activities previously carried out within production industries to the specialist supply sector? Such a division clearly depends on the impact of recession on the attitude of employers towards their non-production workers.

Further, what contribution do services make to the performance of industry? How much evidence is there for the view that the producer service input to client sectors has a critical bearing on their competitivenss? If evidence is available on this point, what are the implications of such a process? Is it possible that efficient service industries (e.g. distribution or finance) may assist the import of goods into an area or country and therefore have a negative impact on their manufacturing industries? On the other hand, is it possible that in an area with uncompetitive or weakly developed services other sectors will be disadvantaged because of the character of the service input? These questions are considered in Chapter 3.

With regard to employment, to what extent can the growth in producer service jobs ameliorate the impact of decline in manufacturing and high levels of unemployment in depressed industrial areas? A related question concerns the quality of employment in producer services. The growth of part-time work (particularly involving female employees) raises questions about the skill level, earnings, conditions of employment, promotion prospects, and job security associated with service work. On the other hand, against this must be balanced a rapid growth of highly paid senior administrative and managerial posts. Thus, an important question considered in Chapter 4 is what type of producer service employment is emerging in local economies throughout the UK?

Such questions cannot be answered without a consideration of the impact of information technology (IT) on the demand for producer service work. This raises the difficult question of labour productivity in services. If the slow growth in labour productivity in producer services is a major explanation for their increasing share of employment, it is possible that new technology, by improving labour productivity, could reduce the ability of producer services to create employment. On the other hand, if slow growth in labour productivity in services, by increasing the price of services relative to goods, has a negative impact on service demand, IT could, by improving productivity growth and ultimately reducing the price of producer services, increase service employment. In addition, IT makes possible a whole range of new service products which could increase demand and create employment so that the answers to all these questions will vary between different types of producer service market.

IT is likely to have an uneven impact over space. Spatial impacts arise partly out of the place-specific character of industries, organizations, and occupations, but also as a consequence of the distribution of the supporting telecommunications infrastructure. Developments in IT are encouraging the growth of entirely new industries, the location of which will have an important bearing on the location of service activities. It is also possible that IT, by substituting for clerical tasks and by creating additional demands for specialists concerned with the operation of information systems, will have an important impact on corporate hierarchies and these are unevenly distributed over space. So a further important issue considered in Chapter 5 is the likely impact of IT on the growth of producer service employment throughout the UK?

Finally, economic history and current evidence suggest that the transition to a service economy is unlikely to be smooth. Notwithstanding the attempts of the Thatcher government in the UK to encourage competition and free trade in services it is clear that, as economies become increasingly complex, market forces alone are unlikely to produce socially desirable or equitable solutions. In the context of prolonged high levels of unemployment we need to ask what contribution national, regional, and urban policy can make to enhancing employment and output growth in services? The UK has had policies towards service activities for more than 20 years, but they have not been conspicuously successful or well co-ordinated. It is difficult to assess whether assistance to firms displaces employment in competitor companies, and to measure how much of assisted employment is actually additional. Many service policies have simply been adjuncts to manufacturing-orientated schemes. We describe in Chapter 7 the history of service policy in the UK and Europe, and consider whether new policy intiatives could assist the development of producer service activity.

Though this study focuses its attention on the UK economy such issues cannot be addressed solely in a national context. Changes in international trade in services, and in particular the growth of financial centres to compete with London, have an important bearing on the dynamics of service activity in London and the South East and by implication the balance between the concentration and decentralization of activities from the capital (see Section 5.1). Attempts to liberalize service trade in the European Community and through GATT, the policies of other nations towards their telecommunications infrastructure, and the assistance provided to attract international service investment are all likely to influence the scale of service investment in the UK. This study, therefore, attempts to analyse producer services in the UK in the context of trends and developments in the international economy.

2

Defining and Analysing Producer Services

2.1. PROBLEMS OF DEFINITION AND THE DEVELOPMENT OF SERVICE STUDIES

Defining producer services and appreciating the characteristics that distinguish them from other services and production is a necessary precondition for an anlysis of their contribution to economic growth and employment creation. In this chapter, previous attempts to classify producer services are reviewed, a classification of such services based on the deliberations of the Producer Services Working Party is presented, and then their contribution to employment is estimated.

Definitional and classifactory problems have plagued the analysis of services. For example, the definition of productive labour as that which adds to the value of material production, with services regarded as ephemeral and largely consumer-orientated, dates back to a misinterpretation of Adam Smith. Smith in fact included merchants amongst the productive classes. Nevertheless, the view that services are non-productive has stuck and this has encouraged their neglect. In 1956 Stigler argued that there was 'no authorative consensus on either the boundary or the classification' of services, and following a 'careful review of subsequent studies' Fuchs (1968) found 'no basis for challenging this conclusion'. Despite a growth of interest in services since, and the pivotal role of services in some economic analysis, questions of classification and definition remain as problematic as ever.

Services are usually defined as activities which are relatively detached from material production and which as a consequence do not directly involve the processing of physical materials. The main difference between manufactured and service products seems to be that the expertise provided by services relies much more directly on workforce skills, experience, and knowledge than on physical techniques embodied in machinery or processes. However, converting this general statement into a practical definition is difficult because of the heterogeneity of service activities.

A number of characteristics have been used to classify services but none alone provides a clear definition. Although non-manual and particularly office-based activities predominate in services, in 1981 42% of male and 30% of female service workers were in fact in blue collar services. Many service products such as advice or training are indeed 'intangible', but some services handle materials or maintain equipment. Most services provide specialist knowledge and expertise, but this may be applied to information processing, materials handling, or to sustaining working conditions. Some service products are ephemeral, but many can in fact be stored, for example on computer tape, and their value may extend over long periods (Greenfield, 1966). While service provision frequently requires personal contact between customers and suppliers, innovations in communication technology are changing this. Finally, while many services are apparently labour-intensive, a judgement on this depends on a proper evaluation of all capital inputs including buildings and infrastructure, and some communications and distribution services are clearly capital-intensive.

The diversity of service activities has encouraged the definition of services by exclusion; services exclude agriculture, mining, or manufacturing production, all activities that are easier to characterize. Unfortunately, such a sectoral definition, conveniently based on the Standard Industrial Classification (SIC), neglects the very different markets served by service industries and their very different behaviour in the course of economic development. The work of Katouzian (1970) and Greenfield (1966) has been influential in differentiating between those business-related or consumer service industries (e.g. research, entertainment, and hotels) that grow in the course of economic development, and traditional personal services (e.g. laundrettes or domestic servants) that decline. Such classifications have also been developed to distinguish between the public and private provision of services and, within private services, between blue collar or physical distribution services and white collar or office-based services (Browning and Singelmann, 1975; Gershuny and Miles, 1983; Noyelle and Stanback, 1984; Stanback and Noyelle, 1982).

While these classifications recognize the diversity of service industries they tend to neglect the extent to which services and other sectors are essentially integrated (Walker, 1985) and the fact that many occupations within the production sector perform service activities. An occupational classification of service work is perhaps more sensitive to the role services play in different sectors. Unfortunately this type of classification is less highly developed than that for service industries. Much of the work has concentrated on information processing activities and has tended to neglect goods-handling services (Gottman, 1961; Porat, 1977). In addition, this approach needs to be combined with a sufficiently detailed functional classification of service markets especially to enable trends in the demand for such service work to be traced.

2.2. DEFINING PRODUCER SERVICES

The starting point for defining producer services in this study is that the production of goods and services are highly interdependent, and ultimately all are consumed together in various combinations as part of final demand. Some services are provided directly to consumers, but they depend heavily upon manufactured goods and infrastructure for their creation and delivery. Other services, sometimes identical in form, supply 'intermediate' input to primary, manufacturing, and other service producers, and these inputs may be critical to the success of such activities in the final market-place. Thus the primary distinction between goods and services is not a matter of the nature of the product (i.e. the type of expertise offered or its difference from goods production), even though, as we shall see later, it is still important to acknowledge such characteristics. The main basis for such a distinction must be in the nature of the markets served.

In this study those services which supply business and government organizations, rather than private individuals, whether in agriculture, mining, manufacturing, or service industries are defined as producer services. Such services can be traded either commercially on the open market or internally within organizations. Some services may even be indirectly tradable through their contribution to the competitiveness of other sectors of the economy. Tradability need not, however, imply a choice of location (e.g. many financial services provided by the City of London are tradable but not footloose). It follows further that producer services are part of the supply capacity of an economy; they influence its adjustment in response to changing economic circumstances. They may help, for example, to adapt skills, attitudes, products, and processes to changes, or to reduce the structural, organizational, managerial, and informational barriers to adjustment.

Based on these criteria, producer services are concerned with financial, legal, and general management, innovation, development, design, administration, personnel, production technology, maintenance, transport, communication, wholesale distribution, advertising, and selling, whether in primary, manufacturing, or service

Table 2.1.   Main Types of Producer Service

Information processing services

Product/process, research and development
Marketing, sales, advertising, market research, photography, media
Engineering (civil, mechanical, chemical, electrical, etc.) and architectural
    design
Computer services, management consultancy, administration
Financial planning, accountancy, investment management, auditing
Banking, other loan institutions
Insurance
Legal
Training/education/personnel and industrial relations
Purchasing
Office services
Property management/estate agency

Goods-related services

Distribution and storage of goods, wholesalers, waste disposal, transport
    management
Installation, maintenance and repair of equipment, including vehicles,
    communications networks, and the utilities
Building and infrastructure maintenance

Personnel support services

Welfare services
Cleaning, catering, security, safety
Personal travel and accommodation

Source: Marshall, Damesick, and Wood (1987).

organizations (Table 2.1). Such producer services are singled out for special study here, in part, because of their neglect in economic analysis, in spite of their evident and growing significance to the volume and efficiency of production. As important is the fact that, like parts of manufacturing, they play a significant role in spatial differentiation because their demand and supply need not be geographically coincident and they are not solely dependent upon the level of economic activity in an area. Further, because of their role in investment, innovation, and technological change they may contribute towards spatial variations in the economic development process.

By concentrating on the markets served by producer services (which will have an important bearing on their development and location) the following sub-categories of producer service can be distinguished.

	Internal Service Trade	External Service Trade	
		'Mixed'	'Pure'
Information Processing Services			
Goods-related Services			
Personnel Support Services			

FIG. 2.1. Classifying producer services.

(1) Services produced by firms for themselves. Here we are concerned with the internalized supply of services within firms. The demand for this component will be influenced by the product, production technology, and organizational characteristics of the firm.

(2) Services produced by firms solely to meet demands from other firms, that is 'pure' specialist producer service suppliers. The degree of service internalization by firms will obviously be an important determinant of the size of this market. However, the characteristics of the service itself may influence barriers to entry into the market, and the degree to which production can be carried out by non-specialist producers.

(3) Services produced for other firms by firms which meet both intermediate and final service demand. In these 'mixed' service activities the business sector and personal consumer demand will both influence the nature of the market.

These sub-categories provide at first a two-fold distinction between producer services which serve markets internal or external to the firm, and additionally organizations supplying external markets can be divided into 'pure' and 'mixed' types (Fig. 2.1).

Having identified the salient market characteristics of different producer services, the nature of the product can be employed to enable further subdivision. A distinction is made in Table 2.1 and Fig. 2.1 between 'information', 'physical' or goods-related, and 'personnel' services. These distinctions partly recognize the different need to locate near markets as a distinguishing characteristic among producer services. In general, goods-handling services are more likely to be closely tied to production industries than 'information' services. The 'personnel' services, on the other hand, are likely to locate in relation to the pattern of all other business activities. The classification also divides services between categories that have experienced different patterns of growth in employment in recent years, most obviously between some of the static or declining 'physical' services and the largely growing information-handling and 'personnel' services. Goods-handling services are also noticeably more capital-intensive than the other categories of service, but this distinction is being blurred by the application of information technology in the office.

All these categories contain a considerable degree of variation within them. For example, it can be argued that financial services, because of their central role in all business investment, should be distinguished from other information processing services. Similarly telecommunications activities bear little relationship in modern circumstances to many other 'manual' services. Within each service there is also likely to be considerable occupational variation and each group will experience differing market demands and pressures. The argument then in presenting this classification is not that it is perfect or sufficiently disaggregated, nor that it is the only possible way of classifying services, but rather that it reflects the different markets served by service activities and the broad categories of expertise they offer (Illeris, 1985). As such it represents a sensible set of general categories with which to analyse service location.

2.3.   CLASSIFICATION AND MEASUREMENT OF PRODUCER SERVICES

Whatever logic supports the adoption of a market-based classification of services, their measurement at present inevitably depends on established data sources. It is useful, therefore, at this point to refer to work which attempts to use these to identify and classify producer services. Such an analysis indicates just how difficult it is to move from the conceptual distinctions made above to a practical classification using conventional government statistics.

There is a notable lack of theory in this area and pragmatism is the order of the day. In the UK, studies of service workers have used the 1970 Classification of Occupations to identify office workers (James, 1978; NRST, 1976), and the 1980 Socio-economic Group classification has been used to distinguish a rough hierarchy of non-manual (white collar) workers within manufacturing (Green and Owen, 1984). Crum and Gudgin (1977) have also used the Census of Population to produce a broader classification of non-production employment which includes some blue collar services.

An updated version of this classification suggests that almost 30% of manufacturing, some 1.8 million jobs, was in service-related work in 1981 (see Chapter 4, Section 5.2 and Appendix 1). These classifications represent a reasonable attempt to deal with the inadequate statistical data sources available. However, they exclude blue collar service workers from study in industries such as construction and utilities because it is impossible to separate these from production workers. Even within manufacturing, arbitrary questions of judgement arise concerning where to draw the line between production and non-production activities and some service workers cannot be adequately identified (see Section 5.2). Also for a truly adequate analysis of service work in different sectors it is necessary to combine occupational data with a classification of service functions or departments.

In the 1968 SIC, service industries were usually defined as orders 22–7, and as groups 6–9 in the 1980 Revision. Public utilities and construction tend to be excluded from the service sector on the rather arbitrary grounds that their product, input, technology of production, and physical plant are more akin to the goods-producing sector. Elsewhere three approaches have been adopted to distinguish private producer from consumer services.

The simplest attempt uses anecdotal evidence (Fothergill and Gudgin, 1982), and a more complex version of this approach allocates employment in Minimum List Headings (MLHs) in the Census of Employment to producer, consumer, and public services, using an 'unclassifiable' or 'mixed' category to resolve difficulties (Hubbard and Nutter, 1982; Northern Ireland Economic Council, 1982). More formally Marquand (1979; 1983) regresses for metropolitan labour markets employment in individual occupations and industries against total population and employment to differentiate producer from consumer services on the basis of variations in their r^2 value. This is supported by analysis of the degree of concentration and dispersion of producer and consumer activities using concentration ratios. The most reliable approach, adopted in a landmark study by Greenfield (1966) in the USA and applied by Wood (1984) and Daniels (1985a) to the UK, uses input–output tables as well as sectoral case studies, to divide service output between intermediate and final demand, and equates output with employment.

These studies highlight a number of practical problems in identifying producer services. (1) The mixture of producer and consumer activities in service industries makes the clear identification of the former difficult. (2) The anecdotal nature of some approaches has limitations, because the division between consumer and producer services can contradict conventional views and the distinction between consumer and producer activities can also change over time. (3) Finally, the division between the public sector and private producer services creates difficulties. Are, for example, nationalized industries in transport and communications to be part of the producer service sector? In addition, parts of central government are clearly intermediate in nature (e.g. business advisory services), and some are currently being privatized. Even medical, sewerage, or education services can be regarded as in part contributing to production. On the other hand political considerations as well as economic factors influence the functioning of public services and for this reason they can be regarded as separate. Nevertheless one should not ignore their value in supporting the private sector economy.

Not surprisingly, given the difficulties described above, there is no satisfactory or wholly acceptable means of identifying private producer service industries using conventional classifications. The technical problems described above have also been compounded by an inconsistent approach to definitional questions by researchers in the field. Table 2.2 presents predominantly UK classifications of producer services using the 1968 SIC, and Table 2.3 adopts a 'lowest common denominator' approach to a definition by simply including services for which there is a majority agreement in Table 2.2. There is clearly a wide divergence in the classifications of producer service industries, partly because individual studies give differing weight to such factors as intermediacy in the production process, exportability, and closeness to production in their definition. The main differences between the classifications arise in those producer service industries where consumer markets are significant, for example transport and distribution. Arbitrary judgements are made. Why, for example, should Road and Passenger Transport (MLH 702) be included as a producer service in Table 2.3 and Railways (MLH 701) excluded? Disagreement over communications and goods-handling services is enhanced because the Northern Ireland Economic Council (1982) allocate nationalized industries to public services, and also because Greenfield (1966) does not break down the industrial classification sufficiently. All studies include insurance, banking, and finance services in a definition of producer services, though several are regarded as 'mixed' producer–consumer services. The latter point is reinforced by Marquand's (1979; 1983) analysis which shows that employment in financial services correlates more strongly with the distribution of population than total employment.

The results nevertheless indicate that there is a core group of industries which are accepted as producer services in most work, and these include services such as advertising, market research, and research and development. These have been included in Table 2.4 which presents a new definition of producer service industries using the 1980 SIC. Here the task of separating intermediate services from those supplying final demand is in some cases made easier by the changes in the industrial classification.

Table 2.4 is based on a simple allocation of the 1981 GB employment data to the four-digit activity categories of the 1980 SIC. Production activities include 6.7 million workers in extractive and manufacturing (of which at least 30% will be non-production employees) and a further 1.7 millions in the utilities and construction (which are, of course, sometimes classified as services). Some 1.8 million workers are in those private services which largely on the basis of previous research, can be fairly unambiguously identified as business-related services. Consumer services including entertainment, transportation, education, health, welfare, recreational, and personal services provided by public and private organizations employed 6.9 million people.

A 'mixed' private producer–consumer category includes those services which, from the point of view of producers, offer either materials-related expertise, or white collar services including banking, other finance, insurance, property management, legal, and accounting functions. These activities deserve special attention because they illustrate an important general characteristic of service activities; namely that while a fairly clear conceptual distinction can be made between the nature of the service provided and whether it supplies producer or consumer markets, in many services patterns of ownership, organization, and distribution increasingly straddle producer and consumer markets. This 'mixed' category also includes a miscellaneous group of functions identified by the SIC, including canteens, vocational training, and laundries, which may also to different degrees be regarded as offering a service to business customers. The 'mixed' group employs 2.7 million workers.

While public services are often excluded from discussions of producer services, and are not the subject of investigation here, clearly some element of the activities of these 1.5 million workers is crucial in supporting production.

In our view a liberal definition of producer services, including both those services which can unambiguously be allocated to the sector and the 'mixed' category, should be employed. Though the responsibility for the transport, storage, and distribution of goods is shared by manufacturers, distributors, and retailers, the economic role of the service supplied is little different. A definition of producer services to include all distribution and transport 'upstream' of the retail outlet

Table 2.2. Definitions of Private Producer Service Industries

MLH		NIEC (1982)	Greenfield (1966)[a]	Gershuny and Miles (1983)[b,c]	Marquand (1979)	Hubbard and Nutter (1982)[a]
	Transport and communications					
701	Railways				•	
702	Road and passenger transport				•	•
703	Road haulage for hire	/			/	/
704	Other road haulage	/			/	/
705	Sea transport	•				
706	Port and inland water transport					
707	Air transport				•	•
708	Postal services and telecommunications				•	
709	Miscellaneous transport	/			•	/
	Distribution					
810	Wholesale distribution, food/drink	•	/		/	/
811	Wholesale distribution, petroleum	•	/		/	
812	Other wholesale distribution	•				/
820	Retail distribution, food/drink	•				
821	Other retail distribution	•				
831	Dealers in builders' materials and agricultural supplies	•	/		/	
832	Dealers in other industrial materials	/	/			/
	Insurance, banking, finance, and business services					
860	Insurance	•	•	/	•	/
861	Banking	•	•	/	•	
862	Other financial institutions	•	•	/	•	/
863	Property owning and managing	•	•	/	•	
864	Advertising and market research	/	/	/	/	•
865	Other business services	/	?	?		
866	Central offices	/	/		/	/

Professional and scientific services

871	Accountancy	/	•	/
873	Legal services	/	•	/
875	Religious organizations	/	/	/
876	Research and development	/	/	/•
879	Other professional and scientific services	/	•	/•

Miscellaneous services

881 Cinemas, theatres, radio etc.
882 Sport and recreation
883 Betting and gambling
884 Hotels and residential establishments
885 Restaurants, cafes etc.
886 Public houses
887 Clubs
888 Catering contractors •
889 Hairdressing
891 Private domestic services
892 Laundries
893 Dry clearing, dyeing etc.
894 Motor repairers, distributors, garages
895 Repair of boots and shoes
899 Other services

[a] These definitions are not totally consistent with the UK SIC.
[b] Based on Browning and Singelmann (1975).
[c] Gershuny and Miles (1983) regard distributive services as a separate category.
[d] Defined as 'basic' services, but excluding consumer activities.
[e] These services though classified as 'mixed' producer–consumer produced a higher r^2 with population than employment.
/ Producer services.
• 'Mixed' producer–consumer services.

Source: Marshall, Damesick and Wood (1987).

Table 2.3.   A Composite Definition of Producer Service Industries Based on the 1968 SIC

SICs	No. times classified producer	MLHs
Transport and communications[a]	3	703, 704, 705, 709
	2	702, 706, 707, 708
Distribution	4	810, 811, 812, 831, 832
Insurance, banking, and finance[b]	5	860, 861, 862, 863
Professional and scientific	5	864, 865, 871, 873, 876, 879
	3	866

[a] This sector is affected by the broad Northern Ireland Economic Council (1982) definition of public service and the lack of detail in Greenfield (1966), therefore MLHs with two mentions are included.
[b] This sector includes services which have a higher r^2 with population than employment in Marquand (1979).

is therefore justified. In the finance industry broadly defined, even those institutions serving consumer demand act as intermediaries in financial markets. As will be argued in Chapter 3, the important influence of the whole finance sector on industrial investment and the UK economy suggests that all financial activities should be included as producer services. The incorporation of services such as canteens, laundries, and vocational education is justified because of their role in supporting and training personnel in the workplace.

Such a classification of producer services is broadly reasonable if the aim is simply to exclude service industries largely serving final demand. It suggests that 4.5 million jobs are in service industries with an important producer component. The national input–output tables help to indicate the possible output of this producer component. Table 2.5 is based on the industry by industry flow matrix from the 1979 input–output analysis for the UK. Column two shows the share of each sector's total output going to intermediate demand (excluding the public sector). If this, when applied to each sectors' 1981 employment can be assumed to represent the degree of 'producer orientation' of the sector, another figure for producer service employment can be computed excluding the consumer employment contained in the 'mixed' activities in Table 2.4. The classification used in the input–output tables is less detailed than in

Table 2.4.   Classification of Activities using the 1980 SIC

SIC	Activity	Great Britain employment, 1981 (000s)
	PRODUCTION ACTIVITIES	
	Extractive and manufacturing industries	
0	Agriculture/Forestry/Fishery	370
11–15	Energy resource supply industries	350
2	Mineral extraction and processing, etc.	891
3	Metal goods, engineering, vehicles	2,797
4	Other manufacturing	2,244
	TOTAL	6,652
	Utilities	
5	Construction	1,074
16	Production/distribution of electricity, gas, etc.	269
17	Water supply	63
92	Sanitary services	280
	TOTAL	1,686
	SERVICES	
	Producer services	
61–3	Wholesale distribution/scrap dealing, etc.	876
723	Road haulage	194
831–2	Auxiliary services to Banking/Insurance	88
837–8	Professional/technical services; Advertising	199
839	Business services	257

Table 2.4.   (*Continued*)

SIC	Activity	Great Britain employment, 1981 (000s)
841–3	Hiring out machinery, equipment, etc.	47
849	Research and development	121
9631	Trade unions, business & professional associations	37
	TOTAL	1,819
	Consumer services	
64–65	Retail distribution	2,060
661	Restaurants, snack bars, cafés	192
662	Public houses and bars	240
663	Night clubs and licensed clubs	132
665	Hotel trade	226
667	Other tourist/short-stay accommodation	36
672	Footwear/leather repairs	5
673	Repair of other consumer goods	23
721–2	Road passenger transport/urban railways	208
846	Hiring out consumer goods	30
931	Higher education	198
932	School education	1,066
936	Driving and flying schools	3
95	Medical/health/veterinary	1,285
96	Welfare/religious/community services	515
97	Recreational/cultural	430
982–9	Personal services	120
	TOTAL	6,869

Mixed producer/consumer services: predominantly private

Code		Value
664	Canteens	113
671	Repair/servicing of motor vehicles	211
71	Railways	174
726	Transport nes	2
74	Sea transport	66
75	Air transport	70
76	Support services to transport	100
77	Miscellaneous transport services nes	168
7901	Postal services	183
7902	Telecommunications	240
814	Banking	368
815	Other financial institutions	111
82	Insurance	225
834	House and estate agents	63
835	Legal services	121
836	Accountants, auditors, tax experts	104
848	Hiring out transport equipment	15
85	Owning and dealing in real estate	98
933	Education nes and vocational training	225
981	Laundries, dry cleaners, etc.	61
	TOTAL	2,718

Public services

Code		Value
91	Public administration, national defence	1,505
	TOTAL EMPLOYMENT IN PRODUCTION AND SERVICES	21,148

Source: Employment Gazette, Supplement No. 1, May 1983.

Table 2.5. Estimated Employment Associated with 'Intermediate Sector' Role of Service Industries

	1 Employment 1981 (000s)	2 %age to intermediate demand	3 Estimated 'producer' employment (000s)
Distribution/repairs	3,175	31.4	997
Hotels/catering	938	5.8	54
Railways	174	42.8	75
Other transport	809	50.2	406
Posts/telecommunications	424	57.6	244
Banking/finance/insurance/business services	1,625	36.4	592
Owning/dealing real estate	98	51.9	51
Other services (estimated)	1,264	59.8	756
TOTAL	8,507	39.7	3,377

Sources: Input–output Tables for UK, 1979, Employment Gazette, Supplement No. 1, May 1983.

Table 2.4. Nevertheless, the calculation suggests than about 3.3 million jobs are producer orientated. Putting this figure together with information on non-production work in manufacturing makes a conservative estimate of producer employment of approximately 5 million jobs or 24% of total employment.

Of course, the input–output tables also suggest that some consumer services in Table 2.4, for example hotels, will serve business to a certain extent. There is also other evidence that the distinction between producer and consumer services is changing. Innovation in the household economy associated with the use of information technology could lead to the further development of intermediate services linked to consumer use of electronics. Consumer services, agriculture, mining, utilities, and construction will also have within them administrative employment which is not tied to the distribution of population. There is no way in which a classification of producer service industries based on the SIC can be integrated adequately with a classification of service work in other sectors of the economy, and this makes it very difficult to identify shifts in service activities between sectors. Thus, our classification in Table 2.4 is only a partial application of the conceptual distinctions made in Figure 2.1, and like the other classifications discussed in this chapter it is limited by the inadequacies of the statistical data base. As a consequence it should be interpreted only as a flexible guide to the scale of different activities within the economy. Indeed this study adopts differing definitions of producer services where this is deemed appropriate.

2.4. PROBLEMS OF ANALYSIS

Clearly the way in which government statistics are collected has enhanced definitional problems and this encourages inconsistencies in academic work (including this study). However, the influence of the statistical sources is even more invidious. For example, the high level of aggregation used in the compilation and classification of government statistics at a national but more especially a local scale restricts enquiry. Another problem is that the Census of Population, the main data source allowing the identification of non-production activities outside the service sector, is probably more bedevilled by changes of definition and classification than any other source.

National indices of output change in constant prices are also an inadequate measure of the growth of service output because employment is used as a proxy for output and because many of the physical indicators of output change ignore changes in service quality (Barras, 1983; Whiteman, 1981). However, the former problem is likely to have been reduced somewhat by the recent incorporation of an assumed labour productivity growth into the national output series.

Finally, adequate input–output tables, a critical source for measuring links between individual sectors of the economy, are only available for Scotland and Wales for single dates and not at all for other regions of the UK. More importantly in the national tables the data on service industries is suspect, not being based on a purchasing enquiry but rather on *ad hoc* surveys, information from major employers, and company reports. Even the data on the service purchases of manufacturing is flawed by the uneven coverage of head offices in the Census of Production where many service purchases are likely to be made. In addition, any analysis over time is confronted by random fluctuations in the input–output relations between service industries which appear to tell us more about the methods of collecting and manipulating the data within the Central Statistical Office than about relations in the economy.

The implications of these limitations in the input–output tables in the UK can be illustrated by an international comparison. In Canada the commodity/industry input–output tables are more disaggregated, and unlike the UK have been produced since the early 1960s on an annual basis. The data are also produced in a standard price form so that, though some problems of interpretation remain, changes in the links between services and other sectors can be traced over a 20 year period. Analysis of this input–output data indicates that, while blue-collar services are largely dependent on goods-producing industries, information processing activities operate relatively independently of the manufacturing base. Nevertheless, over time, an increasingly complex relationship between services and other sectors has been evolving with a growth in the provision of intermediate services to all other activities (Wood, 1985). These trends will be explored, as far as the UK data permits, in Chapter 3.

The work of Postner and Wesa (1984) for the Science Council of Canada also clearly demonstrates the value of good input–output tables (see Section 9.3). To understand adequately the role of services in the economy, it is necessary to measure their contribution to the performance of other sectors. Postner and Wesa exploit the exceptional quality of the Canadian data to explore the efficiency contribution of services to other sectors. This analysis shows that productivity improvements in services have a larger effect on the productivity of other sectors than on the services themselves (Wood, 1985). For the UK, the efficiency contribution of services is an issue which can at present only be considered in a very preliminary way in Chapter 3.

For the future we believe that the activities of the Commission of the European Communities to standardize and improve the quality of the statistical data base in Europe deserve every support in the UK.

3

The Role of Producer Services in the Economy

3.1. INTERPRETATIONS OF STRUCTURAL CHANGE

While classificatory and data problems inhibit precise measurement and analysis, it is clear that the UK has experienced a long-term growth in the extent of service work in the economy, and since 1966 there has been an additional decline in manufacturing production jobs. Both developments suggest important structural changes are occurring in the economy.

It is essential that work on spatial differentiation be based on an understanding of the contribution of services to these changes, because the character of structural changes in the national economy will in the longer term determine the capacity of services to generate jobs, the quality of the jobs created, and the wider impact of service growth on the rest of the economy. Structural changes in the national economy are also integral to the development of existing spatial inequalities and the growth of new patterns of uneven development. In Chapter 1 we described how the beneficial or 'post-industrial' aspects of service development such as the growth of international finance and corporate services were largely concentrated in the south and east of the UK, while in the northern and western areas de-industrialization appeared to be restricting service employment growth. Thus 'post-industrialism' and 'de-industrialization' appeared to represent differing facets of the contemporary space economy. We now wish to explore further the implications of these differing interpretations of structural change for the development of producer services in the UK.

Unfortunately there is no single clear view of the role of services in developed economies. While the UK has been described above both as 'post-industrial' and as experiencing 'de-industrialization', both terms lack unequivocal definition. Nevertheless, they have significantly different connotations for the role of services and the courses of service employment growth, and imply differing views of the economy. At its simplest a 'post-industrial' economy is one in which a majority of the workforce are engaged in service work, but in Bell's (1974) terms it also implies a social change and the prominence of a professional and technical élite in society. Sometimes the term also seems to imply a society in which material needs are largely satisfied and an expansion in recreation and leisure activities is sustained by the increased efficiency of production and a higher income-elasticity of demand among consumers for services compared with goods.

Two main structural changes underlie this view of the development of service work. The first focuses on intermediate demand and the changing pattern of labour inputs to production. Specialist knowledge and skills of various kinds are argued to be key resources, and education and research leading sectors. In Bell's (1974) view: 'A post-industrial society is based on services ... What counts is not raw muscle power, or energy but ... the central person is the professional, for he is equipped by his education and training to provide the kind of skills that are increasingly demanded in a post-industrial society.' An 'information society' viewpoint extends this post-industrial analysis focusing on the role of information processing services in the economy and highlighting the potential of emerging technologies to reduce the cost and improve the quality of information (OECD, 1981; Porat, 1977). The growing importance of activities involved in the production, analysis, and exchange of information in turn leads to the development of an integrated office-based sector of employment, and supports the claim in related geographic writings that the office block has replaced the factory as a symbol of modern urban development (Gottman, 1983). The work of Swedish researchers on contact systems which is reflected in that of Goddard and others in Britain in the 1970s also seems to accept this post-industrial view of the economy (Daniels, 1975; Goddard, 1975; Thorngren, 1970).

The second type of structural change in a post-industrial view of development is basically an extension of the Fisher–Clark model of the changing sectoral distribution of employment. This focuses on the Engel's law proposition that consumers spend proportionately more of their income on services as they become more affluent. This is usually seen as a feature of individual consumption patterns, but equally the trend, until recently, of increasing expenditure on health, education, and welfare services could be interpreted as a collective society-wide expression of Engel's Law.

This is the model of structural change that Gershuny (1978) and Gershuny and Miles (1983) seek to overturn by stressing the substitution of consumer goods for consumer services, and by giving a greater emphasis to the growth of intermediate demand. But in aggregate terms Gersuny and Miles (1983) argue that the growing share of service jobs in the economy is largely a consequence of their slower productivity growth compared with manufacturing. In Gershuny and Miles's (1983) terms, an economy dominated by services does not imply a lesser importance of production industries, and the continued growth of service employment is dependent upon the impact of technological changes on labour productivity and the demand for services. The term 'post-industrial' then, in so far as it implies a dominant role for services in the economy, is in their view a misnomer.

In contrast to the sociological and occupational emphasis in much of the 'post-industrial' literature 'de-industrial' interpretations emphasize the economic and industrial aspects of structural change in the UK. However, de-industrialization is also problematic. At its simplest it can mean an absolute reduction in manufacturing employment (Thirwell, 1982), or a fall in its share of total employment (Blackaby, 1978), but frequently it has been used in ways which seek to signify the causes of manufacturing decline (Singh, 1977). One common connotation in the UK case is a competitive weakness in the manufacturing sector, and an associated failure to maintain a sufficient surplus of manufactured exports over imports. This does have some implications for the demand for services; they may simply be increasing their share of employment because they are less exposed to international competition, and more ominously their growth may be constrained by a lack of manufacturing competitiveness. The important point, however, contrasting with post-industrial perspectives, is that the growth in services is not, in this view of economic change, a positive or progressive development. It has been argued that service employment growth, because much of it is in part-time work offering low wages, is no substitute for a decline in manufacturing jobs (Harris and Taylor, 1978). Other studies take a less benign view of the impact of technology on service jobs than that prevalent in 'post-industrial' work, stressing the potential of computer-based technology to routinize clerical work and disrupt female career hierarchies (Werneke, 1983). The growth in service employment can also be argued to be irrelevant to the main processes of change, which remain firmly centred around the competitive fortunes of manufacturing industry (Cambridge Economic Policy Review, 1982), and the divergence of investment funds into property development and abroad by the finance sector may be argued to act as a constraint on manufacturing performance (GLC, 1985).

There is thus a somewhat confusing array of competing perspectives on the structural changes occurring in the UK economy. It is beyond the scope of this study to produce a definitive view of these changes, but a brief review of the role of producer services in the economy can shed some light on the processes at work.

3.2. THE CONTRIBUTION OF PRODUCER SERVICES TO EMPLOYMENT GROWTH

As might be expected in the 'post-industrial' view of service growth, producer service industries (defined as the composite classification in Table 2.3 plus MLH 701) have made an important contribution to the growth in private service employment, though their contribution to employment growth in the service sector as a whole should not be over-estimated.

Service sector employment grew by 3.4 million jobs between 1959 and 1981.[1] Growth was at an annual average rate of 2.1% during the 1959–66 period, but slowed considerably at the end of the 1960s due largely to Selective Employment Tax (Fig. 3.1). In the 1970s there was a resurgence of employment growth, but at less than the previous rate (an average of 1.5% per annum, 1970–81), with first the oil crisis and then the post 1979 recession acting as a brake on service sector expansion. By the 1980s the increase in service sector employment had slowed again to an average of 0.7% per annum (1978–81).

Producer service industries have broadly followed these trends, though a 'post-industrial' view of their development implying steady employment growth is clearly too simplistic. They were more deeply affected by the general slow-down of employment growth in the service sector in the late 1960s, and actually lost 1,000 jobs between 1965 and 1969. Again producer service industies were more affected by the slow-down in economic activity in the mid-1970s and while service sector employment continued to grow, producer services lost 56,000 jobs between 1975 and 1976. Not surprisingly, then, before 1976 producer service employment growth accounted for only 18.5% of the 2.9 million jobs created in the service sector after 1959, and producer service industries grew more slowly than the service sector as a whole (16.7% versus 29%).

Between 1959 and 1976 a growing demand for health, education, and welfare services resulted in public services being the main source of service employment growth.[2] They increased by almost 1.9 million jobs, accounting for 64.5% of the employment growth in the

---

[1] Service sector employment is defined as orders 22–7 in 1968 SIC and as divisions 6–9 in the 1980 SIC.

[2] Public services are defined as public administration and defence, medical, education, and local authority services.

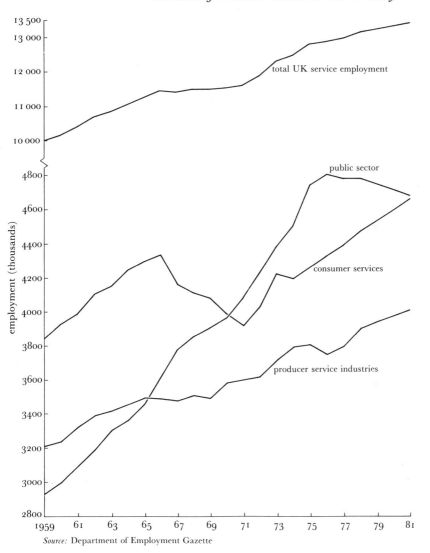

FIG. 3.1. Service employment change in the UK, 1959–1981.

service sector. Between 1976 and 1981, however, producer service industries grew more rapidly (1.8% per annum) than in any previous five-year period since 1959. The public sector declined by 118,000 jobs as successive governments sought to control public expenditure. Thus, producer services helped sustain continued employment growth in private services, accounting for 51% of their employment growth up to 1981.

There has, however, been a considerable diversity of experience of economic change within producer services. Table 3.1 shows that between 1959 and 1981, while other business services increased by 242,000 jobs (341%) and banking by 185,000 jobs (104%), railways lost 229,000 jobs (−54%) and ports and inland transport 89,000 jobs (−59%). There is some support here for the view that 'post-industrial' and 'de-industrial' analysis can be applied to the experience of differing producer service industries, with the goods-related sector experiencing labour shedding and growing capital intensity, while information services, less directly linked to manufacturing, continue to expand. Thus, differing views of the role of producer services in the national economy can easily be grounded in differing definitions of that sector, or on generalizations based on the experience of only part of it. But clearly there is no inexorable process of growth in producer services, and the analysis so far suggests that it is necessary to differentiate between the experiences of individual parts of the sector.

A growth of part-time employment also places a question mark over the quality of jobs being created in producer services. In 1981 the Census of Employment indicates that there were approximately 557,000 part-time workers in producer service industries and the bulk of these (80.4%) were female. Though in office-based business services[3] part-time employment accounts for 25.3% of total employment, the proportion of part-time workers in total producer service employment (13.2%) is rather low by the standards of the service sector. In contrast some 43.1% of consumer and 31.6% of public service employees work part-time.

Between 1971 and 1981 part-time work accounted for 44% of employment growth in producer service industries and part-time jobs grew by 65.8% compared to 8.3% for full-time employment. Converting to full-time equivalents reduces employment growth in producer activities by three percentage points to 10.5%. Part-time work grew faster for females (70.1%) than males (50.2%) during the period. For both sexes, however, part-time employment grew faster in producer services than in other parts of the service sector; by 65.8% in producer services as a whole, compared to 52.3% and 34.1% in consumer and public services. In business service offices part-time employment for both males and females actually grew by more than 100% between 1971 and 1981.

Part-time working has contributed to an increased participation of married women in the workforce, although the salary level, degree of security, and general conditions of employment can be poorer in part-time than full-time employment. Part-time workers are more

---

[3] Intermediate office-based services outside the financial sector.

Table 3.1. Employment Change in Producer Service Industries, 1959–1981

MLH	Thousands			MLH	%
		Ten fastest growing services			
865	242	Other business services	Other business services	865	341
861	185	Banking	Air transport	707	158
709	108	Miscellaneous transport	Property owning and managing	863	158
879	101	Other professional and scientific services	Miscellaneous transport	709	140
708	99	Postal services and telecommunications	Advertising and market research	864	117
863	87	Property owning and managing	Other professional and scientific services	979	110
832	73	Dealers in other industrial materials	Other financial institutions	862	110
860	73	Insurance	Banking	861	104
863	69	Other financial institutions	Research and development	876	86
707	57	Air transport	Accountancy	871	75
		Ten slowest growing/fastest declining services			
701	−229	Railways	Port and inland transport	706	−59
706	−89	Port and inland transport	Railways	701	−54
702	−88	Road and passenger transport	Sea transport	705	−51
705	−71	Sea transport	Road and passenger transport	702	−31
831	−16	Dealing in coal, oil etc.	Dealing in coal, oil etc.	831	−10
703	−9	Road haulage	Road haulage	703	−5
704	+1	Other road haulage	Wholesale dealers in petroleum	811	+3
811	+1	Wholesale dealers in petroleum	Other road haulage	704	+6
866	+13	Central offices	Wholesale distribution of food and drink	810	+15
864	+21	Advertising and market research	Other wholesale distribution	812	+19

Source: DE Continuous Employment Series and Census of Employment.

Table 3.2. Percentage Employment Change in Manufacturing and Service Industries in the Developed World, 1974–1984

	Manufacturing	Trade, restaurants, and hotels	Transport, storage, and communications	Finance and business services	Community, social, and personal	Total services
UK						
1974–84	−28.9	+19.0	−10.8	48.0	+5.2	+12.0
1974–79	−8.4	+5.1	+0.8	+11.8	+10.2	+7.7
1979–84	−22.4	+13.3	−11.5	+32.5	−4.6	+4.0
USA[a]						
1974–84	−0.1	+26.0	+28.8	+61.4	+26.2	+30.5
1974–79	+6.8	+15.2	+13.7	+26.7	+16.8	+17.2
1979–84	−6.5	+9.3	+13.2	+27.4	+8.0	+11.3
Canada[b]						
1974–84	−0.5	+32.1	+7.8	+58.7	+38.2	+34.9
1974–79	+4.7	+20.9	+15.1	+36.9	+18.7	+21.2
1979–84	−5.0	+9.2	−6.4	+15.9	+16.4	+11.3
Japan[c]						
1974–84	+0.8	+20.2	+3.0	+135.0	+15.7	+23.4
1974–79	−6.6	+11.9	+5.4	+90.2	+3.3	+12.6
1979–84	+7.9	+7.4	−2.3	+23.5	+11.9	+9.6
Belgium						
1974–84	−30.8	−1.4	+0.1	+18.9	+32.5	+15.7
1974–79	−18.8	+0.6	+2.6	+11.7	+18.3	+9.7
1979–84	−14.7	−2.0	−2.3	+6.5	+12.0	+5.4
Denmark						
1974–84	−13.3	+7.0	+6.6	+28.5	+30.5	+21.4
1974–79	+2.2	+4.1	+1.2	−2.8	+11.6	+6.9
1979–84	−13.1	+2.8	+5.3	+32.1	+16.9	+13.6
Spain[d]						
1974–84	−26.4	−6.0	−12.1	+10.9	+3.5	−2.1
1974–79	−9.7	+2.6	−7.8	+5.8	−6.3	−1.2
1979–84	−18.5	−8.3	−9.6	+4.8	+27.5	−1.0

France	1974–84	−16.2	+0.9	+8.7	+37.1	+29.6	+18.6
	1974–79	−7.4	−1.7	+5.5	+23.1	+18.4	+10.8
	1979–84	−9.5	+2.7	+3.1	+11.4	+9.5	+7.0
W. Germany	1974–84	−16.4	+3.2	−6.9	+20.0	+18.1	+8.2
	1974–79	−7.1	−1.1	−4.9	+8.3	+11.5	+5.6
	1979–84	−10.1	+4.2	−2.1	+10.8	+6.0	+2.4
Holland	1975–84	−15.9	+6.4	+10.6	+40.5	+28.2	+21.6
	1975–79	−7.4	+3.2	+2.8	+21.3	+9.9	+8.7
	1979–84	−9.2	+3.2	+7.5	+15.9	+16.6	+11.9
Italy	1974–84	—	—	—	—	—	—
	1974–79	—	—	—	—	—	+15.5
	1979–84	−9.1	+14.9	−4.4	+34.6	+19.0	+15.5
Ireland	1974–84	—	—	—	—	—	—
	1974–79	+8.0	+8.7	+7.9	+37.0	+19.4	+15.0
	1979–84	—	—	—	—	—	—
Luxemburg	1974–84	−22.0	—	—	—	—	+28.0
	1974–79	−14.0	+6.1	+10.0	+33.3	+28.6	+17.3
	1979–84	−9.3	—	—	+25.0	—	+9.1
Portugal*e*	1974–84	+2.2	+35.7	+9.8	+119.6	+69.4	+51.9
	1974–79	+4.0	+12.7	+5.2	+35.7	+25.2	+18.6
	1979–84	−1.7	+20.4	+4.3	+61.8	+35.3	+28.1

a Hotels are included in Community, Social, and Personal Services, and Sanitary Services are excluded.

b Repair and Maintenance Services are included in Manufacturing, some Business Services are excluded from Finance and Business Services.

c Finance and Business Services includes Hotels and in 1974 Blue Collar Distribution Services.

d Repairs are classified to Trade, Restaurants, and Hotels rather than Community, Social, and Personal Services.

e Before 1984 persons aged 10 and over included, in 1984 persons aged 12 and over included.

Source: International Labour Organization.

likely to be concentrated at the lower end of the salary scale and promotion prospects are limited. There is less provision for occupational pensions, sickness benefit, holiday pay, training, and promotion for part-timers, and they tend to be discriminated against in redundancies (Robinson and Wallace, 1984a, b). The increase in part-time working may be interpreted as part of a growing 'casualization' of service work as employers seek to reduce labour costs and increase their flexibility to deal with uneven work loads in producer services (Foord, 1985).

It is also revealing to view changes in UK service employment in an international perspective (Table 3.2). Notwithstanding some notable exceptions (e.g. Luxemburg and W. Germany) there is a broad association between employment change in the manufacturing and service sectors in the EEC, North America, and Japan. Those countries such as Portugal, Canada, Japan, and the USA in which manufacturing has grown or remained stable during the last decade have among the strongest service sector growth records and in all of these apart from Japan, service employment has grown by more than 30%. In contrast, in Belgium and the UK, where manufacturing employment declined by approximately 30% between 1974 and 1984, employment growth of only 15.7% and 12% respectively was recorded in service industries. This would seem to imply that a dynamic economy, including manufacturing, is a prerequisite for rapid service industry employment growth, and that the poor performance of manufacturing is a constraint on UK service growth.

However, not surprisingly, in each nation individual service industries show considerable variability in performance relative to manufacturing change. Employment change in producer services such as transport, storage, and communications, and finance and office-based business services are most strongly related to manufacturing performance, while employment in community, social, and personal services which are dominated by the public sector reflect the political and social decisions of each state.

The UK after 1979 combines a disastrous manufacturing performance with a decline in social and welfare service employment, and as a consequence its employment growth in services at 4% is less than half of that in Portugal, the USA, Japan, Canada, Denmark, Holland, and Luxemburg. However, the UK is atypcial in that after 1979 the decline in manufacturing which is reflected in transport, storage, and communications is matched by a strong employment performance in trade, restaurants, hotels, and intermediate office services. Employment growth in consumer and in business services at 13.3% and 32.5% respectively is only bettered by Portugal and Italy, both of which have an expanding population encouraging consumer services. Italy, like the UK, has a dynamic finance and business service office sector despite a modest manufacturing performance, and this appears to imply that in both countries an expansion in intermediate services may be related more to a growth in consumer service markets than manufacturing industry. In the UK a major erosion of the manufacturing base has coincided with a consumer-led boom. There is little evidence, with the possible exception of leisure sevices, of a growth in the share of private service purchases in consumer expenditure (Gershuny, 1978; Gershuny and Miles, 1983). The growth in consumer demand for services appears to be sustained by a reduction in restrictions on consumer credit, a *laissez-faire* government attitude towards the rapid growth of incomes in the private sector, and a supportive cushion of North Sea oil financing welfare payments to the unemployed. Once more, to understand the growth of producer services in the UK, a careful consideration of the markets they serve is required.

3.3. PRODUCER SERVICES AND MANUFACTURING INDUSTRY

The growing share of producer service industry employment in total employment suggests that (1) over time a given level of national output requires an increasing level of intermediate service inputs, and/or (2) that slower labour productivity growth has occurred in office-based producer services compared with other sectors of the economy, especially manufacturing.

It is difficult to assess the relative importance of the second of these possibilities. Some producer services, particularly of the goods-handling type, have shown substantial labour productivity growth and job loss but, in general, productivity growth appears to be slower in office-based services than manufacturing. Nevertheless, the importance attributed to labour productivity explanations for service employment growth depends on the reliability of the constant price series for service sector output (Barras, 1983). Those studies which argue that the slow growth of labour productivity is an important explanation for service growth accept the conventional statistics at face value (Gudgin, 1983). However, excluding the public sector and professional and scientific services from comparisons of service and manufacturing productivity growth, because employment data are used to estimate output in these services, reduces substantially the gap in productivity growth between the two sectors (Whiteman, 1981). Furthermore, there does seem to be some evidence that the conventional output statistics under-represent improvements in the quality of service output (Barras, 1983). In addition, even on relatively pessimistic assumptions about producer service productivity growth, an important share of employment growth appears to be due to an above average increase in demand for intermediate service inputs in relation to overall output.

Thus, Gershuny and Miles (1983) have shown that the level of intermediate service inputs needed for a given level of primary and manufacturing industry output increased in the UK between 1963 and 1973. The usual explanation for this trend is that the pace and complexity of economic and technical change have necessitated greater utilization of more specialized and sophisticated services by the production sector, for example in research, design and develop-ment, marketing, training, finance, and investment. Essentially competition in the modern industrial system requires firms to be adaptive and responsive, depending upon elaborate intelligence gathering and the ability to process and act upon specialized information effectively. Hence Marquand's (1983) comment, 'In an age of rapid technological change, what is particularly important about certain producer services is that these provide the source and mediators of that change'.

The growth of producer service industry employment can thus be explained by the changing input requirements of manufacturing industry. This is clearly part of the story; the national input–output tables suggest 18.5% of service industry output goes to manufactur-ing, with over 30% of other services (including education, training, research and development, and welfare services) and railway output going to the manufacturing sector. Manufacturing of course is even more important in terms of its share of intermediate demand for particular service products, accounting for as much as 74.2% and 58.6% respectively of the intermediate output of railways and distribution. There also appears to have been a growth of 6.2% in the share of services in the domestic purchases of mining and manufacturing industry between 1968 and 1979, largely as a consequence of a growth of 4.8% in the share of distribution in total purchases (Table 3.3). Though it is worth bearing in mind that these figures may overestimate this growth because they take no account of changes in relative prices, it is clear that there has been a reorganization of the distribution function resulting in an increased tendency to use specialist suppliers of this service (see also Section 5.3).

But what has been the impact of a decline in manufacturing employment and at times output on producer services? This can be highlighted by focusing on the other component of intermediate

Table 3.3.   The Service Purchases of Mining and Manufacturing Industry, 1968–1979

	Share of domestic purchases(%)	
	1968	1979
Transport and communications	6.0	6.8
Distribution	4.0	8.8
Miscellaneous	9.5	10.1
TOTAL	19.5	25.7

Source: Input–output tables.

service activity, non-production activities in manufacturing (see also Section 5.2).

Administrative, technical and clerical staff (ATCs) in British manufacturing reached a peak of 2.3 million jobs in 1970 (see Fig. 3.2)[4] and between that year and 1984 declined by approximately three-quarters of a million (33.6%). Furthermore, the rate of decline increased after 1979, some 63.1% of the decline in ATCs being recorded after that date. Notwithstanding this absolute decline there has been a moderate increase in the share of ATC employment in total manufacturing employment (from 26.4% in 1970 to 28.4% in 1984 (Fig. 3.3). However, this increase slowed during the 1970s. Only a 2.6% increase was recorded between 1969 and 1979 compared with 4.9% in the previous decade. There was also a slight actual decline in the proportion of ATCs during the early 1970s and a sharper decline after 1980. The proportion of ATCs in manufacturing employment declined from 30% in 1980 to 28.4% in 1984. It will be interesting to see if this development continues.

There are a variety of possible contributing factors to these trends. The decline in ATC jobs is clearly in the main a response to the decline that has taken place in production employment. The slower growth in ATC proportions and their decline during the last few years is less easy to explain. One factor here could be an increase in the capital intensity of non-production activities during the 1970s associated with the application of information technology. The intensified decline in ATC proportions in recent years could also

[4] The data on ATCs in manufacturing make no allowance for the change to the 1980 SIC in 1983. The total number of ATC employees in 1983 is 3.3% greater under the new SIC than under the 1968 SIC. Thus, the data probably understate the decline in ATC employment. There is no change in the proportion of ATCs in manufacturing employment as a result of the introduction of the new SIC classification.

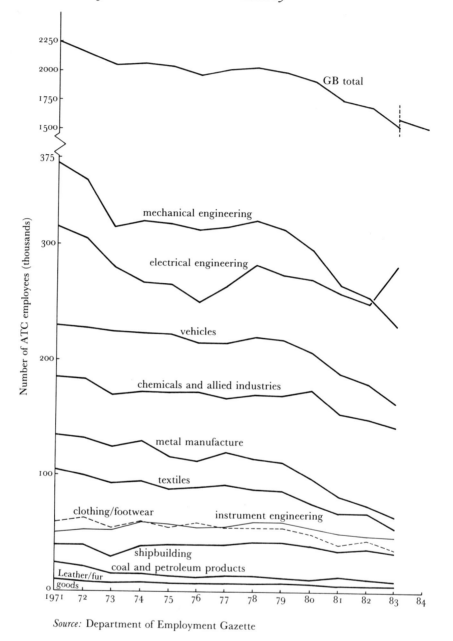

Source: Department of Employment Gazette

FIG. 3.2.   The change in ATC employment in GB manufacturing 1971–84.

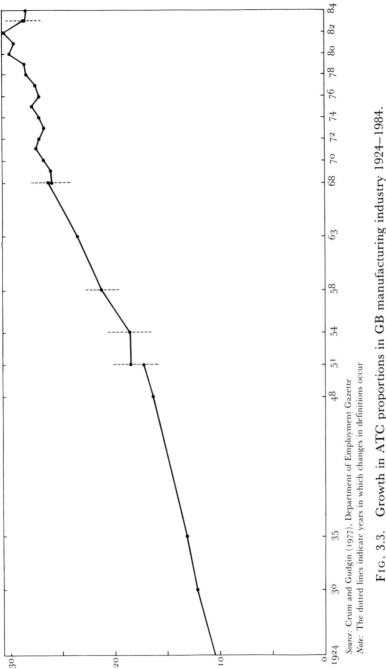

Source: Crum and Gudgin (1977), Department of Employment Gazette
Note: The dotted lines indicate years in which changes in definitions occur

FIG. 3.3. Growth in ATC proportions in GB manufacturing industry 1924–1984.

Table 3.4.   Producer Service Employment Change in the UK, 1959–1981

	1959–70		1970–81		1959–81	
	Absolute (000s)	%	Absolute (000s)	%	Absolute (000s)	%
Producer service industries[a]	372	11.6	502	14.0	874	27.2
ATCs in manufacturing[b]	474	25.3	−576	−24.5	−102	−5.4
TOTAL	846	16.6	−74	−1.2	772	15.2

[a] The definition of Producer Service Industries is that contained in Table 2.3 plus Railways (MLH 701).
[b] ATCs for Northern Ireland have been estimated by assuming that they account for the same proportion of total employment as in GB.

Source: DE Continuous Employment Series, Census of Employment and Survey of ATCs in Manufacturing.

simply be a catching up process after a slower response by ATC employment to the recession after 1979. However, it is also possible that we are witnessing a changing attitude towards non-production activities in manufacturing with closer scrutiny of 'overhead' costs generally and also perhaps an increased tendency to subcontract out service work. This would certainly be consistent with the evidence that large firms are attempting to improve their responsiveness to change by segmenting their activities into an indispensible 'core', insulated from economic change by more expendable functions (often contracted out) which are flexible enough to expand and contract with economic circumstances (Atkinson, 1984). If such evidence is part of a more general trend, much of the growth in producer service industries could be the product of a growing transfer of activities from within production to the specialist supply sector (Rajan and Pearson, 1986). Indeed there is supportive evidence in the distributive trades case study to follow (Section 5.3) that such a reorganization has taken place.

Finally, returning to the relationship between manufacturing and producer services more generally, if data on employment in ATCs within manufacturing are combined with employment in producer service industries to create an approximate measure of total producer service employment change (i.e. excluding manual services in manufacturing), between 1970 and 1981 UK employment in that sector actually declined by 74,000 jobs (Table 3.4). In only three of the eleven years in that period did producer services record an increase in employment. This places the role of intermediate services as a generator of jobs in a wider context and appears to support the 'de-industrialization view' that the poor performance of manufacturing industry is the main constraint on employment growth, whatever compensating expansion may occur in producer service industries.

3.4. PRODUCER SERVICES AND FINAL DEMAND

A 'de-industrialization view' is not, however, the complete picture, since services are not simply dependent on manufacturing demand. In fact slightly more of the output of private service industries goes to other services (including the public sector) than to manufacturing (21.8% compared to 18.5%). In particular financial and business services, which are clearly producer activities, supply only 11% of their output to manufacturing industry, while 34.6% goes to other services. Not surprisingly also, posts and telecommunications supply 50% of their output to service industries (including the public sector). Thus, some of the change in producer services employment and output is likely to be only indirectly related to material production. The input–output tables suggest that a growing share of service output is going to serve intermediate demand and that there is a parallel decline in the share of output going directly to consumers (Table 3.5). In part this simply reflects the multiplier effects of reorganization in the distribution service and is, thus, indirectly related to changes in manufacturing demand. But the scale of the growth of miscellaneous service output directed to the service sector itself (an increase from 6.2% to 18.1%), combined with evidence of an increase in the share of services purchased by the distributive and miscellaneous service industries (Table 3.6), implies that an increasing indirectness of supply to final consumer demand is an important stimulus to intermediate service output growth.

This conclusion can be taken further using employment statistics which allow a more disaggregated analysis. Table 3.7 presents the contribution of selected service industries to employment growth, and indicates that a change occurred during the 1970s and 1980s in the character of employment growth in producer service industries. Between 1959 and 1973 the producer services, other business services, and central offices in business grew in percentage terms more rapidly than any other non-public service. But between 1973 and 1984, central offices were no longer among the ten most rapidly growing services in percentage terms, and business services had dropped out of the top three places. Three of the four fastest growing services after 1973 were consumer services compared to one in the 1959–73 period; and four consumer services are represented in the top ten in the latter period compared with two in the former. Of course producer service industries are still the majority of industries in the top ten services, but half of these supply 'mixed' producer–consumer markets and these have risen in the rankings relative to 'pure' producer services. Caution is necessary here because we have no disaggregated information on output and productivity trends, but it does seem, as earlier work by Gershuny and Miles (1983) and the analysis of international statistics carried out in Section 3.2 implied, that the demand of consumer service industries for intermediate services and the expansion of 'mixed' producer–consumer markets have made an important contribution to the increase in producer service employment during the 1970s and 1980s.

It is often argued, of course, that the growth of consumer demand for many services is dependent on manufacturing trading perfor-mance since manufacturing accounts for 62% of UK exports, compared to 23% for service industries. However, the strategic

Table 3.5. Changes in the Markets for Service Output, 1968–1979

Service industry		Markets as a proportion of total output							
		Mining and manufacturing	Private services	Other industry	Total intermediate demand	Consumer demand	Exports	Other final demand	Total final demand
Transport and communication	1968	20.9	23.3	3.5	47.7	21.0	24.3	7.0	52.3
	1979	21.2	27.2	3.2	51.6	18.2	22.9	7.3	48.4
Distribution	1968	12.4	1.4	2.1	15.9	75.7	4.8	3.6	84.1
	1979	19.1	7.1	5.2	31.4	55.7	6.5	6.4	68.6
Miscellaneous	1968	20.2	6.2	5.9	32.3	41.6	7.9	18.3	67.7
	1979	18.6	18.1	3.1	39.8	34.3	12.4	13.4	60.2

Source: Input–output tables.

Table 3.6.   Backward Linkages of Service Industries, 1968–1979

Purchasing industry	Share of domestic purchases of client industry (%)							
	Transport and Communication		Distribution		Miscellaneous		Total	
	1968	1979	1968	1979	1968	1979	1968	1979
Transport and communication	8.8	4.0	11.7	8.5	7.1	7.9	27.6	20.4
Distribution	1.1	1.7	0.3	2.8	0.6	3.3	2.0	7.8
Miscellaneous	2.8	4.0	3.9	8.2	8.9	11.1	15.6	23.3
TOTAL	12.7	9.7	15.9	19.5	16.6	22.3	45.2	51.5

Source: Input–output tables.

Table 3.7.   Percentage Employment Change in Non-public Service Industries, 1959–1984[a]

The fastest growing services in rank order

1959–73 (%)	1973–81 (%)	1981–4 (%)[d]
Other business services 193[b]	Sport and recreation 72	Other tourism 73
Central offices 128[b]	Property 61[c]	Renting consumer goods 29
Air transport 117[c]	Other miscellaneous services 61	Retailing footwear 23
Other miscellaneous services 116	Catering 51	Business services nes 21[b]
Miscellaneous transport 78[b]	Other business services 51[b]	Services auxiliary to banking 20[c]
Advertising 78[b]	Clubs 50	Renting transport, etc., goods 20[c]
Other financial institutions 76[c]	Professional and scientific services 44[b]	Dealing in scrap 19[b]
Betting and gambling 72	Miscellaneous transport 35[b]	Other finance 17[c]
Banking 60[c]	Accountancy 34[c]	Retail distribution of furnishing 16
Property 60[c]	Banking 27[c]	Advertising 16[b]

[a] Producer services defined as in Table 2.3 plus MLH 701, and Table 2.4.
[b] 'Pure' producer service.
[c] 'Mixed' producer–consumer service.
[d] Based on estimates.

Source: DE Continuous Employment Services, Census of Employment and Gazette.

nature of export sectors should not blind us to the fact that economic growth occurs not only through exports but also through innovations in manufacturing and service activity creating new demands. In any case, not only are the financial and distributive trades sectors significant exporters (see Section 5.1) but more importantly, as shown in the input–output tables, each 100 units of manufacturing output requires 19 units of service industry inputs so that (together with non-production activities within manufacturing) such services could contribute to the performance of the exporting sector. Given the importance of such a question it is to this subject we now turn.

3.5. THE CONTRIBUTION OF PRODUCER SERVICES TO THE PERFORMANCE OF OTHER SECTORS OF THE ECONOMY

We have a very limited understanding of the contribution of producer services to the performance of manufacturing and other sectors in the UK economy. The Canadian evidence (see Section 2.4) suggests that better data might indicate that not only is manufacturing highly dependent on service inputs but that the efficiency contribution of services to manufacturing performance is substantial. Figure 3.4 makes a preliminary attempt, in very simple terms, to describe the complex nature of the likely relationship between service use and firm performance in the UK. It shows that the influence of services on firm performance will be contingent upon such factors as the type of market it is in, the technology used, and product or service supplied. For example, in highly competitive markets where consumer tastes influence demand, the image of the product or service may be important, and this will encourage advertising, while in markets where technological innovation is important more resources will need to be devoted to development work.

Organizational factors will also have an influence on service use; more complex, larger, and multi-site firms will have greater service needs (for example communication management) than simple smaller organizations, though this could also be balanced by economies of scale associated with the use of more standardized service inputs. Of course firms will respond to market pressures in differing ways. Some may adopt, in response to market demands, a strategy of product improvement which could influence the level of research and development. Others may concentrate on price competition which would focus attention on production efficiency, perhaps leading to the use of works methods services. Firms will also

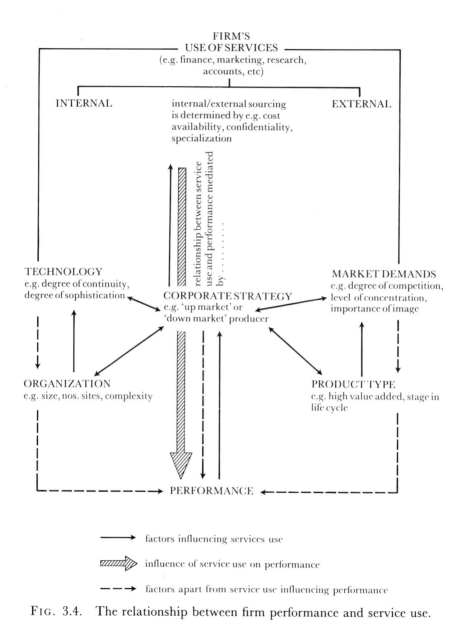

FIG. 3.4. The relationship between firm performance and service use.

decide whether to carry out such services 'in-house', or whether to employ specialist suppliers. Important considerations will be the confidentiality required in a service, its relative cost inside and outside the firm, and the degree of specialist skill and knowledge required for its production (see Sections 5.2 and 6.2). It is the appropriateness of such value judgements and the strategy towards service use which, together with competition in the market place, will influence company performance.

The argument that the service input to production can have a positive impact on the competitiveness and tradability of industry is based on largely circumstantial evidence. The importance of services which provide accurate, up to date, and complete information to management (Knight, 1982), the value of service functions such as marketing to the firm (Rabey, 1977), the leading role of service firms such as civil engineers in the organization and selling of goods production (OECD, 1983), and the contribution of research, development, and technical competence to innovation (Freeman, Clarke, and Soete, 1982; Rothwell and Zegweld, 1979) are all emphasized in the literature as positive aspects of the contribution of services to firm performance.

Research relies on a limited number of largely qualitative examples. However, there have been a small number of quantitative studies of the non-production component within manufacturing firms, which show that industries and firms employing more service workers perform better on output per head and productivity growth measures (Delehanty, 1968; Gershuny, 1978; Gudgin, Crum, and Bailey, 1979). A further study of 604 contracts carried out by management consultancy firms uses the job summaries, completed by consultants at the end of a contract with a client, to measure the contribution of specialist producer service suppliers to customer performance (Johnstone, 1963). Many of the contracts were not suited to quantitative assessment, others had no impact on the client firm because the consultant's advice was not taken, the implementation was left up to the client, or the contract was terminated. In the remaining 47% of cases productivity increases of 53% were recorded, and on average the net return on fees to the firm was 206%. Both varied by sector with chemicals, clothing and footwear, textiles, bricks and pottery, and engineering experiencing above average benefits.

However, the activities of producer services need not be unequivocally beneficial to client industry. For example, the efficiency and structure of retail distribution in the UK, with large retailers and distributors controlling much of sales, storage, and delivery can be argued to aid the country's overseas industrial competitors in penetrating the domestic market (see Section 5.3). The activities of the financial sector can also illustrate the ambiguous relationship between producer services and domestic industry.

Services associated with the City of London are subject to trends and forces which are to an extent independent of and indifferent to the fortunes of domestic industry. For example, financial institutions are able to invest in commercial property abroad as well as in domestic industry, and imported goods are just as easily bought by credit card or hire purchase as the home produced item. Such a view, shared by such commentators as Glyn and Sutcliffe (1972), Lever and Edwards (1981) and the authors of the GLC's London Industrial and Financial Strategies (1985), emphasizes the perceived failure of the UK financial services sector to support domestic industry. The search for short-term returns is argued to cause adverse terms and conditions to be attached to the finance available to industry. The tendency of the City to ignore high-risk ventures or for investment to be subject to changes in fashion is argued to mitigate against the long-term profitability of industry. The financial institutions have also been criticized for their role in the large-scale export of capital and in the 'excessive' diversion of investment funds into property development and house purchases.

However, it is not simply that the financial sector has failed to 'channel' funds through in a satisfactory manner to industry. Some survey evidence indicates that there is no shortage of funds for investment on the part of large firms. Rather the limited technical capacity and poorly developed managerial practices in British business have limited their demand for investment funds (Urry, 1986). The relationship between industry and finance also needs to be seen in a long-term perspective. London developed into a world commercial and financial centre before the industrial revolution and industrialization in Britain occurred largely independently. The 'separation' of finance and industry is grounded in commercial practices which have a lengthy history and reflect the prominent role of London in the international financial system (see Section 5.1).

Nevertheless, important structural changes have taken place in the financing of British industry since the 1960s (Rybczynski, 1982) associated with changes in manufacturing itself. In particular, the decline of heavy industries, which typically had a significant part of their working capital financed by equity capital and long-term loans, has tended to increase the share of overall working capital financed by shorter-term borrowing from banks. Industry's financial needs were also affected by the general decline in profitability, from around an 11% rate of return in the early 1960s to just over 2% in 1981; this increased the demand for external funds, mainly short-term bank loans. Changes in the methods of financing, with the growth of leasing and availability of medium-term bank loans, have added to the shift towards shorter-term bank finance as opposed to permanent funds raised through the capital markets. Rybczynski argues that this shift has important wider implications. One is that industry has become more reliant on outside funds which form part of the M3 definition of money supply. They are thus more likely to be affected by government monetary policy and by associated vagaries of interest rates. Second, the relative decline of the capital markets as a source of finance for British industry has contributed to the Stock Exchange moving into new areas of activity, including more involvement in dealing in foreign securities.

Clearly, then, relationships between the producer services sector and industry require interpretation. Key questions remain unanswered.

(1) In which direction does the causality work; the characteristics of firm performance will influence the use of services, when is the opposite relationship likely to hold? (2) Many studies are partial and concentrate on particular services and on the provision of services either within or outside user firms. Which factors influence the level of service use and the degree of 'internalization' or 'externalization' of service use by clients (see Section 5.2)? It is only by considering such factors that a bench-mark can be established showing what service use can be expected in a given firm, and what impact variations in service use can have on performance. (3) Finally, it is worth remembering that very simplistic measures of financial performance are used in most studies, a clearer conceptualization and a more subtle measurement of the relationship between service use and firm performance is needed.

3.6. DO SPATIAL VARIATIONS IN PRODUCER SERVICES MATTER?

A line of argument related to the above has recently gained ground; namely that the availability, range, and quality of producer services in an area can have a significant effect upon the competitiveness and capacity for successful adjustment to change of local industry.

Perhaps the most explicit statement of the relationship between producer services (in this case offices) and area economic development comes from the work of the Northern Region Strategy Team (1976). They argue that:

Offices make a vital contribution to the generation of new economic activity, to the search for and development of, new processes, markets and management systems. It is generally in offices too that decisions are taken as to how, when and where ideas for new goods and services should translate into action. It follows that an area deficient in office activity and thus lacking these crucial skills and capabilities will find it difficult to increase and sustain economic growth.

Research at the Centre for Urban and Regional Development Studies has provided empirical support for some of NRST's analysis. It is argued that the innovative performance of industry is an important determinant of its long-term commercial success. Spatial variations in the industrial innovation and diffusion processes have been established, with some peripheral regions lagging behind the Greater South East in the take-up and development of new products (Oakey, Thwaites, and Nash, 1980). Spatial variations in the distribution of research and development in small and medium sized enterprises is argued to make an important contribution to these differences in innovative performance. A second argument suggests that business information, obtained largely via personal contact in producer service occupations, has an important impact on the innovation process. Therefore, remoteness from specialist centres of such producer services, by reducing the supply of commercially relevant information, will act as a constraint on the innovative performance of peripheral areas (Goddard, 1980).

Evidence from the Northern Region (James, Marshall, and Waters, 1979) shows that business travellers (even those employed in manufacturing) from the North usually attend meetings in service establishments in London. This data, together with the under-representation of producer service employment in the region, *could* suggest a shortfall in the local supply of business services in the Northern Region. There is supportive evidence from an establishment survey in the Northern Region that those establishments which communicated further afield performed more successfully on measures of labour productivity and output growth. Those establishments which communicated locally attached little importance to communications as a managerial tool, and local communicators with a poor financial performance tended to be small or medium sized, local, single-site enterprises which did not have access to advanced communications technology. These firms in other analysis show a poor innovative performance in regions like the North.

Other work examining the relationship between accessibility and economic development in Europe has identified an association between peripherality and relatively low incomes per head. The core regions of the European Community possess more dynamic and buoyant economies, and economic disparities between the core and periphery of Europe have increased during the 1970s (Keeble,

Owens, and Thompson, 1981). Related evidence suggests that limited local supplies of information in peripheral areas of Europe add to communication costs. These costs come about directly where distance-related charging is operated by the telecommunications authority. New and more efficient data communications services are volume based, but they are demand led, and are frequently introduced into core areas, thus helping to enhance spatial variations in communications costs (Gillespie *et al.* 1984).

A study of the computer service industry in the UK also indicates that some non-local firms which sell services to distant regions charge more for their service. This may indicate that in areas with few local services, using non-local services may add to firm costs. In computing, some supplier firms do not sell their service outside the local area because of problems of servicing non-local contracts or lack of knowledge of markets outside the host region (Green, 1982). So a shortfall in local services could mean lack of service provision in some instances, and this again could have implications for the performance of small and medium sized firms which rely on local suppliers (Marshall, 1979).

On the other hand, a recent study exploring the relationship between the location of specialist suppliers of marketing, technical, and research services and their use by small engineering firms did not find any distinctive spatial variations in service use which might influence firm performance (ECOTEC, 1985). Firms which exported more tended to use services more regularly, thus supporting the argument for a positive relationship between service use and firm performance. But neither suppliers nor users indicated that there were any important spatial variations in the quality or quantity of services available to them. Of course, some services were only supplied by firms outside the region, but the use of local subcontractors by non-local firms, and the lack of any locational dimension to firms' pricing policies minimized cost penalties. The main conclusion of the research was that very few of the manufacturing firms actually used the relatively sophisticated services studied.

A number of caveats are worth recording about this study. Firstly, the locations examined, namely the North East, North West, and South West, did not include a service rich area of southern Britain. The study focused solely on the external provision of services and neglected 'in-house' activities. Perhaps also the expected spatial variations in service use which affect performance would be prevalent in larger firms which used services more regularly.

Nevertheless, given the negative conclusions of this survey it is legitimate to enquire whether the studies of the relationship between producer service location and industry performance have been unduly concentrated on a narrow range of office-based services. Work on business service linkages suggests that the most regularly used local services are distribution and financial services, neither of which have been the subject of much study (Marshall, 1982a; Polese, 1982; Wood, 1985). For the latter at least, the expansion of the local authority Enterprise Boards in the UK which seem to have filled a market niche by providing long term equity and loan finance for medium and small size firms, suggests that the local financial system may not be satisfying all the needs of industry.

While there may still be an association between producer service location and user performance, we are unclear as to how such a relationship operates. As at the national level the evidence does not indicate clearly the direction of causality—when do producer services lead other sectors and when the reverse? The information and innovation studies are based on good empirical information about the first commercial application of products and processes, but infer the economic processes that may produce the observed spatial patterns. In particular, there has been no study of spatial variations in the distribution of information, nor the role of producer service firms in supplying this. Nor has there been any investigation of how spatial variations in information availability affect innovative performance. So far research has used simplistic measures of organizational structures and focused largely on research and development. What aspects of other activities such as financial control, corporate strategy, or market research contribute to firm performance?

It is still an open question whether there are actually spatial variations in the availability and quality of producer services which affect firm performance. Does a shortfall in the local supply of producer service industries add to client costs or reduce the quality of the service provided, and if so how do user firms respond? Does a shortage of local services encourage users to internalize their producer services, and does this mean they are performed less well? Finally, assuming any of these factors affect client performance, how important is the impact relative to that of other influences on performance?

4

The Location of Producer Service Employment

4.1. WHICH SERVICES ARE UNEVENLY DISTRIBUTED?

Notwithstanding the ambiguous conclusions of the work examining the relationship between the availability of producer services and firm performance, it is clear that producer services can make an important contribution to uneven development. In particular, disparities in tradable producer service endowments affect the size and diversity of the export base in different areas, and also have a significant impact on occupational structures and thus on the range and quality of employment opportunities in different areas. This may in turn encourage differences in new firm formation so that spatial disparities may become cumulative and self-perpetuating.

The proposition that producer services, unlike many private consumer services, are unevenly distributed is tested in Table 4.1. This presents the results of a location quotient analysis of employment in service and manufacturing industries in the regions of the UK.[1] The standard deviation from the regional mean on the location quotient is presented for each industry and provides an indicator of their uneven distribution relative to regional employment. Of course, since there are only 11 regions, the standard deviation may be distorted by extreme values, and for this reason a second measure, the mean deviation, which does not square deviations has also been included to support the results.

The low score for the standard and mean deviations for service industries as a whole in Table 4.1 confirms the view that, in contrast to manufacturing, services are distributed in much the same way as total employment, and this would seem to imply that their location is determined by the level of demand in the local economy. However, breaking down service industries to look at their constituent parts shows that, while many consumer services do indeed

[1] $LQ = (E_{ij}/E_i)(R_j/N)^{-1}$ where E_{ij} = employment in industry i in region j
E_i = employment in industry i in nation
R_j = total employment in region j
N = total national employment.

Table 4.1.   The Uneven Location of Service Industries by Region, 1981

Producer services	SD	MD	Consumer services	SD	MD	Public services	SD	MD
Unevenly distributed services[a]								
Air transport	0.645	0.411	Clubs	0.646	0.530	Public administration	0.451	0.359
Sea transport	0.549	0.467	Hotels	0.539	0.440			
Central offices	0.546	0.382	Religious institutions	0.468	0.426			
Advertising	0.524	0.333	Cinemas, etc.	0.358	0.209			
Ports	0.480	0.374	Betting and gambling	0.357	0.281			
R&D	0.475	0.400	Repairs of boots & shoes	0.330	0.250			
Wholesale distribution of oil and petroleum	0.357	0.271	Public houses	0.306	0.250			
Other road haulage	0.355	0.245						
Other business services	0.340	0.259						
Insurance	0.325	0.276						
Miscellaneous transport	0.304	0.205						
Evenly distributed services[b]								
Wholesale distribution of food and drink	0.195	0.172	Motor repairs	0.192	0.178	Medical services	0.181	0.140
Post & communications	0.193	0.144	Hairdressers	0.144	0.121	Local government	0.178	0.149
Accountancy	0.185	0.127	Sport	0.138	0.121	Education	0.130	0.095
Legal	0.169	0.143	Other retail distribution	0.106	0.093			
			Restaurants	0.105	0.082			
Summary								
Producer services	0.179	0.127						
Consumer services	0.075	0.063						
Public services	0.178	0.127						
All services	0.089	0.071						
Manufacturing	0.194	0.169						

[a] Service industries with a standard deviation more than 0.3.

[b] Service industries with a standard deviation less than 0.2.

Source: Census of Employment.

follow the distribution of regional employment very closely, producer and also public service employment have standard and mean deviations which are more similar to manufacturing.[2]

Examining individual producer service industries, only a few have low standard deviations. However, producer industries are not the sole contributors to the spatial concentration of service activity, a significant number of entertainment and leisure services have high standard deviations and many of the unevenly distributed producer service activities serve 'mixed' producer–consumer markets. In addition, the conventional concentration on office activities as the main contributors to the uneven location of employment is modified by the evidence in Table 4.1. Several blue collar services have high standard and mean deviations. As we will explore later the difference between office and blue collar, as well as consumer services, is that offices tend to be over-represented predominantly close to the capital, while the other service industries are more likely to be over-represented in a variety of provincial locations.

4.2. THE REGIONAL DISTRIBUTION OF PRODUCER SERVICE EMPLOYMENT

The pattern of over-concentration in office-based activities is reflected in the concentration of all producer service employment in the South East of the country. Table 4.2 is based on Census of Population data, which includes non-production activities in manufacturing and producer service industries, and this shows that the South Eastern Economic Planning Region has 40.3% of GB producer service employment, with the North West (11.3% of GB employment) and the West Midlands (8.8% of GB employment) providing secondary concentrations (column one). East Anglia, Wales, and the Northern Region have the smallest concentrations of producer service employment at 3.3, 3.4, and 4.3% of GB employment respectively. This evidence suggests an urban bias in the location of producer service activities, and this is confirmed by the fact that 45% of GB's producer service employment is contained in Greater London and the former Metropolitan Counties, London accounting for almost half of this. In addition, these conurbations contain more than half of the producer service employment in the South East,

---

[2] The definition of producer service industries is that contained in Table 2.3 plus MLH 701. Public services include national government and defence, local authorities, medical, and educational services.

Table 4.2. Location of Producer Service Employment, 1981[a]

	Percentage of national producer employment			Deviation from expected given share of national total employment (000)			(7) NPEM/1000 Manufacturing employees	(8) PSIE/1000 Total employees
	(1) PSE	(2) NPEM	(3) PSIE	(4) PSE	(5) NPEM	(6) PSIE		
North	4.3	4.9	4.0	−73.1	−8.1	−65.0	254	223
Yorks and Humberside	7.7	8.3	7.4	−72.2	−8.1	−64.1	259	247
E. Midlands	5.9	7.7	5.3	−64.7	+13.0	−77.6	261	242
E. Anglia	3.3	3.2	3.3	−7.0	−3.7	−3.3	290	274
South East	40.3	33.9	42.8	+461.7	+15.3	+446.5	364	345
South West	7.2	7.1	7.2	−33.8	−11.9	−22.0	305	264
W. Midlands	8.8	12.1	7.5	−40.0	+48.4	−88.4	274	264
North West	11.3	12.6	10.8	−18.1	+17.5	−35.6	277	277
Wales	3.4	3.1	3.5	−71.0	−25.2	−35.6	232	214
Scotland	7.9	7.1	8.2	−82.1	−37.3	−44.9	259	244
GB TOTAL	100	100	100				295	284

[a] The data excludes producer service employment within primary industry, construction, and utilities due to classificatory problems.
PSE = Total producer service employment.
NPEM = Non-production employment in manufacturing.
PSIE = Producer service industry employment.

Source: Census of Population, adapted from Marshall, Damesick, and Wood (1987).

Yorkshire and Humberside, West Midlands, and North West Economic Planning Regions.

Table 4.2 shows the expected level of producer service employment for each region given its share of national employment (column four). It indicates that there are 461,700 more producer service jobs in the South East than expected. The largest deficits are in Scotland (−82,100), the Northern Region (−73,100), Yorkshire and Humberside (−72,200), and Wales (−71,000).

A significant feature of Table 4.2 is that the pattern of over- and under-representation in most regions is largely a result of the distribution of producer service industry employment (PSIE). This reflects not only the greater size of this component of producer service employment, but also the fact that it is more spatially concentrated than non-production employment in manufacturing (NPEM). Thus, while the South East contains 42.8% of national PSIE it has only 33.9% of NPEM, little more than its share of national employment. As a result 96.7% of the excess in producer service employment in the South East is accounted for by producer service industries. The greater decentralization of NPEM relative to regional shares of total employment is further highlighted by the excess of non-production employment in the West Midlands, North West, and East Midland regions. These regions all have a large manufacturing sector and not surprisingly the West and East Midlands have the largest deficits in PSIE relative to their share of total employment.

In columns seven and eight Table 4.2 takes account of the relative size of the various sectors in the regional economy by presenting the number of non-production staff per 1,000 employees in manufacturing and the number of producer service industry jobs per 1,000 workers for each region. It further emphasizes the concentration of both NPEM and PSIE in the South East. Notwithstanding the predominance of manufacturing in the East Midlands, West Midlands, and North West, in common with all provincial regions apart from the South West, they have fewer non-production staff than expected given their manufacturing employment. Column eight also shows that relative to the size of the regional workforce PSIE is least developed in Wales, the North, East Midlands, and Scotland.

There is some variation in the composition of producer service employment within regions, NPEM being less concentrated in the main conurbations than PSIE (41% of NPEM being in Greater London and the former Metropolitan Counties compared to 46.7% of PSIE). However, this urban pattern tends to be masked by regional variations. There is no consistent tendency for conurbations to display a lower proportion of non-production workers in producer

Table 4.3. Producer Service Employment in Conurbations and Regions, 1981[a]

Location	Employees (000s)	Proportion of national PSE	Proportion of regional PSE	Proportion of area PSE	
				NPEM	PSIE
Tyne and Wear	113.9	1.8	41.7	30.9	69.1
Northern Region	272.9	4.3	—	32.8	67.2
S. Yorks.	122.9	1.9	25.0	32.9	67.1
W. Yorks.	220.9	3.4	44.9	32.9	67.1
Yorks. and Humberside	491.6	7.7	—	30.7	69.3
East Midlands	381.7	5.9	—	36.4	63.6
East Anglia	210.2	3.3	—	27.4	72.6
Greater London	1415.2	22.0	54.7	18.4	81.6
South East	2587.8	40.3	—	23.8	76.2
South West	459.6	7.2	—	27.7	72.3

W. Midlands C.	341.2	5.3	60.3	39.3	60.7
W. Midlands R.	566.0	8.8	—	38.8	61.2
Greater Manchester	322.9	5.0	44.3	32.8	67.2
Merseyside	167.4	2.6	23.0	24.9	75.1
North West	728.0	11.3	—	31.3	68.7
Wales	220.2	3.4	—	25.9	74.1
Clydeside	194.7	3.0	38.2	28.0	72.0
Scotland	509.9	7.9	—	25.5	74.5
Total Conurbation	2898.1	45.0	—	25.7	74.3
GB	6427.9	100	—	28.2	71.8

PSE
NPEM } As in Table 4.2.
PSIE

[a] The data excludes producer service employment within primary industry, construction, and utilities due to classificatory problems.

Source: As in Table 4.2.

service employment than their region (Table 4.3). The share of producer service employment taken by NPEM is lowest in Greater London where it accounts for 18.4%. The South East, South West, and East Anglia as well as Wales and Scotland including Clydeside all have a lower share of NPEM in total producer employment than GB as a whole. In contrast, all peripheral regions and their conurbations in England except for Merseyside have a larger proportion of non-production staff than the GB average.

4.3. THE URBAN CHARACTER OF PRODUCER SERVICE INDUSTRIES

Further analysis of the location of NPEM is constrained by classificatory and area changes in the Census of Population, which is the sole source of occupation data by industry. The remainder of the analysis, therefore, concentrates on only producer service industries.[3]

An exploration of the urban character of producer services can be taken somewhat further for producer service industries using Census of Employment data. The areas used are the 280 Centre for Urban and Regional Development Studies (CURDS), Local Labour Market Areas (LLMAs), defined through extensive analysis of 1971 population, employment, and commuting data (Coombes *et al.*, 1982), which form the basis of a hierarchy of urban-centred Functional Regions (Fig. 4.1). The Functional Regionalization provides the key elements of a classification of LLMAs into 19 categories, according to their regional setting (i.e. northern and western v. southern and eastern), functional status (dominant v. sub-dominant, metropolitan v. free-standing, and between service, commercial, and manufacturing towns) and urban size status (distinguishing on the basis of the population size the more urbanized parts of the LLMAs, and between rural and urban areas, towns and cities). The 19 categories are listed in Table 4.4, with example LLMAs shown.

The distribution of producer industries between the 19 LLMA groups in 1981 is shown in Fig. 4.2 and summarized in Table 4.5.[4] The London LLMA contains 1.2 million producer service industry jobs, fully 29.6% of the GB total. While 19.5% of GB employment is classified as within these producer service industries, in London this

---

[3] The definition of producer service industries being used is that in Table 2.3 plus MLH 701.

[4] The analysis uses the Manpower Services Commission's National On-Line Manpower Information System (NOMIS).

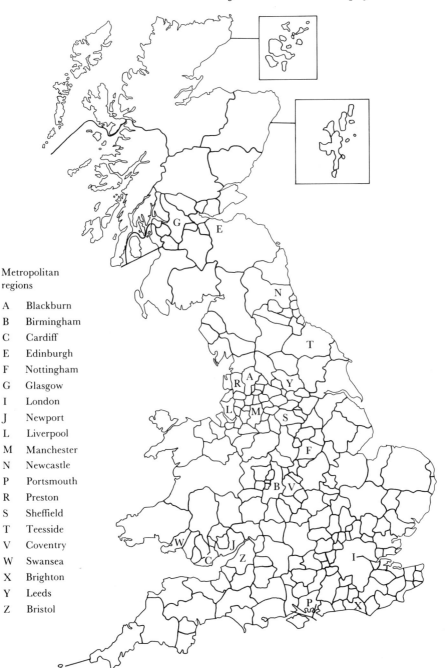

Metropolitan
regions

A   Blackburn
B   Birmingham
C   Cardiff
E   Edinburgh
F   Nottingham
G   Glasgow
I   London
J   Newport
L   Liverpool
M   Manchester
N   Newcastle
P   Portsmouth
R   Preston
S   Sheffield
T   Teesside
V   Coventry
W   Swansea
X   Brighton
Y   Leeds
Z   Bristol

FIG. 4.1.   The location of local labour markets (functional regions and
metropolitan regions).

Table 4.4.   A Classification of Local Labour Market Areas

Class	Title	No. of LLMAs	Example
1	London Dominant (L)	1	London
2	Conurbation Dominants (CD)	5	Manchester
3	Provincial Dominants (PD)	5	Edinburgh
4	Subregional Dominants (SD)	9	Portsmouth
5	London Sub-dominant Cities (LSC)	7	Southend
6	London Sub-dominant Towns (LST)	23	Maidenhead
7	Conurbation Sub-dominant Cities (CSC)	13	Motherwell
8	Conurbation Sub-dominant Towns (CST)	22	Northwich
9	Smaller Northern and Western Subdominant (SNWS)	24	Rugby
10	Southern and Eastern Freestanding Cities (SEFC)	12	Norwich
11	Northern and Western Freestanding Cities (NWFC)	13	Derby
12	Southern and Eastern Service Towns (SEST)	22	Canterbury
13	Southern and Eastern Commercial Towns (SECT)	14	Trowbridge
14	Southern and Eastern Manufacturing Towns (SEMT)	13	Wellingborough
15	Northern and Western Service Towns (NWST)	12	Llandudno
16	Northern and Western Commercial Towns (NWCT)	19	Hereford
17	Northern and Western Manufacturing Towns (NWMT)	14	Scunthorpe
18	Southern and Eastern Rural Areas (SERA)	19	Penzance
19	Northern and Western Rural Areas (NWRA)	34	Penrith

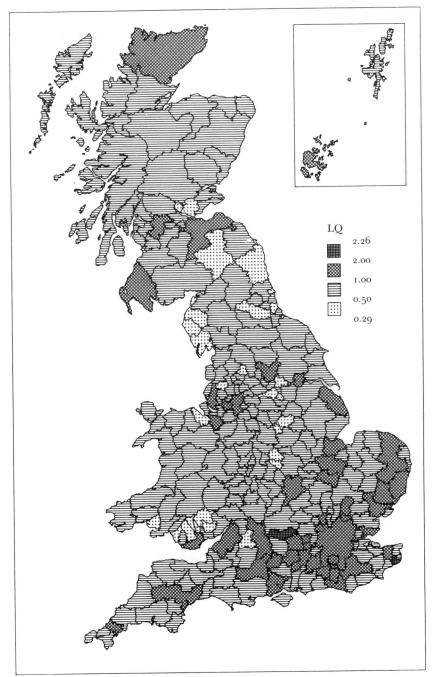

LQ

■ 2.26
▨ 2.00
▤ 1.00
▥ 0.50
▦ 0.29

Source: Census of Employment (NOMIS)

FIG. 4.2. Location quotients for producer service industries in local labour markets, 1981.

Table 4.5.   The Relative Distribution in 1981 of Producer Services, All Services, and Business Service Industries

Class	LLMA[ab]	Producer services Abs. Emp. (000s)	LQ	All services LQ	Business service offices LQ
1	L	1219	1.61	1.19	1.85
2	CD	488	1.06	1.02	1.07
3	PD	288	1.01	1.00	0.99
4	SD	193	0.91	1.01	0.84
5	LSC	129	1.04	1.07	1.21
6	LST	200	1.03	0.99	1.05
7	CSC	153	0.69	0.85	0.58
8	CST	123	0.74	0.89	0.69
9	SNWS	107	0.54	0.76	0.40
10	SEFC	305	0.99	1.01	0.94
11	NWFC	229	0.78	0.91	0.63
12	SEST	133	0.81	1.10	0.84
13	SECT	125	0.94	1.01	0.78
14	SEMT	63	0.76	0.88	0.77
15	NWST	65	0.74	1.08	0.67
16	MWCT	94	0.64	0.87	0.50
17	MWMT	62	0.56	0.75	0.45
18	SERA	58	0.93	0.95	0.89
19	NWRA	77	0.75	1.00	0.63
GB TOTAL		4111	1.00	1.00	1.00

[a] If using aggregations of employment.
[b] For the definitions of areas see Table 4.4.
Source: Census of Employment (NOMIS).

proportion is considerably higher, at 31.3% (Location Quotient = 1.61). Many of the Subdominant Cities and Towns within the London metropolitan region also display a relative over-representation, as do the Conurbations and Provincial Dominants. In all of the remaining LLMA groups, producer service industries are under-represented in relation to overall employment. At each level of the urban hierarchy (i.e. cities, towns, and rural areas), the degree of under-representation is greater amongst LLMAs in the north and west than amongst those in the south and east.

For comparative purposes the second part of Table 4.5 shows the LQs for the service sector as a whole. The distribution of producer services between the 19 groups is seen to be considerably more polarized than is the case for services as a whole; thus London's degree of over-representation is much greater for producer services than for all services (LQs of 1.61 and 1.19 respectively). Thus for all but one of the 19 labour market groups, the LQ for services is nearer to unity than the LQ for producer services. In a number of instances, LLMA groups with a relative service specialization, such as the Southern and Eastern Service Towns (with a LQ of 1.10), are seen to have a marked under-representation of producer services (a LQ of 0.81). It should be noted that with the major exception of the capital there is no general tendency for producer services to be more concentrated at higher levels of the urban hierarchy than services as a whole. Although the Conurbation Dominants do have marginally greater over-representation in producer service in-dustries than in all services (LQs of 1.06 and 1.02 respectively), the essential point is that every other level of the urban hierarchy has a lower representation of producer services than it does of all services, such is the degree of over-concentration of producer services in the London LLMA.

The final column in Table 4.5 indicates the spatial distribution of a sub-set of producer services which might be best described as *business, information, or office-based services*. These are insurance, banking, financial, business, and professional services, which form a distinctive group of producer service industries along with the goods-related industries of transport, communications, and dis-tribution. As Table 4.5 indicates, in 1981 these business service offices are even more concentrated close to the capital than other producer service industries. Fourteen of the 19 groups have a more marked relative under-representation of business than of overall producer services; of the remaining groups, the Conurbation Domi-nants and the London Sub-dominant Towns have a fractionally greater over-representation in business services than in all producer services, while the London LLMA and the London Sub-dominant Cities have a markedly greater over-representation in business services than in producer services (with London's LQ being 1.85 and 1.61 respectively, and the London Sub-dominant Cities' being 1.21 and 1.04). Thus, business or information services are heavily over-represented in the capital and in the larger cities within its immediate sphere of metropolitan influence. The London LLMA alone possesses over 40% of GB employment in business service offices.

Table 4.6. Changes in Service Industry Employment by Region, 1971–1981

	South East		East Anglia		South West		West Midlands		East Midlands		Yorkshire & Humberside	
	Absolute (000s)	%	Absolute (000s)	%	Absolute (000s)	%	Absolute (000s)	%	Absolute (000s)	%	Absolute (000s)	%
1971–8												
Producer services	94.2	5.7	25.9	30.8	62	33.6	33.6	13.4	40.3	27.2	27.2	11.4
Consumer services	105.9	7.4	26.2	22.5	90.3	33.0	32.8	10.4	54.5	28.3	67.3	22.1
Public services	135	9.2	19.3	17.0	70.9	25.2	64.4	19.1	81.5	38.0	71.5	22.9
1978–81												
Producer services	94.2	5.4	8.9	8.1	16.6	6.7	5.6	2.0	10.2	5.4	15.9	6.0
Consumer services	79.8	5.1	6.1	4.3	12.7	3.5	22.9	6.6	21.1	8.5	-3.8	-1.0
Public services	-35.3	-2.2	2.4	1.8	-3.8	-1.1	-10.8	-2.7	-21.9	-7.4	-12.1	-3.2
1971–81												
Producer services	188.4	11.4	34.8	41.3	78.6	42.6	39.2	15.6	50.5	34.1	43.1	18.1
Consumer services	185.7	13.0	32.2	27.8	103	37.6	55.7	17.6	75.6	39.3	63.5	20.8
Public services	99.7	6.8	21.7	19.1	67.1	23.9	53.6	15.9	59.6	27.8	59.4	19.0

Table 4.6. (Continued)

	North West		North		Wales		Scotland		Northern Ireland		United Kingdom	
	Absolute (000s)	%	Absolute (000s)	%	Absolute (000s)	%	Absolute (000s)	%	Absolute (000s)	%	Absolute (000s)	%
1971–8												
Producer services	-11.6	-2.7	14.1	10.3	6.7	5.7	13.4	4.6	4.8	8.2	310.6	8.6
Consumer services	50.8	11.4	23.5	10.5	33.5	21.8	54.4	14.4	15.3	19.6	554.5	14.2
Public services	73.1	16.0	27.8	12.4	44.6	22.3	69.3	18.3	43.6	42.4	701	17.2
1978–81												
Producer services	10.8	2.6	-3.4	-2.2	1.7	1.4	11.4	3.7	-0.2	-0.3	171.7	4.4
Consumer services	17.3	3.5	-0.1	0	4.5	2.4	20.0	4.6	5.3	5.7	185.8	4.2
Public services	-24.7	-4.7	-15.8	-6.3	-2.4	-1.0	11.1	2.5	12.2	8.3	-101.1	-2.1
1971–81												
Producer services	-0.8	-0.2	10.7	7.8	8.4	7.2	24.8	8.4	4.6	7.9	482.3	13.4
Consumer services	68.1	15.3	23.4	10.5	38.0	24.7	74.4	19.7	20.6	26.4	740.3	18.9
Public services	48.4	10.6	12.0	5.4	42.2	21.1	80.4	21.2	55.8	54.2	599.9	14.7

Source: Census of Employment.

4.4.   REGIONAL CHANGES IN THE LOCATION OF SERVICE INDUSTRY AND MANUFACTURING EMPLOYMENT

While there was a general growth in producer and other service industry employment more or less throughout the country between 1971 and 1981 there was a relative decentralization of these activities from the South East Economic Planning Region (Table 4.6). The South East's producer service employment grew by 11.4% between 1971 and 1981, less than the national average (13.4%). There was, however, considerable variability in the performance of the other Economic Planning Regions, the most pronounced growth being recorded in areas adjacent to the South East; the South West (42.6%), East Anglia (41.3%), and East Midlands (34.1%). In contrast, producer service employment declined in the North West (−0.2%) and growth was substantially below the national average in Scotland (8.4%), Northern Ireland (7.9%), the North (7.8%), and Wales (7.2%).

The growth in East Anglia, the South West, and East Midlands is underestimated by focusing only on aggregate employment. While most producer service industry employment growth in these regions between 1971 and 1981 was in full-time work (71–82.1%), in the South East, North West, North, Wales, and West Midlands at least half of the growth was in part-time employment (Table 4.7). These

Table 4.7.   Part-time Employment Growth in Producer Service Industries by Region, 1971–1981

	Part-time workers as % of employment change		
	Males	Females	Total
South East	48.5	68.2	64.2
East Anglia	3.1	39.9	19.9
South West	5.3	38.1	17.9
West Midlands	14.8	61.6	50.0
East Midlands	6.8	52.4	29.0
Yorks. and Humberside	19.6	48.7	41.9
North West	6.4	87.4	109.0
North	25.6	70.1	56.3
Wales	169.4	45.8	51.2
Scotland	33.3	90.1	68.1
Northern Ireland	18.9	37.6	32.6

Source: Census of Employment.

differences in the type of employment being created reflect the unequal growth of part-time female work. Part-time employment has grown more rapidly for both males and females in the poorer performing regional economies (Table 4.7), but part-time female employment made the major contribution to part-time employment growth in all regions. In contrast, two less dynamic regions, the North West and Wales, actually recorded a decline in full-time male producer service employment between 1971 and 1981 and in the former case this was sufficient to cause a decline in all producer service employment.

Analysis of the two sub-periods 1971–8 and 1978–81 reveals that, even allowing for the shorter time span of the second period, the decentralization of producer service industry employment from the South East declined. Regional variations from the national average are much less marked in the second period. After 1978 there was a resurgence in the South East's relative growth performance, producing a 5.4% employment increase compared to a national average of 4.4%. The position of the North West, Yorkshire and Humberside, and Scotland also improved; employment in the first, for example, increasing by 2.6% between 1978 and 1981 in contrast to a decline in the earlier period. In contrast, producer service industry employment fell in the North (− 2.2%) and Northern Ireland (− 0.3%), while the rate of growth in regions adjacent to the South East declined (in the case of the South West from an average of 4.8% per annum 1971–8 to 2.2% per annum 1978–81).

As a result of these patterns of employment change in producer service industries many peripheral regions relied on consumer service employment to sustain growth in service industries (Table 4.6). Thus, while between 1971 and 1981 producer services grew more rapidly than consumer services in the Greater South East, the position was reversed elsewhere, most notably in the North West, where consumer services grew by 15.3% in contrast to a decline in producer service employment, and in Wales, Scotland, and Northern Ireland, where the growth in consumer services was three times that in producer activities. This dependence on consumer services in the provinces outside the Greater South East tended to increase during the latter part of the 1970s when the contribution of public services to employment declined in most regions. Even where growth was retained, most notably in Scotland and Northern Ireland, its rate declined significantly.

It is interesting to compare these regional changes in the service sector with the employment performance of manufacturing (Table 4.8). This confirms the aggregate evidence for the UK that manufacturing is not the sole economic base of the economy (see Section 3.2). By ranking the performance of each region in terms of

Table 4.8. Employment Change by Region, Ranked by Percentage Change, 1971–1981

Manufacturing			Producer service industries			Consumer service industries			Public sector industries		
Region	Absolute (000s)	%	Region	Absolute (000s)	%	Region	Absolute (000s)	%	Region	Absolute (000s)	%
E. Anglia	−6.9	−3.6	S. West	78.6	42.6	E. Midlands	75.6	39.3	N. Ireland	55.8	54.2
S. West	−25.7	−6.3	E. Anglia	34.8	41.3	S. West	103.0	37.6	E. Midlands	59.6	27.8
E. Midlands	−68.8	−11.6	E. Midlands	50.5	34.1	E. Anglia	32.3	27.8	S. West	67.1	23.9
North	−105.9	−23.6	Yorks. & Humb.	43.1	18.1	N. Ireland	20.6	26.4	Scotland	80.4	21.2
S. East	−532.7	−24.2				Wales	38.0	24.7	Wales	42.2	21.1
Scotland	−173.8	−26.0	W. Midlands	39.2	15.6	Yorks. & Humb.	63.5	20.8	E. Anglia	21.7	19.1
Yorks. & Humb.	−205.3	−26.3	S. East	188.4	11.4	Scotland	74.4	19.7	Yorks. & Humb.	59.4	19.0
			Scotland	24.8	8.4	W. Midlands	55.7	17.6			
Wales	−86.1	−26.6	N. Ireland	4.6	7.9	N. West	68.1	15.3	W. Midlands	53.6	15.9
W. Midlands	−308.3	−27.9	North	10.7	7.8	S. East	185.7	13.0	N. West	48.4	10.6
N. West	−354.0	−30.4	Wales	8.4	7.2	North	23.4	10.5	S. East	99.7	6.8
N. Ireland	−54.7	−31.9	N. West	−0.8	−0.2				North	12.0	5.4

Source: Census of Employment.

percentage employment change 1971–81 by sector, Table 4.8 highlights the diversity of service industry response to manufacturing performance. Care in interpretation is required because percentage changes need to be viewed in the context of the size of individual sectors in the regional economy. For this reason absolute changes in employment are also shown in Table 4.8.

Bearing this caution in mind, it is clear that while East Anglia, the South West, and East Midlands had a consistently strong employment performance by national standards across all the private sectors of the economy, there were stark contrasts in performance in other regions. Most notable is the case of Northern Ireland where a disastrous manufacturing performance and sluggish producer service growth were redeemed by public sector employment growth, also possibly reflected in a growth in consumer services. In contrast, in the Northern Region a modest decline in manufacturing coincided with less strong producer, and poor consumer service growth. It is possible that the limited growth of the public sector acted as a constraint on the other service sectors. There are also other examples of divergent sectoral growth performance; reasonable producer service growth in the West Midlands and Yorkshire and Humberside seems out of tune with the ranking of the rest of their economies. Although the South East, because of its size, would dominate any ranking of absolute changes in employment, in relative terms the position of that region also varied considerably across the sectors.

4.5. THE CHANGING LOCATION OF PRODUCER SERVICE INDUSTRIES IN LOCAL LABOUR MARKETS

Of course the Economic Planning Region is a very coarse spatial unit with which to measure locational change. The location of producer services needs to be considered not only at the regional scale but also in terms of broad 'core–periphery' divisions of the national territory, in which the London metropolitan region clearly constitutes the core area, and between dominant and sub-dominant labour markets within metropolitan areas.

Table 4.9 and Fig. 4.3 present changes in the location of producer service industry employment between 1971 and 1981 using the CURDS classification of LLMAs. They confirm the impression of the previous section that at the national scale, *some limited spatial concentration took place during the 1970s. At each level in the urban hierarchy, LLMAs in the southern and eastern half of the country performed more*

Table 4.9. Change in Producer Service Industry Employment, 1971–1981

Class	LLMA[a]	Absolute change (000s)	Percentage change
1	L	2.8	0.2
2	CD	−38.1	−7.2
3	PD	42.7	17.4
4	SD	20.6	12.0
5	LSC	34.7	37.1
6	LST	61.3	44.1
7	CSC	20.6	15.6
8	CST	35.1	40.0
9	SNWS	24.8	30.0
10	SEFC	83.9	38.0
11	NWFC	27.8	13.8
12	SEST	31.0	30.4
13	SECT	28.4	29.5
14	SEMT	21.8	52.5
15	NWST	6.6	11.4
16	NWCT	10.7	12.9
17	NWMT	7.4	13.7
18	SERA	17.4	43.2
19	NWRA	12.6	19.7
GB		452.8	12.4

[a] For the definition of areas see Table 4.4.

Source: Census of Employment (NOMIS).

impressively in job generation terms than did their northern and western counterparts. Thus the London Dominant and Sub-dominant LLMAs out-performed their Conurbation counterparts, the Southern and Eastern Free-standing Cities and Towns did better than the Northern and Western Free-standing Cities and Towns, and the Southern and Eastern Rural Areas did better than the Northern and Western Rural Areas.

At the intra-regional scale, however, the pattern of change is both much more dramatic and involves a very marked relative deconcentration within metropolitan regions, frequently spilling over into the Free-standing Cities and Towns which surround them. In the case of the London area, the dominant LLMA experienced an increase in producer service industry employment between 1971 and 1981 of just 0.2%

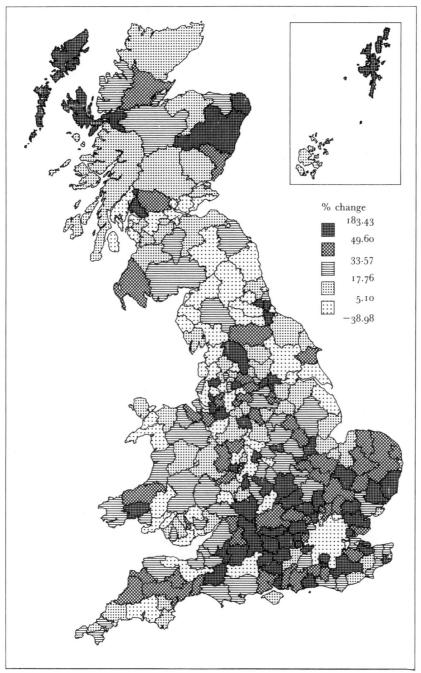

% change
183.43
49.60
33.57
17.76
5.10
−38.98

Source: Census of Employment (NOMIS)

FIG. 4.3. Percentage change in producer service industry employment by
local labour market, 1971–1981.

(compared with a GB average growth of 12.4%); the Sub-dominant Cities and Towns, however, grew by 37.1% and 44.1% respectively, adding 96,000 new jobs compared with less than 3,000 in the London LLMA itself. In the metropolitan regions based on the other conurbations, deconcentration was absolute as well as relative, with the dominants shedding more than 38,000 producer service jobs (−7.2%) while their sub-dominants grew by 55,700 employees (representing a 15.6%) growth in the Sub-dominant Cities and a 40% growth in the Towns. Taking these metropolitan areas as a whole, although both the London Metropolitan Region and the Conurbation Metropolitan Regions recorded overall growth in producer service employment (by 6.8% and 2.4% respectively), in both cases the national growth rate was not attained. Thus not only at the scale of the largest city LLMAs, but also when their functionally defined metropolitan regions are included, London and the Conurbations failed to maintain their share of national producer employment. While the Free-standing Cities and Towns in the north and west of Britain experienced growth very similar to the national average, in the south and east, similar places around London all recorded vibrant growth in producer industry employ-ment (Fig. 4.3). The Southern and Eastern Free-standing Cities grew by almost 84,000 jobs (38%), while an even higher growth (52.5%) was enjoyed by the Southern and Eastern Manufacturing Towns (a group which includes Milton Keynes).

Thus far we have considered urban changes in the spatial distribution of producer services in isolation from distributional trends in other types of employment. Table 4.10 attempts to provide this broader perspective by showing, firstly, the share of total employment in each LLMA group which is accounted for by producer service industries in 1971 and in 1981 and, secondly, by showing the changing pattern of over- and under-representation of producer service industry employment as measured by the location quotient. Although it was noted above that producer service employment change varied widely between the 19 LLMA groups (from a decline of 7.2% in the Conurbation Dominants to a growth of 52.5% in the Southern and Eastern Manufacturing Towns); relative to total employment producer service employment change was far less marked. In each of the 19 LLMA groups the producer service share of total employment grew. Nationally the share increased from 16.9% of total employment in 1971 to 19.5% in 1981. The increase in share varied between the 19 groups from only 0.3% in the Northern and Western Service Towns to 4.9% in the London Sub-dominant Towns.

In the London Dominant LLMA the share of total employment

Table 4.10. Change in Producer Service Industry Employment in Relation to Total Employment, 1971–1981

Class	LLMA[a]	%age of total		%age point change	LQ change	
		1971	1981		1971	1981
1	L	28.5	31.3	2.8	1.68	1.61
2	CD	19.4	20.6	1.2	1.15	1.06
3	PD	16.3	19.7	3.4	0.96	1.01
4	SD	15.0	17.7	2.7	0.88	0.91
5	LSC	16.4	20.4	4.0	0.97	1.04
6	LST	15.2	20.1	4.9	0.90	1.03
7	CSC	10.4	13.6	3.2	0.61	0.69
8	CST	10.0	14.5	4.5	0.60	0.74
9	SNWS	7.9	10.5	2.6	0.47	0.54
10	SEFC	15.3	19.3	4.0	0.90	0.99
11	NWFC	13.1	15.3	2.2	0.78	0.78
12	SEST	13.6	15.8	2.2	0.80	0.81
13	SECT	15.7	18.3	2.6	0.93	0.94
14	SEMT	10.8	14.8	4.0	0.64	0.76
15	NWST	14.1	14.4	0.3	0.83	0.74
16	NWCT	10.8	12.5	1.7	0.64	0.64
17	NWCT	8.9	11.0	2.1	0.53	0.56
18	SERA	13.3	18.1	4.8	0.79	0.93
19	NWRA	13.4	14.6	1.2	0.79	0.75
GB		16.9	19.5	2.6	1.00	1.00

[a] For the definition of areas see Table 4.4.

Source: Census of Employment (NOMIS).

accounted for by producer services grew more than the national average (from 28.5% to 31.3%), even though the capital was considerably more dependent on producer service employment than was the nation as a whole at the beginning of the period. As measured by the LQ, London's over-representation of producer service employment fell only marginally between 1971 and 1981 (from 1.68 to 1.61). In contrast, growth in the producer service industry share was much more sluggish in the Conurbation Dominant LLMAs, and their relative over-representation of producer service industry employment fell markedly over the period (from 1.15 in 1971 to 1.06 in 1981).

Other notable changes include the transition of the London

Sub-dominant Cities and Towns from under- to over-representation during the period. Their counterparts elsewhere, whilst also improving their position, remain severely under-represented in producer services (the LQ for the London Sub-dominant Cities stood at 1.04 in 1981, for example, compared with 0.69 in the Conurbation Sub-dominant Cities). In the non-metropolitan areas, considerable contrasts exist in the changing pattern of producer service representation between the north and west, and south and east of Britain. Although all of the non-metropolitan LLMAs in 1971 and 1981 had producer service LQs below 1.0, in the south and east of the country the degree of under-representation became less marked. In the north and west very little change was apparent. To provide one example, South Eastern and North Western Rural Areas had identical producer service LQs in 1971 (0.79); by 1981, however, the under-representation had diminished considerably in the Southern and Eastern case (LQ of 0.93), but had increased amongst the Northern and Western Rural Areas (LQ of 0.75).

In summary then, the main features of interest in the changing patterns of over- and under-representation of producer service industry employment are that:

(1) the London Metropolitan Region as a whole maintained its very marked over-concentration. A slight decline in the over-concentration of employment in the dominant LLMA was compensated for by the Sub-dominant LLMAs moving into a position of over-representation.

(2) the Conurbation Dominant LLMAs experienced declining levels of over-concentration in producer services; although the Sub-dominant Cities and Towns reduced their marked under-representation, the Conurbation Metropolitan Regions as a whole continue to have a lower share of producer service than of total employment;

(3) the degree of under-representation in producer services amongst non-metropolitan LLMAs was reduced substantially in the south and east of the country, while in the north and west there was no consistent pattern of change.

4.6. THE CHANGING LOCATION OF INDIVIDUAL PRODUCER SERVICE INDUSTRIES

It was observed above that in 1981 the business or information service sub-group was more unevenly distributed than producer services as a whole. Table 4.11 extends the change analysis to this sub-group. A number of comparisons can be made between the pattern of change in business service offices and in producer service industries as a whole. First, the decline of the London LLMAs' over-representation is more marked for business than for all producer services, although the level of concentration was higher to start with and remained higher throughout the period. Secondly, the fall in the over-representation of producer services in the Conurbation Dominants, which was observed in the previous section, does not apply to business services in which representation increased slightly in the Conurbation Dominants. For business services, like producer services at large, however, there was a similar trend towards intra-metropolitan region deconcentration. The sub-dominant LLMAs experienced an improving representation, although the Conurbation Sub-dominants displayed marked under-representation in 1981 especially of business services while London's Sub-dominants display over-representation (particularly of business services).

Table 4.11 also highlights the considerable diversity of producer service industry experience. Notwithstanding the considerable changes in producer service location between 1971 and 1981, insurance, banking, accountancy, legal services, and dealing in oil, coal, and building materials displayed few significant changes in their levels of under and over-representation. In the case of banking, for example, only 6 of the 19 groups experienced a change in LQ in excess of ±0.1.

The changing location of the financial sector deserves further comment because these industries are explored in a case study in Section 5.4. Insurance and banking became increasingly over-represented in Metropolitan Regions between 1971 and 1981, while the representation of other financial institutions in these areas tended to fall. In banking, London's LQ remained unchanged between 1971 and 1981, and though London's over-representation fell in insurance (LQ of 1.93 in 1971 and 1.73 in 1981) in both industries London's Sub-dominant LLMAs experienced an increasing representation of employment. The Conurbation Dominants increased their representation in banking and in both industries Provincial Dominant Cities increased their representation. This coincided with falling representation in locations outside metropolitan areas, particularly in the north and west. In contrast, the representation of other financial institutions (which includes building societies) in Free-standing Towns and Rural Areas, as well as Metropolitan Sub-dominants, has been growing while over-representation in Metropolitan Dominants has tended to fall.

In business services, property owning and managing, advertising,

Table 4.11. Changing Patterns of Over and Under-representation of Employment Amongst Individual Producer Service Industries, 1971–1981 (see key for explanation)[ab]

LLMA[c]	Business services sub-group		Business service offices	Insurance	Banking	Other financial institutions	Property own & management	Advertising and market research	Other business services	Central offices	Accountancy services	Legal services	Research and development	Other professional & scientific services	Wholesale distribution of food and drink	Wholesale distribution (petroleum products)	Other wholesale distribution	Dealing (coal, oil, builders materials)	Dealing (other industrial materials)
	1971	1981																	
L	2.04	1.85																	
CD	1.04	1.07																	
PD	0.92	0.99																	
SD	0.68	0.84																	
LSC	1.17	1.21																	
LST	0.99	1.05																	
CSC	0.44	0.58																	
CST	0.55	0.69																	

SNWS	0.35	0.40																	
SEFC	0.84	0.94																	
NWFC	0.59	0.63																	
SEST	0.82	0.84																	
SECT	0.78	0.78																	
SEMT	0.61	0.77																	
NWST	0.75	0.67																	
NWCT	0.48	0.50																	
NWMT	0.39	0.45																	
SERA	0.72	0.89																	
NWRA	0.72	0.63																	

[a] 'Up' arrows indicate an *increase* in representation, as reflected in the location quotient, equal to or in excess of 0.10. 'Down' arrows indicate a *decrease* in representation, equal to or in excess of 0.10 on the LQ.

[b] Solid arrows indicate LLMA groups with over-representation in the service in 1971 (i.e. LQ in excess of 1.0). Open arrows had an under representation in 1971.

[c] For the definition of areas see Table 4.4.

Source: Census of Employment (NOMIS).

and other business services there is a trend towards decentralization out of their core in the London metropolitan region into other metropolitan and non-metropolitan areas. Accountancy and research and development also display a process of deconcentration from larger urban areas, but this is contained largely within southern Britain. In contrast, in central offices London's position has remained stable while the Conurbation Dominants have experienced a sharp decline and moved from a position of over- to under-representation.

Again there is no simple pattern of change in distributive trades, though there is a decentralization of employment from locations of over-representation and a growth in under-represented areas. In wholesale distribution of food and drink, other wholesale distribution, and dealing in other industrial materials there is a decline in over-representation in major conurbations, but while this decentralization spills over into smaller centres and Rural Areas in the case of other wholesale distribution and dealing in other industrial materials, the representation of wholesale distribution of food and drink has declined in Southern and Eastern Rural Areas. Wholesale distribution of petroleum products is somewhat unusual in that only London and some southern and eastern labour markets and Northern and Eastern Rural Areas are over-represented in this service, but there has been an increase in its concentration in southern Britain between 1971 and 1981.

4.7. CHANGE IN THE URBAN DISTRIBUTION OF PRODUCER SERVICE INDUSTRIES BY SUB-PERIOD

Previous sections have considered the changing patterns of employment and of over- and under-representation for the 1971–81 period as a whole. In this final section we split the period into two, with 1978 constituting the break (Table 4.12). The relative deconcentration of producer service industries within the London and Conurbation Metropolitan Regions is seen to be considerably more apparent in the period up to 1978 than in the period following it. The vibrant growth of producer service industries in the Sub-dominant Cities and Towns, which had supported broad inter-regional concentration, is also primarily a feature of the first period. Between 1978 and 1981 growth in producer service employment slowed considerably in the southern and eastern LLMAs, while the modest growth rates experienced by the northern and western LLMAs tended to be maintained.

The national economic recession would seem to have put a brake

Table 4.12. Changes in Producer Service Industry Employment, 1971–1978 and 1978–1981

Class	LLMA[a]	Percentage change		Location quotients		
		1971–8	1978–81	1971	1978	1981
1	L	−1.8	2.0	1.68	1.68	1.61
2	CD	−4.8	−2.6	1.15	1.08	1.06
3	PD	12.6	4.2	0.96	1.01	1.01
4	SD	6.5	5.2	0.88	0.89	0.91
5	LSC	31.2	4.4	0.97	1.09	1.04
6	LST	31.5	9.6	0.90	1.02	1.03
7	CSC	13.4	1.9	0.61	0.66	0.69
8	CST	26.0	11.0	0.60	0.68	0.74
9	SNWS	18.1	10.0	0.47	0.50	0.54
10	SEFC	25.6	9.9	0.90	0.97	0.99
11	NWFC	7.8	5.5	0.78	0.77	0.78
12	SEST	20.6	8.1	0.80	0.81	0.81
13	SECT	21.8	6.3	0.93	0.96	0.94
14	SEMT	33.6	14.1	0.64	0.72	0.76
15	NWST	3.7	7.4	0.83	0.75	0.74
16	NWCT	6.5	6.0	0.64	0.62	0.64
17	NWMT	13.5	0.2	0.53	0.54	0.56
18	SERA	31.0	9.3	0.79	0.92	0.93
19	NWRA	8.3	10.5	0.79	0.74	0.75
GB		7.8	4.2	1.0	1.0	1.0

[a] For the definition of areas see Table 4.4.

Source: Census of Employment (NOMIS).

on those areas which had been experiencing rapid growth in producer service industry employment up to 1978. We can speculate that the recession resulted in many new projects—whether major *in situ* expansions, new ventures, or relocations—being temporarily shelved, producing the marked slow down in expansion in those investment destination areas—such as the Free-standing Towns and Cities of the south and east—which would otherwise have continued to grow. By dampening down the process of changing location through growth, the recession would thus appear to have slowed down the trend towards intra-metropolitan region deconcentration and to have all but halted the growth in southern and eastern LLMAs which created the broader concentration of producer service industries in the southern and eastern half of the country. The results of the 1984 Census of Employment will be needed to determine whether the changes after 1978 represent a temporary trend.

5

Case Studies of Producer Service Location

The previous chapter has emphasized the concentration of producer services in conurbations and especially the London metropolitan area. It also showed that there was a decentralization of these services during the 1970s, predominantly from conurbations to their hinterlands, but at a broad core–periphery scale there was also a modest increase in the concentration of producer services in the south and east of the country. There were, though, considerable differences in the degree of concentration of individual producer services and in their experience of decentralization. This suggests a disaggregated analysis of the locational experience of the sector is appropriate. In this chapter we present case studies of producer service activities based on literature reviews and interviews with dominant employers, professional associations, and trades unions. These aim to place the locational trends described in Chapter 4 in their economic, organizational, and technological context.

Producer Services in an International Context. Here we argue that producer service location should be understood in an international context. The activities of the City of London in international trade have an important bearing on the growth of producer services in the capital and surrounding areas and ultimately influence the balance between the concentration and decentralization of services to the provinces.

Non-Production Employment in Manufacturing. In Chapter 3 we described a symbiotic relationship between manufacturing and producer services. Here we develop this theme, concentrating on the implications of changes in corporate structure within manufacturing firms for the location of producer services.

Physical Distribution. Blue collar or physical distribution services are often neglected in studies of service location. We have argued in previous chapters (3 and 4) that goods-related services are unevenly distributed and that traditional explanations for service location which concentrate on variations in manufacturing demand seem most appropriate to these services. Here we explore the development of distributive trades and the factors influencing their location.

The Financial Sector. Financial services operate in relative independence from manufacturing. Here the organization and reorganization of major firms and the way they service consumer and related business markets is shown to have an important influence on the location of employment. The way information technology may change the demand for employment and the location of work is also explored.

Business Service Offices. These services have been the subject of most recent research. While firms are smaller than in financial services, we show that acquisition activity and subsequent reorganization have had an important influence on the location of these activities.

5.1. Producer Services in an International Context[1]

There can be little doubt that it is impossible to comprehend the role of producer services in the UK without an exploration of offshore markets. Yet frequently the role of international trade in the growing demand for services is ignored (Riddle, 1986). This case study provides an international context for Chapter 3 on structural change in the UK and for the case studies which follow, especially those devoted to the financial sector (Section 5.4) and to business service offices (Section 5.5). An increasing proportion of the output and organization of these services is devoted to international trading and there is some evidence, yet to be properly articulated, that increasing external orientation has significant locational consequence within the UK.

After considering in broad terms some of the trends in international trade in services, there follows a more detailed examination of the pivotal role of the City of London, using accounting services as an example. The deregulation of the financial, securities, and other markets in the City in October 1986 (the so-called 'Big Bang') has introduced uncertainties about whether the recent trend towards expansion of employment in producer services in the City of London will continue. The exposure of the UK financial and other services to competition and take-over by overseas firms could lead to a decline of their role as employers, both in the UK and international financial markets. On the other hand the injection of foreign capital could open up new markets and provide new management expertise for UK companies. It is clearly not possible to explore these issues in this case study but they would certainly be worth closer scrutiny in any programme for further research on producer services, the City, and the development of the UK space economy.

International trade in services

Figures on international trade in services are notoriously unreliable (Petit, 1986; Noyelle, 1986). However, it has to be assumed that the available figures do reflect underlying trends. Given that this is the case the data suggest that the internationalization of the output of producer services is a relatively recent phenomenon. Services as a whole remain the least internationalized sector in world trade (Table 5.1) even though their overall share of world GDP exported

[1] This section has been prepared as part of an ESRC project (Grant HR D0023 2194) on the 'Location Behaviour of Large Professional Producer Service Firms in Britain'.

Table 5.1.   Internationalization of the World Economy

Sector	1970		1980	
	World GDP (billion $)	Exports as % of GDP	World GDP (billion $)	Exports as % of total GDP
Agriculture	181.9	31.8	602.8	45.3
Mining and manufacturing	726.7	29.9	2,769.5	55.0
Services	1,457.6	6.9	5,644.0	10.8
TOTAL	2,366.2	15.9	9,016.3	26.7

Source: Clairmonte and Cavanagh (1984), (UNCTAD data).

increased from 16% to 27% between 1970 and 1980 (Clairmonte and Cavanagh, 1984).

Service *exports* expanded from 6.9% to 10.8% of the service sector's GDP during the same period. Producer services as a sub-group tend to have the largest foreign income as a share of total revenues in countries such as the USA. In 1981, 23% of US financial services revenues had foreign origins; some 15% of computer and data processing; 9% of insurance; 7% of consulting and management; and 22% of equipment lending and rental.

Just six countries (USA, France, UK, W. Germany, Belgium/Luxemburg) accounted for more than 50% of the $585 billion worth of service exports in 1981. The UK and USA have the largest surpluses, and Japan, W. Germany, and Saudi Arabia the largest deficits on service accounts.

Estimates suggest that 18% of world *trade* in 1983 was in services with 7.5% of all trade taking place in 'other' services i.e. financial, consultancy, and similar services (Key, 1985). The average annual growth of trade in the latter between 1968 and 1983 (current dollar prices) has also been higher than for any other trade (Table 5.2).

Clairmonte and Cavanagh (1984) argue that aggregate statistics like these cannot provide much assistance in improving our understanding of the growth and prospects of trade in (producer) services. They suggest that this understanding can only be achieved by examining changing institutional power relations in the global service economy. Certainly it is clear that the internationalization of producer services is not just a product of the growth/marketing strategies of specialist national suppliers. It is intimately associated with the development of multinational corporations (MNCs) with interests spanning primary, secondary, and teriary sectors. These corporations are primarily a product of the period since the early 1960s when manufacturing and service MNCs at first grew in

Table 5.2.   World Trade in Services, 1983

	Goods		Services[a]		
	Manufactures	Other	Transport	Travel[b]	Other[c]
% total world trade in goods and services	49.0	33.0	6.0	4.5	7.5
Average annual growth rates (%) 1968–83[d]	11.0	11.8	10.8	11.5	14.3

[a] Excluding government transactions.
[b] Including business travel and tourism.
[c] Including financial services, consultancy.
[d] Current dollar prices.

Source: Key (1985).

parallel (but at different rates) and then more recently, have begun to coalesce. By 1982 the world's top 200 MNCs had combined sales exceeding $3 trillion (or equivalent to one third of the world's GDP) with 82 service MNCs (Schwamm and Mericia, 1985) accounting for $1.2 trillion of these sales revenues (Table 5.3).

Table 5.3.   The Top 200 Manufacturing and Service MNCs, 1982[a]

Country	Service MNCs		Manufacturing MNCs	
	Number	% of total revenues	Number	% of total revenues
United States	30	32.9	50	49.1
Japan	21	40.9	14	9.2
United Kingdom	9	8.4	9	8.9
W. Germany	4	3.8	13	8.8
France	9	7.8	7	4.8
Netherlands	—	—	4	4.6
Italy	1	0.8	4	4.0
Canada	5	3.2	2	0.9
Brazil	1	0.7	1	1.0
Spain	—	—	2	1.2
Switzerland	—	—	2	1.1
Israel	2	1.3	—	—
Others	—	—	10	6.4
TOTAL	82	100 ($1,192,067)	118	100 ($3,045,679)

[a] A service MNC derives over half its revenues from services; a manufacturing MNC derives half its revenues from manufacturing.

Source: Clairmonte and Cavanagh (1984).

MNCs have diversified as corporate capital seeks new outlets to sustain profitability; and three main types can now be identified: (1) multinational service corporations specializing in one service product; (2) multinational service conglomerates involving banking, insurance, and other financial services or advertising, public relations, the media and telecommunications which are beginning to develop and finally; (3) multinational integral conglomerates (MICs) such as R. J. Reynolds Industries Inc. (US) with interests in cigarette production from plantation to marketing, in shipping, in petroleum, and in lending money to any strong, well-established business are the ultimate in national and international corporate organizations (Clairmonte and Cavanagh, 1984).

International trade in services from a UK perspective

A useful starting point in relation to the UK is the paper by Key (1985) which, although suggesting that services as a whole have performed less well in recent years, indicates that producer services (especially financial services) made a significant contribution to the surplus of trade in the UK services between 1960 and 1980. While a decline in this surplus set in after 1981, banking and 'other' services increased their net exports.

For the UK the growth in the value of service *exports* was greater than that for imports until the late 1970s; thereafter import values have grown faster. However, when the figures are disaggregated (Fig. 5.1) the trends are less consistent. Note that financial and 'other' services have steadily increased their contribution to the account. A more detailed breakdown of UK exports and imports of services is given in Table 5.4.

The UK's share of world exports (by value) of other services (financial services, consultancy, etc.) has declined from 13.9% in 1968 to 8.2% in 1983 (Key, 1985). This surprising trend almost exactly matches the rate of decline in the share of world exports of manufacturing; the main difference being that imports of services have grown more slowly than for manufactures.

But since 1974 the UK's surplus of trade in non-transport producer services has grown rapidly and by 1984 was equivalent to almost 3% of GDP (£6 billion). That said, the value of total UK exports of financial services (about 3.1%) was much the same in 1984 as in 1974. In real terms, Key shows that exports of financial services may have risen by only 0.1% per annum (but it is important to recognize that volume measures in these areas are inevitably unreliable) (Table 5.5).

The contribution of different producer services to exports can be

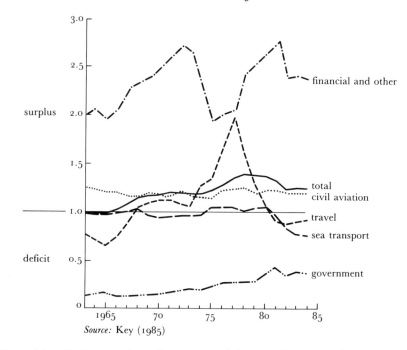

FIG. 5.1. Relative value of exports and imports in categories of services.

Table 5.4. UK Exports and Imports of Services, 1974 and 1985

Services	Exports			Imports		
	1974[a]	1984	Average annual real growth[b]	1974	1984	Average annual real growth
Sea transport	12	4	−8.7	10	5	−5.6
Air transport	3	3	6.3	2	3	8.1
Tourism	4	3	0.2	3	5	10.0
Financial and other	10	11	2.4	4	5	1.5
Government	—	—	1.9	2	2	1.4
TOTAL	29	23	—	21	19	1.5

[a] Share of total value (%).
[b] It is difficult to obtain entirely satisfactory measures of volume in services. Little significance should therefore be attached to small differences in real growth rate.

Source: Key (1985).

Table 5.5.   UK Exports of Financial Services, 1974–1984[a]

Financial service	'Real' average growth rate, % per annum
Insurance	−3.9
Banking[b]	6.8
Commodity trading	−5.0
Export houses	1.9
Other brokerage	0.9
TOTAL	0.1

[a] Earnings net of overseas expenses of institutions concerned.

[b] Excluding earnings on services provided to related firms overseas.

Source: Key (1985).

broadly assessed. UK banks have achieved a steady increase in export earnings and London continues, but only just, to be holding its position in the major world financial markets (Reed, 1983). The future for bank export earnings will depend on a number of factors such as: the extent to which the banks will be prepared to take on business with countries which have international debt problems; the effect of tighter supervision of capital requirements (this has ecouraged more off balance sheet business, so making market share measurement more difficult); the extent to which the banks move into the provision of new services, encouraged by the opportunities offered by information technology.

Overseas earnings from the services provided by insurance and other brokerage have been lower than in banking for the last decade. Increased foreign competition from 'Lloyds-type' exchanges and protectionism abroad are thought to be contributory factors (Manser, 1985). The UK share of securities trading has also diminished as part of the market for the shares of large UK companies has moved to the USA where they are traded as American Depository Receipts (absence of stamp duty means that transaction costs are lower).

The market for UK consultancy services seems to have peaked in 1978 and has now levelled out at a £1.4 billion contribution to the current account in 1983 (at current prices). With many of these exports going to Middle East and developing countries, the decline in OPEC oil revenues may limit the scope for any return to the level of performance recorded in 1978.

The scale of international trade in, mainly, UK producer services should not be overstated; 'only a fairly small proportion of the services sector is internationally traded' (Key, 1985). Nor should it be assumed that (producer) services will provide a growing trade surplus to replace any decline in revenues from oil or domestic manufacturing. Certainly, the UK's surplus on international trade in services has increased steadily (especially during the late 1970s) but we should not assume that this is an inexorable trend or a fixed component in UK international trade. Just as trade in goods is affected by fluctuations in the exchange rate, so services are similarly affected. Hence, although the surplus in value terms increased between 1978 and 1982; it deteriorated in volume terms because of the rise in sterling's real exchange rate.

The impact of international trade in services on the UK: the City

The geographical questions arising from the relatively recent emergence of international trade in producer services revolve around its impact on occupational structure, employment, and location of economic activities in the countries participating in such trade. In the case of the UK there is already some evidence to suggest that London and the South East experience the most tangible impacts (e.g. Dunning and Norman, 1983; Thrift, 1985; Daniels, 1986). Most of these impacts will be filtered through the City of London.

The City of London is a major participant in international trade in producer servies. It is especially important as a node in the circulation of commercial capital which mediates the circulation of commodities for a fee. Thrift (1986*a*) identifies four main groups of organizations and practices comprising commercial capital: commodity exchanges (including real estate) and the more recently developed futures markets; monetary exchanges; dealers in securities (often via stock exchanges), and the sale of corporate services of which the most important is non-life insurance and reinsurance. The role of the City as the premier national centre for the activities representing commercial capital has recently been boosted by the growth of international commodity, monetary, securities dealing, and insurance services. This internationalization has been encouraged by earlier trends in the same direction by industrial and banking (or interest-bearing) capital. These points are expanded upon below.

The City has reigned supreme amongst centres of international commercial capital since the eighteenth century (see McRae and Cairncross, 1984). By 1832 the City had already taken on much of its present form with, for example, the discount houses in place as well as several of the 'classical' fixed markets. Already in that year Nathan Rothschild could observe that 'this country in general is the Bank for the whole world ... all transactions in India, in China, in

Germany, in Russia, and in the whole world, are guided here and settled through this country' (cited in Ingham, 1984). The City's international role meant that it was becoming divorced from the British domestic economy—it had little to do with the industrial revolution or subsequent developments. And by the turn of the century this divorce was almost complete. From 1865 to 1913, 'income from interest and dividends on foreign investments, from shipping credits, insurance, banking, and the financing of foreign trade increased from a total of around £80 million to £340 million' (Ingham, 1984), moving the UK's balance of payments into surplus. The City's earnings declined relatively before the Second World War, mainly because of the worldwide depression. They then increased again after the War was over, mainly because of an increasing foreign presence in the City. The form of the City's institutions is not immutable but Table 5.6 attempts to summarize its present state. Numerous introductions to the City exist, which would make a longer summary superfluous (e.g. Wilson Committee, 1980; Coakley and Harris, 1983; McRae and Cairncross, 1984; Harris, 1985; Plender and Wallace, 1985; Clark, 1986; De Montfort Publishing, 1986).

By 1983 the total overseas earnings of the City stood at £5,378 million, with £2,754 million of this amount coming directly from the fee-earning activities of commercial services. The City controlled assets double the size of Britain's GDP (Harris, 1985). Arguably, the City is still the world's leading international financial centre, despite a strong challenge from New York in the 1970s and 1980s (Table 5.7). The City has been able to retain its supremacy as the chief nexus of a number of markets including:

1. *The insurance market.* London is still the major international insurance centre in the world, despite a strong challenge from New York (which is still mainly concerned with domestic insurance). It has retained its position by actively developing the world re-insurance market and encouraging, to a limited degree, foreign names and insurance companies (see Manser, 1985). Already, by 1978 the City's annual premium income had overtaken the gross domestic product of New Zealand (McRae and Cairncross, 1984).

2. *The money and capital markets.* London is one of the largest of the foreign exchange markets handling about $90 billion worth of currencies per day. It is also the major node of the Eurocurrency market. Of the $2,500 billion of Eurocurrency extant in the world in September 1985, 31% was on the books of banks based in London (Table 5.8). The City is also a major centre for the issuing of Eurobonds, and it also commands 75% of secondary trading in these bonds (Montagnon, 1986).

Table 5.6. The Structure of the City of London: Basic Commercial Practices and Institutions

Commodity	Practices	Institutional structure	Organizations
Money	Arranging loans, clearing	Wholesale money markets; foreign exchange markets, etc.	Overseas banks Discount houses Merchant banks (including accepting houses); Arms of clearing banks, Foreign exchange dealers
Securities	Issuing, broking, jobbing	Stock Exchange, Eurobond market, etc.	Issuing houses; Stockbrokers and jobbers
Commodities	Merchanting, broking	Various commodity markets and exchanges (e.g. LIFFE, LME) and other more diffuse markets	Brokers associates Merchant banks, etc.
Services (a) Insurance	Underwriting, broking, marketing	Lloyds and other more diffuse markets	Lloyds, Insurance companies
(b) Freight	Chartering, Lloyds Shipping Register etc.	Baltic Exchange	Chartering companies
(c) Accountancy, legal services, advertising, public relations, tax consultants and advisers, management consultants, etc.	Adjudicating, publicizing, minimizing costs of exchange, etc.	Diffuse markets	Relevant companies

Source: Derived from Ingham (1984).

Table 5.7.   Status of the Three Major Financial Centres

	No. foreign banks	No. foreign stock exchange members	No. foreign dealers in government banks	Share international banking market (%)	Share foreign exchange turnover (1984)	Stock market turnover (£bn)	Stock market capitalization (£bn)
London	399	22	12	24.9	32.6	52.8	244.7
New York	254	33	2	15.0	22.3	671.3	302.2
Tokyo	76	6	29	9.1	5.3	271.5	648.7

Source: Price (1986).

Table 5.8. The Growth of London as a Banking Centre, 1970–1986

	1970	1975	1980	1984
Number of foreign banks directly represented through a representative office, a branch office, or a subsidiary	163	263	353	400
Number of foreign banks, indirectly represented through a share in a joint venture or a consortium bank	—	72	50	47
Total number of foreign banks directly or indirectly represented	163	335	403	447
Number of foreign securities houses (dealers in bonds and securities)	—	—	—	104
Numbers employed by foreign banks and foreign securities houses in London	11,813	20,881	31,132	53,833

Source: The Banker, various issues.

3. *The commodity markets.* London still leads the other international financial centres in a number of commodity markets such as gold bullion. However, the largest commodities markets now are futures markets. Of these futures markets, the largest is the Chicago Mercantile Exchange but this is still mainly a domestic market, although its International Monetary Market, dealing in financial futures, has had enormous influence. The largest international futures markets are in New York and London. London has the edge in cocoa, sugar, and coffee futures but New York has taken the lead in many other futures. For example, COMEX in New York is easily the largest market in the world for gold futures. In the early 1980s, however, London responded to the challenge of Chicago and New York by setting up a range of new futures exchanges including the London Gold Futures Market and The Lonon International Financial Futures Exchange (LIFFE).

4. *The service centre.* As a centre of services, especially accountancy and legal services, the City of London is still pre-eminent. The fortunes of many people in Britain now rely on the continuing success of the commercial activities of the City of London (Table 5.9) (King, forthcoming). The judicious use of social exclusion, the constant creation of new credit money markets (such as Eurocurrency markets), and allowing the selective entry of foreign institutions have so far enabled the City to retain its position as the leading international financial centre, unbolstered by any significant

Table 5.9.   Employment in the City of London, 1981

SIC[a]	Employment	
	No.	%
Forestry	20	0.005
Fishing	18	0.005
Coal extraction and manufacturing of solid fuel	27	0.007
Extraction of mineral oil and natural gas	1,346	0.345
Mineral oil processing	850	0.218
Production and distribution of electricity	2,648	0.679
Water supply industry	10	0.003
Extraction and preparation of metalliferous ores	6	0.002
Metal manufacturing	189	0.055
Manufacture of non-metallic mineral products	301	0.077
Chemical industry	609	0.153
Manufacture of metal goods nec	196	0.077
Mechanical engineering	1,238	0.316
Other machinery and mechanical equipment	458	0.117
Manufacture of office machinery and data processing equipment	1,027	0.263
Electrical and electronic engineering	1,540	0.395
Manufacture of motor vehicles and parts	7	0.002
Manufacture of other transport equipment	396	0.102
Instrument engineering	399	0.103
Food, drink and tobacco manufacturing industries	1,312	0.385
Textile industry	107	0.027
Manufacture of leather & leather goods	144	0.036
Footwear and clothing industries	904	0.232
Timber and wooden furniture industries	137	0.036
Manufacture of paper and paper products, printing, and publishing	31,055	7.954
Processing of rubber and plastics	378	0.096
Other manufacturing industries	268	0.069
Construction	3,514	0.899
Wholesale distribution	13,343	3.416
Dealing in scrap and waste materials	19	0.005
Retail distribution	6,900	1.791
Hotels and catering	10,059	2.576
Repair of consumer goods and vehicles	106	0.412
Other inland transport	2,034	0.521
Supporting services to transport	1,421	0.620
Miscellaneous transport services and storage	7,612	1.950
Postal services and telecommunications	35,509	9.095
Banking and bill discounting	76,865	19.694
Other financial institutions	8,768	2.246

Table 5.9.   (*Continued*)

SIC[a]	Employment	
	No.	%
Insurance, not compulsory social security	25,916	6.638
Activities auxiliary to banking and finance	10,731	2.748
Activities auxiliary to insurance	15,814	4.050
House and estate agents	952	0.244
Legal services	13,852	3.548
Accountants, auditors, tax experts	14,264	3.653
Professional and technical services (other)	5,401	1.383
Advertising	2,676	0.685
Business Services	19,075	4.885
Computer services	2,928	0.740
Business services nec	8,068	2.060
Central offices not allocable elsewhere	8,079	2.070
Renting of moveables	280	0.071
Public administration, national defence, and compulsory social security	21,215	5.432
Sanitary services	10,436	2.472
Education	5,083	1.302
Medical and other health services, veterinary services	4,479	1.146
Other services provided to general public	4,414	1.131
Recreational services and other cultural services	1,936	0.495
Personal services	540	0.137
Diplomatic representation	47	0.012
Unclassified by industry	229	0.059
TOTAL	390,444	100.0

[a] Standard industrial classification, 1980.
Source: Census of Employment, 1981.

national market. As Manser (1985, p. 115) points out with respect to the London insurance markets:

It is important to distinguish between the 'UK market' and the 'London market'. The UK market is no more than a market of national insurers ... The London market is much more than a geographical expression. It is an international insurance centre which, apart from certain advantages of language and communications, is based in London largely by historical accident ... The speciality of London is (international) finance, where that of Detroit is motor manufacture and that of Dusseldorf is steel.

But as some of the examples above make clear, London is feeling the chill winds of competition from other international financial centres.

These have already forced it to deregulate many of its activities, as shown by the changes in the domestic securities markets brought about by the 'Big Bang'. It can never expect to again be unambiguously the world's major international financial centre. It is no surprise then that just as foreign firms based in other international financial centres have moved their operations into the City or bought into City firms in the lead up to the 'Big Bang' (Table 5.10); so City based firms are moving their operations into other international financial centres abroad or buying into them to ensure that they are not left behind in the race for these centres' business. The City firms are trying to make sure that they are represented in each and every significant international financial centre.

The City's major commercial firms have been internationalizing since the turn of the century. But it has been in the 1970s and 1980s that they have seriously moved overseas. The impacts of this movement on other international financial centres have been quite substantial and have actually rebounded on London. New York, for example, owes much of its success as a foreign exchange trading centre to an influx of British-owned broking firms, with their expertise and contacts, into the city in the 1970s. In another example, London's major corporate lawyers (43 in the City, 101 in London as a whole)[2] have extensively internationalized in the last fifteen years with a resultant concentration of their offices in particular international financial centres (*Investors Chronicle*, 1984). Stone James Stephen Jaques now has offices in New York, Sydney, Perth, and Canberra, while Linklaters and Paines has offices in New York, Paris, Brussels, and Hong Kong. In Singapore 23 foreign law firms now have offices. Nine of these firms are based in the City of London. Thus pockets of the City of London can now be found in all major international financial centres.

Clearly, however, there is a need for more detailed case studies of particular forms of internationalization (see Thrift, 1985; 1986*b*). The next section provides a survey of the internationalization of one key sector of the City—accountancy.

Accountancy

The accountancy profession adjudicates exchange for a fee. It informs shareholders of an industrial or banking company what they have received in exchange for their investment. It allows creditors to

---

[2] Numbers noted here relate to firms that serve one or more of *The Times* 500 companies.

Table 5.10. Foreign Purchases of City Stockbrokers and Stockjobbers, 1981–1985

Banks and financial groups	Brokers	Jobbers
Citicorp (US)	Vickers da Costa (11/83)	
	Scrimgeour Kemp Gee (8/84)	
	J. & E. Davy (7/85)	
Chase Manhattan (US)	Laurie Millbank (11/84)	
	Simon and Coates (11/84)	
Shearson Lehman/ American Express (US)	L. Messel (7/84)	
Security Pacific (US)	Hoare Govett (6/82)	C. T. Dulley (7/84)
Merrill Lynch (US)		A. B. Giles & Cresswell (6/85)
Dow Scania (US)	Savory Miln (9/84)	
North Carolina National Bank (US)	Panmure Gordon (12/84)	
Canadian Imperial Bank of Commerce (Can.)	Grenfell & Colegrave (4/85)	
Orion Royal Bank (Can.)	Kitcat & Aitken (2/85)	
Hong Kong & Shanghai Bank	James Capel (8/84)	
Union Bank of Switzerland (Switz.)	Phillips and Drew (11/84)	
Credit Suisse First Boston (US/Switz.)	Buckmaster & Moore (1/85)	
Bank Centrade (Switz.)	R. Nivison (6/85)	
Banque Bruxelles Lambert (Belg.)	Williams de Broe Hill Chaplin (12/84)	
BAII (Lux.)	Sheppards & Chase (5/85)	
National and City (—)	Dillon and Waldron (9/84)	
FBD Insurance (Ire.)	Maguire McCann Morrison (5/85)	
Smurfit Paribas (Ire.)	Doak & Co. (7/85)	
Credit Commercial de France (Fra.)	Laurence Prust (6/85)	
Paribas (Fr.)	Quitter Goodison (9/85) (from Skandia, Sweden)	
Gironzentrale (Aus.)	Gilbert Eliott & Co. (5/85)	

Note: Figures in brackets denote the date of purchase of brokers/jobbers by banks and financial groups.

Source: Hamilton, 1986, compiled from table 10, pp. 138–9.

assess the security of their claims. It also helps the state to decide whether the revenues it receives from the company are sufficient.

The profession of chartered or public accountancy is relatively recent. Originally, it came into being as a profession in Great Britain from the 1850s onwards as a result of state action; the introduction of the companies acts and the bankruptcy acts. But it was not formally recognized as a profession by Royal Charter until 1880 (Jones, 1981). The industry internationalized early on. In the decades following the US Civil War, British chartered accountants crossed the Atlantic to monitor British capital investment in the United States:

By protecting shareholders and maintaining investor confidence, account-ants performed the primary service of stimulating capital accumulation in the United States in the early twentieth century. The (British) firm of Marwick Mitchell helped J. P. Morgan avert a bank collapse and restore investor confidence in the Knickerbocker Trust Co., thereby ending the panic of 1907. The State's ratification of an income tax constitutional amendment in 1913 led to a substantial increase in demand for professional accountacy services, as did the call for official accounting standards and guidelines by the Federal Trade Commission and the Federal Reserve Board. But it was the stock market crash of 1929 and the Securities Acts of 1933 and 1934 that produced the largest growth in the demand for accountants. Peat, Marwick, Mitchell's experience provides some indica-tion of the magnitude of this growth. In 1947, the firm's revenues stood at less than $10 million; by 1981 revenues had reached $979 million. British accounting experienced a comparable growth as a result of the 1948 Companies Act; Britain today (with some 100,000 chartered and certified accountants) has more accountants per head than any other advanced capitalist county. (Tinker, 1984)

Other overseas links were also forged by British chartered accountants at an early date. For example, by 1939 the ancestors of the modern-day firm of Ernst Whinney had made arrangements with accountancy firms in Australia, New Zealand, South Africa, Canada, France, Germany, Spain, Gilbraltar, Malta, Turkey, South America, and the Far East (Jones, 1981). Most of these links had been forged in order to keep contact with the expansion of British companies abroad.

The core of the accountancy business is still the audit. An audit is a summary of the economic transactions of a firm made for a fee. Typically, a large corporation makes millions of transactions in any year, so audits are concerned with designing a sample frame that captures the significant features of these transactions. This requires a three phase exercise. The first phase involves the assessment of the quality of the internal controls of corporations to check if the corporation can be audited. The second phase consists of tests for errors in the corporations recording of transactions (e.g. matching shipping documents to invoices). In the final phase additional testing is carried out (Stevens, 1982). The fees involved are substantial and £1 billion of fee income are on offer in Britain alone each year, so competition is harsh.

Recently three trends have touched the accountant's world. The first trend has been automation (Barras and Swann, 1984a). Computers and modern telecommunications have affected both the work performed for clients (for audit, etc.), and the internal organization of the firm (through the adoption of word processors and other office machines which have the effect of increasing the ratio of professional to administrative staff). The second trend is diversification out of auditing into other services. Tax consultancy was an early favourite. Management consultancy and related business services (e.g. insolvency) are the current major areas of expansion in Britain since it is but a short step from auditing a firm to offering advice on financial management and corporate strategy (Table 5.11). The success of these large accountancy firms in these markets can be gauged by the fact that Coopers and Lybrand now claims to be, on the basis of the number of professional staff employed, the largest management consultancy firm in the UK (*Investors Chronicle*, 1985). But the largest accountancy firms are now diversifying even further. In the UK, Deloitte Haskins and Sells

Table 5.11. Fee Income of UK Accountancy Firms

Firm	Practice area (%)				
	Audit	Tax	MAS[a]	Insolvency	Other
Coopers & Lybrand	32	14	23	11	20
Peat Marwick Mitchell	53	12	10	7	20
Arthur Young	45	27	9	7	12
Touche Ross	60	20	12	8	0
Arthur Anderson	48	27	25	—[b]	0
KMG Thompson McLintock	62	17	10	5	6
Spicer and Pegler	56	19	5	7	13
Binder Hamlyn	50	22	10	4	14
Deardon Farrow	48	25	—[c]	4	2
Grant Thornton	53	18	14	15	0
MEAN	51	20	13	8	9

[a] Management Advisory Services.
[b] Included in audit total.
[c] Member of Annan Impey Morrish, Management Consultants group.

Source: UK Accounting Bulletin (1985) Table 2.

has set up a financial services division and many of its activities are now close to those of merchant banking. Other avenues opened up include services to central and local government, development consultancy, charity consultancy, and so on.

The third trend is litigation. Most accountancy firms are run as partnerships but this form of organization is now coming under considerable strain as they become subject to more and more law suits from creditors alleging careless auditing practice after companies go bust. In the United States suits against accountants are running at one a day. But even in less litigious countries accountants are now being sued. The result is that insurance cover is becoming increasingly hard to obtain and much more expensive. It is quite possible that, as a result of this pressure, the larger accountancy firms may become limited companies, so protecting the partners from personal bankruptcy.

The accountancy profession is dominated worldwide by a few very large firms operating in most of the significant national markets. These accountancy multinationals dominate the game and have a significant market share in most countries around the world. The largest accountancy multinationals are often referred to as the 'big nine'. In 1984 the big nine firms audited 78% of the 250 leading international companies (Cairns, Lafferty, and Mantle, 1984). The big nine have extensively penetrated many national markets (Tables 5.12 and 5.13) including the UK (Table 5.14). In 1981 the big nine employed 170,000 people worldwide in some 2,000 offices in more than 100 countries (Table 5.15). In the United States alone the big nine had over 15,000 partners and employed 30,000 Certified Public Accountants. The firms employ enough lawyers to be regarded as some of the largest firms in the world and enough management consultants to be regarded as amongst the world's largest management consultancy firms (Stevens, 1985; Tinker, 1984). In other words, they are all 'multinational service conglomerates' (Clairmonte and Cavanagh, 1984).

Most of these conglomerates have become multinational via a process of merger with firms in other countries, or via arrangements to refer business to firms in other countries rather than through straightforward takeover, or establishment of an office in a country from scratch. For these reasons, the largest accountancy firms operate a number of modes of organization of their worldwide operations. At one end of the spectrum, some firms strive for their integration via an overarching 'world firm', which integrates the flow of world services and partners on secondment, and offers a common name in all countries. At the other end of the spectrum, other firms operate as loosely structured federations, referring

Table 5.12. The Big Nine Worldwide, 1985

Firm	Fee income ($m)	No. of countries	No. of offices	No. of partners	No. of professional staff	All other Staff	Total staff
Arthur Anderson	1,574	47	191	1,630	21,336	6,836	29,802
Peat Marwick Mitchell	1,445	89	335	2,533	20,482	6,849	29,864
Coopers and Lybrand	1,410	98	519	2,850	N.A.	N.A.	36,000
Price Waterhouse	1,234	95	378	2,113	20,656	7,603	30,372
Ernst and Whinney	1,185	77	359	2,199	17,201	5,600	25,000
Arthur Young	1,060	68	370	2,560	17,640	6,600	26,800
Touche Ross	973	90	463	2,550	17,550	5,950	26,000
Deloitte Haskins and Sells	953	63	433	2,125	16,621	5,266	24,012
Klynveld Main Geordler	N.A.[a]	73	487	3,215	19,300	12,817	29,766

[a] In 1983, fee income was estimated as $1m (International Accounting Bulletin, 1983).

Table 5.13. Markets Controlled by the Big Nine, 1971–1980

| | Proportion of audit clients served by Big 9 (%) | | |
	1971[a]	1976[a]	1980
Australia	32	37	71
Canada	42	58	99
UK	72	76	86
US	95	96	99

[a] Figures for 1971 and 1976 refer to 'Big 8' as Klynveld Main Goerdler was not formed until 1978/9.

Source: Bavishi and Wyman (1983).

business internationally to other firms in the network as and when that business arises. But the primary reason for the setting up of an international network of firms has not changed. It is still essentially a matter of orientation to clients.

More and more, bidders with the strongest presence in all the world's commercial centres win the multinational accounts. For this reason there is great pressure ... to expand internationally by passing money and talent into overseas offices or by merging with established firms in Europe, Asia and the Americas. (Stevens, 1982)

Thus, it is vital for an accountancy firm dealing with a large multinational corporation to be able to offer a worldwide network of offices and especially offices in the big international financial centres where most of the corporate action still is. Bids for audit accounts often stress the layout of office locations. Thus Stevens (1982) discusses a Peat Marwick Mitchell bid for the Caltex audit:

The proposal was designed in fourteen sections. Key segments covered the greater glory of Peat Marwick International, the firm's oil industry experience, an overlay map of Peat and Caltex locations worldwide a review of the audit scope, and a description of PMM's consulting and tax services.

Alternatively, the overseas experience of partners within a large accountancy firm can be useful reservoir of experiences. Thus:

When Ernst and Whinney won the National Coal Board audit this year, it produced back-up documentation which outdid many a glossy US corporate offering in its style and presentation. And the firm also pulled in US partners with experience at coal audits over there (*Investors Chronicle*, 1985).

Table 5.14. The top 20 Accountancy Firms in the UK, 1986

Firm	Fee income (£m)	No. of offices	No. of partners	No. of professional staff	No. of other staff	Total staff
Coopers & Lybrand[a]	119.4	37	267	3,245	1,192	4,704
Peat Marwick Mitchell[a]	114.4	42	259	3,600	867	4,728
Price Waterhouse[a]	108.9	20	247	2,722	NA	NA
Deloitte Haskins & Sells[a]	99.3	28	251	3,002	888	4,141
Ernst & Whinney[a]	82.9	23	202	2,476	866	3,544
Touche Ross[a]	76.5	22	205	2,040	62	2,807
Arthur Young[a]	75.0	23	205	2,313	733	3,151
Arthur Anderson[a]	67.1	16	121	1,555	505	2,181
Grant Thornton	58.0	55	255	2,139	672	3,066
KMG Thompson McLintock[a]	52.5	22	148	1,811	453	2,412
Spicer & Pegler	44.8	29	156	1,459	539	2,154
Binder Hamlyn	36.2	24	137	1,291	383	1,721
Pannell Kerr Forster	31.2	36	166	1,220	194	1,580
Clark Whitehill	23.5	13	188	1,151	293	1,632
Stoy Hayward	21.2	8	83	789	213	1,085
Deordon Farrow	19.7	17	93	615	203	911
Neville Russell	18.8	21	75	552	250	877
Moore Stephens	17.5	34	108	602	221	991
Robson Rhodes	17.5	14	77	580	NA	NA
Hodgson Impey	16.5	22	84	561	214	859

[a] Representatives of the big nine.

Source: The Accountant (1986).

Table 5.15. Number of Offices and Total Number of Partners of the Top 13 International Firms by Location, 1981

City	No. of offices	No. of partners
New York	16	1104
London	19	823
Toronto	17	574
Chicago	12	549
Los Angeles	12	329
Sydney	13	315
Paris	21	288
Montreal	13	286
Houston	12	280
Washington	14	265
Tokyo	14	258
Philadelphia	12	245
Dallas	14	240
Melbourne	11	229
Johannesburg	14	227

Source: Bavishi and Wyman (1983).

Of the largest accountancy firms a number originated within the City of London. There is, however, some difficulty in judging the nationality of ownership of partnerships. Historically, City accountancy firms have tended to expand in the UK and overseas by merging with other accountancy firms to form a loose alliance of country partners all operating under the same name. Since in the majority of these firms the United States practices are much larger in terms of number of partners than any other and partners have, nominally at least, equal voting rights, ownership and control of these City firms is a problematic concept. Whatever the case, currently there are 30 major accountancy firms based in the City of London and 63 in London as a whole (*Investors Chronicle*, 1984).

One of the largest of these is Price Waterhouse. 'It is blue chip and proud of it. A Wykehamist senior partner is likely to keep it this way' (*Investors Chronicle*, 1985). The firm was founded in the City of London in 1849 by S. H. Price and E. Waterhouse. The firm was able to attract distinguished partners, including Knights of the Realm, and with this social background was quickly able to find impressive accounts. It has used social networks to economic gain ever since.

The firm went multinational early on in its history. At the turn of the century it joined with the New York firm, Jones, Caesar and Co.

By the mid-1930s the firm already had 57 branch offices around the world and employed 2,500 employees in all (Stevens, 1982). By 1985 its complement had grown to 30,372 employees (including 2,113 partners) working in 95 countries. In 1985 Price Waterhouse as a whole earned £1,234 million in fees (*International Accounting Bulletin*, 1986). The office structure of Price Waterhouse is extensive, both internationally (Figure 5.2) and in the UK (Figure 5.3). Price Waterhouse's main activities continue to be in audit. In both the United States and the UK, for example, about 70% of its chargeable hours come from this source. However taxation services are growing fast (18% of chargeable hours in the United States, 16% in the UK), as is management consultancy (about 10% of chargeable hours in both the United States and the UK). The firm is also involved in businesses like insolvency, business services to small firms, and services to central and local government. The movement into new services has come about partly through organic growth and partly through merger. For example, in 1983 Price Waterhouse UK merged with Urwick Orr and Partners, one of the City of London's major management consultancy firms. The firm has tried to merge on a larger scale than this with other accountancy firms. For example, also in 1983 it tried to merge with another of the big nine, Deloitte Haskins and Sells but partners in the two firms threw the proposal out (a problem of the partnership form).

Over time, the company has tried to act more and more like a centralized multinational corporation by adding a world tier of administration—the 'world firm' based in the City of London. The world firm co-ordinates the operations of each of the country partnerships (which are organized as 20 member firms responsible for major markets like the United States, Canada, Australia, South Africa, Asia, and so on) at the world scale. It is run by a nine member policy committee, a twenty member council of firms and a council of partners. The world firm is responsible for international marketing, promotion of a world image, the development of computerized auditing and other systems able to be used by each of the member firms. It would certainly be an exaggeration to say that the company is entirely run from the City, but it is subject to centralized control of a sort.

The firm has become international for two main reasons. The first is a constant search for new markets offering profit opportunities for accountancy. The second is the fact that its clients have become international and in order to continue to obtain work it was necessary to be able to display an international office network likely to match their own locational pattern. This is also vital in obtaining new audits. On a worldwide basis 40% of all clients audited by the

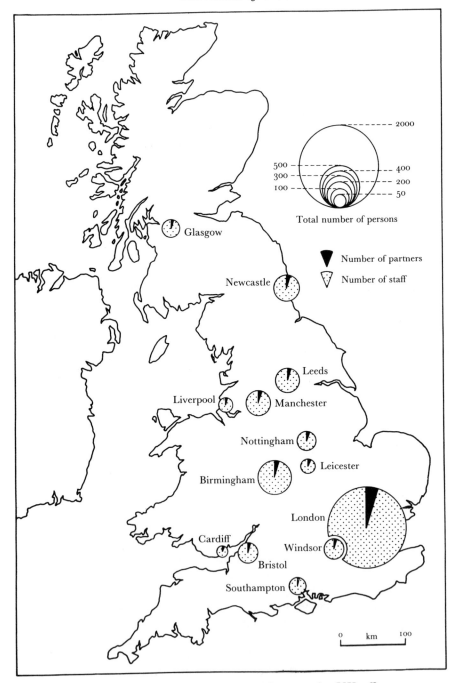

FIG. 5.3. Price Waterhouse: employment by UK office.

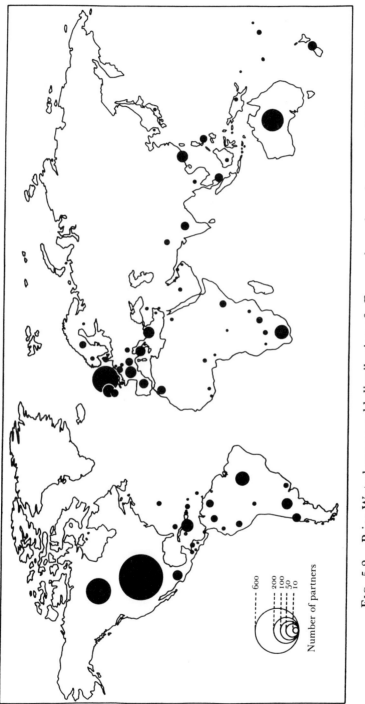

Number of partners

600
200
100
50
10

Fɪɢ. 5.2. Price Waterhouse: world distribution of offices and number of partners, 1985.

firm have international operations. The result of these factors is that Price Waterhouse has an employment structure which matches closely the pattern of international corporate and financial centres (Table 5.15) for that is where custom is to be found and that is where the existing clients are.

Conclusion

This brief case study has highlighted the way in which international processes influence producer services in the UK. The location of the main offices of large financial and professional firms close to London and in a few large provincial centres is encouraged by the international operation of these companies and their need for access to international financial markets and corporate complexes in world cities. The growth of activities related to the City of London has done much to sustain the concentration of producer service employment in the south and east of the country and the competitiveness of these services in international trade is likely to have an important bearing on the capital's future prospects. Decisions concerning future investment associated with the 'Big Bang' are also likely to have an important impact on the location of producer services within the UK.

5.2. Non-production Employment in Manufacturing

The significance of non-production employment in manufacturing

The view of producer services taken by this study recognizes that one of their principal roles, although not the only one, is to support and facilitate production as a result of the 'externalization' of many non-production functions by manufacturing firms. This role, however, is complemented by the contribution of 'internal' non-production activities sustained by manufacturing itself. Indeed, the inputs to production made, for example, by the engineers, financial advisers, or legal experts employed by a manufacturing firm, together with their technical and clerical support staff, or by its building and equipment maintenance staff, may be very similar to those of workers for specialist outside firms. The two groups of activity are often interchangeable, with developments in each affecting the other. Thus it is necessary to consider trends in non-production employment in manufacturing (NPEM) in any analysis of the relationship between producer services and manufacturing.

While the proportions of non-production workers employed by manufacturing firms has tended to grow in recent decades, so has their dependence on outside expertise. The reasons for both trends lie in the growing technical complexity of production, the associated substitution of processing work by more capital intensive methods, and the development of a growing range of support functions such as research and development, production engineering, technical monitoring, and maintenance activities. Financial, personnel recruitment, purchasing, and sales functions have also become more complex, while the increased uncertainty of the commercial and technological environment has involved more staff in external monitoring and development of corporate strategies, for example in relation to technical innovation or merger activities.

Like similar patterns of producer activity, the uneven regional distribution of NPEM, demonstrated in Section 4.2, attracted interest during the 1970s, when a number of studies revealed an apparently growing concentration of high-level administrative, technical, and research functions in the South East (Buswell and Lewis, 1970; Evans, 1973; Goddard and Smith, 1978; Oakey, Thwaites, and Nash, 1982; Parsons, 1972; Thwaites, 1982; Westaway, 1974). These trends were commonly associated with the increasing domination of British manufacturing by large, multi-plant companies, including multinationals. A clear distinction seemed to be emerging within such companies between the functions performed by their corporate and divisional headquarters and their various branch production centres. The latter in particular seemed to be increasingly specializing in routine production and support activities, lacking both the autonomy of decision-making and the quality of jobs offered by independent companies or by their own parent plants. Much of the evidence reviewed here suggests in fact that more complex processes of change are taking place in the role and distribution of service support for production than this rather simple 'hierarchical' view would indicate. One important element of this complexity is undoubtedly the changing policy of manufacturing firms towards the employment of support staff, as opposed to outside expertise.

Non-production employment in manufacturing: the current evidence

In Sections 3.3 and 4.2, the contribution of administrative, technical, and clerical (white collar) employment in manufacturing to producer service employment was estimated as far as was possible from aggregate national and regional data. Major national trends were also examined between 1959 and 1981. The most comprehensive earlier studies of the scale, functioning, and distribution of NPEM have been undertaken by Goddard (1979), Crum and Gudgin (1977) and Gudgin, Crum, and Bailey (1979) although all focused heavily on white collar activities (as does Section 3.3), excluding much consideration of the important blue collar ancillary functions in manufacturing. Goddard, developing Swedish research ideas, emphasized the information and planning needs of large companies to explain the growing proportions of non-production activities in manufacturing, and their geographical concentration into the 'information rich' London Region. An increasing need was seen for regular face-to-face contacts by senior staff, both within firms and with outside organizations, to monitor change and make informed strategic decisions about the future.

According to Table 4.2 this geographical concentration appears to have been almost as marked for NPEM as in specialist producer services, although there is some evidence for the retreat of manufacturing from high-cost headquarter locations in London (Goddard and Smith, 1978). The South East as a whole nevertheless remains favoured not only by the need for large manufacturing firms to have at least a minimal corporate presence in the region, but also by the relative prosperity of its industries, its high proportion of national research and development activity and the continuing consolidation of control in the region as a result of mergers and takeovers. Goddard's study, although providing a framework for explaining the locational needs of high-level manufacturing functions, did not explore the employment patterns of non-production work, including the wide range of more routine support functions found throughout manufacturing firms.

In these respects Crum and Gudgin provided a more comprehensive analysis of the structure and distribution of non-production work in UK manufacturing. They showed, from Census of Population data, that over one third of manufacturing employment in 1971 was in NPEM including, among white collar occupations, 5.8% in managerial and professional, 5.9% in scientific and technical, and 12% in clerical activities. They also noted that the blue collar groups contributed 7% in distribution and 3.3% in other support services. In their organizational survey they found a great variety of non-production functions and a wide dispersal of employment among them (Table 5.16). The main support functions represented in branch plants were in general management, office services, security and maintenance, production planning, quality control, and distribution. On average, these employed 18.5% of the local workforce, compared with 19% in head office sites. The activities that were more typical in headquarters were finance, purchasing, product design, R&D, market research, and especially sales and servicing. These functions made up 18.1% of employment in head office sites compared with only 8.2% in branch plants. Only 1% of the surveyed manufacturing employment was in detached headquarters, but general management, finance, and sales were particularly concentrated there in such cases.

Many functions were therefore quite evenly distributed, especially those with high proportions of clerical and technical staff and a significant local role, although more strategic elements of each were likely to be found at head offices. It should also be noted from Crum and Gudgin's data that the main blue collar categories identified (security and maintenance, and distribution) employed a higher proportion of branch plant staff than most of the white collar categories, amounting to 8.2% of total employment, and 27% of non-production workers in branches. This suggests that the data on non-production employment used in Table 4.2, in so far as they do not cover all blue collar workers, may exaggerate the degree of concentration of NPEM as a whole in the South East and South West.

In their analysis of the factors influencing the distribution of white collar workers in manufacturing, Crum and Gudgin particularly

Table 5.16.   Average NP Function Proportions by Status of Establishment

Department (or functions)	% of total employment		
	Branch	Production site including head office	Detached head office
Number of observations	352	64	32
1. General management	2.1	2.0	12.0
2. Public relations	0.03	0.09	1.3
3. Data processing	0.3	0.9	5.5
4. Office services	2.0	2.2	10.1
Subtotal: General Management	4.5	5.2	28.9
5. Wages and salaries	0.9	1.0	1.1
6. Accounts and finance	1.9	3.4	11.9
7. Legal, insurance, etc.	0.1	0.2	2.3
8. Purchasing	0.8	1.2	2.3
Subtotal: Specialist Services	3.7	5.8	17.6
9. Personnel, etc.	0.6	0.8	3.1
10. Health, welfare, etc.	1.1	1.4	1.9
11. Security and maintenance	4.4	4.6	1.4
Subtotal: Personnel and maintenance	6.2	6.9	6.4
12. Product design	1.4	2.1	2.7
13. Production planning	4.1	4.1	3.7
14. Quality control	2.1	2.2	0.7
Subtotal: Production-related departments	7.6	8.4	7.1
15. Research and development	0.7	1.7	5.4
16. Market research, etc.	0.5	1.6	5.6
17. Sales	2.4	6.2	14.7
18. Sales servicing	0.5	1.9	3.8
19. Distribution	3.8	3.9	5.9
Subtotal: Marketing and distribution	7.2	13.3	30.0
20. Other	0.6	0.4	0.6
TOTAL: NP functions	30.4	41.7	100.0

Source: Crum, Gudgin, and Bailey (1979).

highlighted:

(i) the type of product and processes undertaken (i.e. the industrial sector), as they affect technical, sales, and clerical employment needs.

(ii) the organizational status of plants, whether headquarters or branch, independent or subsidiary, in relation to various forms of organizational hierarchy. They noted however that, as long as some degree of shared responsibility with head-quarters decisions is retained by branch plants, their proportions of non-production work may remain as high as in many autonomous plants.

(iii) more or less random variations between companies, based upon the degree to which they may contract out support tasks, their inherited pattern of organization and their efficiency.

Crum and Gudgin's analysis confirmed the general domination of NPEM by the South East, especially for the higher-paid and growing managerial and professional functions. They estimated that in 1971, compared with what might have been expected from the region's industrial structure, it benefited by over 250,000 non-production jobs (defined in this case to include blue collar distribution and service functions). The explanation of this was clearly organizational, rather than sectoral, deriving from the corporate and divisional structures of multi-regional companies. Crum and Gudgin concluded that these disparities have arisen from the history of industrial development in the UK, and are associated especially with the greater prosperity of manufacturing in the South East over a long period. They were not, however, able to examine regional trends, or to discover how far and in what direction the concentration of NPEM in the South East has changed in recent decades.

Concern about these trends, of course, has been linked to the supposed benefits imparted by NPEM on local communities. Crum and Gudgin associated these with the relatively stable, high wage employment it provides (at least, compared to manual work), and the fact that the high level decision makers included amongst non-production workers may favour nearby locations when deciding to invest. Both of these assumptions need to be qualified, of course. As Crum and Gudgin themselves demonstrate, many non-production workers are not highly paid, especially in the clerical, junior sales, and manual occupations that make up a large proportion of the jobs. In current conditions of rapid technological and organizational change, they are also vulnerable to displacement by various forms of automation. Similarly, the notion that regions containing headquarter activities may be favoured by employment-creating investment for that reason alone, neglects the impact of many other factors that are likely to be important in location decisions.

Recent trends

Little recent research has been carried out to compare with Crum and Gudgin's analysis, or more specifically considering the effects of technological and organizational changes on the numbers, functions, or spatial patterns of NPEM. Nevertheless, significant and perhaps diverse influences have undoubtedly been at work increasing the need for skilled managerial, financial, and technical expertise while also creating pressures to reduce the numbers in more routine support activities. It is also unlikely that the turmoil of British manufacturing over the past decade has left non-production work unscathed.

The further examination of aggregate data presents some difficulties. Classification changes in 1980 prevent direct comparison of the occupational structure of manufacturing in 1971 examined by Crum and Gudgin with that revealed by the 1981 Census. Table 5.17 shows that 1981 structure in terms of the 1980 classification. On the basis of a broad classification[3] of non-production work (see Appendix 1) 29% of male and 40% of female workers in manufacturing (32% overall) were occupied in white collar functions, comprising 2,119,000 workers. Some 6.5% of manufacturing workers were managers, 5.4% were various forms of non-scientific professionals, and 6.1% were in scientific and technical occupations. Clerical work constituted 12% of the total and a further 2.5% were in sales activities. The identified blue collar support services, including catering, cleaning, personnel support services, and construction activities, made up a further 4%, and transport and storage 6%. This brings the total representation of non-production work in manufacturing in 1981 up to no less than 43%, considerably higher than the 32% identified by Crum and Gudgin from the 1971 Census. But 43% is probably an over-estimate of manufacturing employment in non-production activities because it is difficult to exclude all production workers and it is best interpreted as an upper estimate for comparison with the conservative estimates in Chapter 2, Section 4.2, and elsewhere in the literature. However, the difference between this figure and that obtained by Crum and

---

[3] This classification is not consistent with that used in Table 4.2—see Appendix 1 for details.

Table 5.17. Non-production Employees in Manufacturing in the UK, 1981

	Male		Female		Total	
	No. (000s)	%	No. (000s)	%	No. (000s)	%
Professional (managerial, welfare, artistic)	281	6.0	73	3.8	354	5.4
Professional (scientific, technical)	377	8.0	22	1.2	399	6.1
Managers	376	8.0	49	2.6	425	6.5
Clerical	204	4.4	574	30.7	778	11.9
Sales	126	2.7	37	2.0	163	2.5
		29.1		40.3		32.4
Catering, cleaning, personal services, security	76	1.6	127	6.7	199	3.1
Construction	55	1.2	1	—	56	0.9
Transport and storage	383	8.2	25	1.3	408	6.2
		11.0		8.0		10.2
Processing, repair, assembly, packaging, general labouring, etc.		59.9		51.7		57.4

Source: Census of Population

Gudgin shows how definitional problems can have a major impact on the analysis of non-production activities. Nevertheless, the proportion of white collar work in Table 5.17 does agree quite closely with the evidence of the Department of Employment's ATC data discussed in Section 3.3.

From this ATC employment data Crum and Gudgin showed that in the post-war period up to the early 1970s the share of white collar staff in manufacturing had expanded more rapidly than before. They related this to growing manufacturing productivity, associated with the higher capital intensity of production, more emphasis on sales and distribution, and increased technical sophistication. Figure 5.4 pursues these white collar trends into the 1980s (see also Figs. 3.2 and 3.3). In 1971, at a time when the numbers were near their historical peak, Crum and Gudgin noted that 26% of manufacturing workers were ATC staff. Since then, as noted in Section 3.3, there has been a marked absolute decline, following the general contraction of manufacturing employment. Compared with a value of 2.3

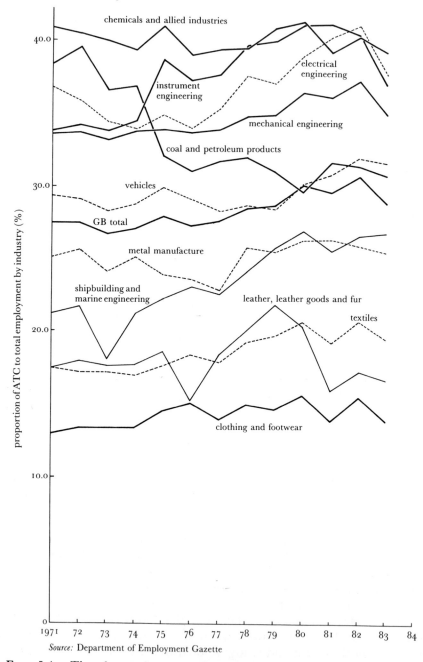

Fig. 5.4.   The change in proportion of ATC to total employment over time by industry.

millions in 1970, ATC staff were only 1.75 millions in 1981 and 1.5 millions in 1984, a fall of one third over 13 years. In spite of this, the share of manufacturing jobs in ATC occupations grew; hardly at all in the early 1970s but quite appreciably thereafter, to over 31% by 1982. There was, however, a marked drop after this date, to less than 29% in 1984, much sharper than the temporary relapses of 1973 and 1976.

The ATC data also show the variation between different manufacturing industries in the proportions of white collar workers. The highest proportions in 1982 were around 40%, in chemicals and in electrical and instrument engineering; in the latter two the share had grown markedly over the previous decade. Growth was also appreciable in mechanical engineering (to 37% in 1982) and vehicles (32%), although coal and petroleum products showed a sharp fall, presumably in the aftermath of the development phase of the North Sea oilfields. Most other sectors showed a drift upwards, but the effect of the post-1982 slump seems to have been greatest on industries with the highest levels of ATC workers. The main contributors to the total of ATC workers in 1983 were electrical (18.4% of the total) and mechanical (14.9%) engineering, vehicles (10.5%), paper, printing and publishing (9.9%), and chemicals (9.3%), together accounting for 63% of the total.

These data confirm Crum and Gudgin's description of the most significant influences on the share of white collar work in different sectors; productivity related to capital intensity, economies of scale, the degree of sales effort, and technological sophistication. They also make clear, however, that sectoral structure has little influence on the distribution of non-production workers. Here, as we have seen, the impact of organizational factors are paramount.

The diversity of corporate structure and NPEM[4]

Although patterns of business organization have attracted a good deal of attention in industrial location studies over the last decade, as we have seen there has been a tendency to rely upon rather simple 'hierarchical' models of corporate structure when considering the spatial organization of non-production functions. Such a structure certainly characterizes some large companies, typically those with a single dominant product. Many, however, show a much more complex pattern, involving divisional structures (both product and geographically based), profit centres, holding companies, and complex ownership and management arrangements.

---

[4] This section is based on an account prepared by Peter Damesick, using information provided by John Salt, University College London.

To take some illustrative examples, Courtaulds has a structure in which one division is itself a holding company and several others are companies with their own divisions. Ferranti has a combination of product and geographically based (Scottish) divisions, with the latter involved in several products. The company has also shown organic evolution of its structure; parts of two divisions were merged to form a new one specializing in a particular branch of weapons manufacture. These corporate structures reflect company history as much as any other influence.

Product technology, the nature of the product, and market characteristics also have an effect. A comparison of Rolls-Royce and IBM illustrates the point. Both are in high technology sectors; aero-engines and computers, but the technologies and markets differ widely. Rolls-Royce has a London head office but a substantial proportion of its white collar staff are located in Derby. In this case, the nature of the product demands close contact between research, design, and development functions and production. In IBM's operations research and development can be separated from the production and assembly of components. Also, a critical part of the company's production is a 'service'—software development. The nature of the products and the markets served by IBM also necessitate an extensive network of offices concerned with sales and customer service.

The pattern of NPEM therefore reflects the dynamic character of corporate development. At any time it may include elements surviving from formerly separate companies before acquisition or merger. Later, consolidation and rationalization may produce a different pattern (Leigh and North, 1978). The creation of new subsidiaries or divisions and new corporate strategies may lead to new patterns. In the 1980s many companies have undertaken significant restructuring of their activities to adapt to changing market and technological needs. The result has often been a reappraisal and dispersal of over-concentrated patterns of control inherited from the 1950s and 1960s. Thus purely functional descriptions of the pattern of NPEM ignore the wider corporate context in which patterns develop and continually change.

Unfortunately, of course, evidence is lacking about the overall effects of these types of adjustment on the regional distribution of NPEM in recent years, in spite of the likely impact of the recession and technological change. This is perhaps where up-to-date research is most needed. Such inquiry should nevertheless take place within a framework of analysis that recognizes the complexitites of changing patterns of NPEM in relation to trends in independent producer service functions (see Section 6.2).

Producer service trends in relation to non-production employment in manufacturing

Without more information about the modern scale and distribution of NPEM, a number of important questions about the functions and growth of producer services cannot be fully answered. The issues in question are raised here to indicate significant research needs. These may be summarized as:

1. How far, in fact, are the functions of non-production activities in different forms of manufacturing capable of being substituted by independent producer services? How far also are they regarded as such by managers?

2. What is the general policy of manufacturing firms in current circumstances with regard to the contribution of non-production work? In recent years, the most technically progressive branches of manufacturing have employed most non-production workers. Since the early 1980s recession, however, and perhaps even before, the proportion of non-production employment has come under close scrutiny in the endeavour to cut overhead costs. The scope for doing this has, of course, increased with the automation of some functions. The impact of further technical changes, especially in new forms of information collection and processing, may accelerate these trends. Does the evidence of Figure 5.4 since 1982 therefore reflect a permanent change in the employment of white collar staff, or at least the achievement of a 'ceiling' to its growth?

3. What will be the future balance of different non-production functions within large manufacturing firms? Although this will be affected by the services offered by outside firms, as Crum and Gudgin conclude the internal organizational needs of different-sized manufacturing firms in different sectors, and with different management structures, are probably the most important determinants of the scale and structure of their non-production functions. The proportion of skilled managerial and technical support staff is likely to grow in relation to the routine clerical, sales, and technical functions. Among manual workers, non-production work has probably been sustained more than direct production employment. Certainly, skilled repair and maintenance activities remain of critical significance even while employment, for example in storage and transportation functions, may continue to fall.

4. Is it possible to derive better indicators of the efficiency contribution of non-production work in manufacturing? Clearly, effective technical innovation, design, sales, market intelligence, financial management, quality control, and even personnel management are critical to the success of any manufacturing operation.

The evaluation of such functions is, of course, a more-or-less continuous process within business. Many of the benefits of such activities, however, are felt only in the relatively long-term, and can often only be achieved with the indirect support of the more routine functions within a firm. The assessment of each activity's distinctive contribution to efficiency is therefore not easy.

The same question may seem to be less applicable to the buying-in of outside expertise, since the competitive contractual process should impose some criterion of efficiency. For this reason, more manufacturing firms may in fact increasingly favour independent service suppliers over 'in-house' departments. On the other hand, some producer service functions are nowadays supplied only by relatively few firms. A tendency towards 'cartel' practices, with associated price increases, may be expected to intensify as markets for producer service functions become more specialized and subdivided, partly in defence against competitive pressures. Meanwhile specialist corporate divisions of some large manufacturing firms have been encouraged to tender for outside work as well as serving internal needs, which they also sometimes do under competitive tender. In these circumstances, comparison of the effectiveness of NPEM with that of outside producer services may become more difficult as the distinction between the two breaks down. Perhaps also, however, new opportunities for making such comparisons may present themselves.

5. What market factors are influencing the balance between the roles of NPEM and producer services? It seems that, while non-production activities have increased their importance within manufacturing, producer service activities have expanded even more rapidly. The latter, of course, are not dependent only on stagnant manufacturing markets, and their ability to serve the growing needs of consumer and other producer service activities is a major advantage over most related 'in-house' functions in manufacturing firms. In spite of the oligopolistic tendencies mentioned above and the involvement of large manufacturers in offering services to other firms, the increasing subdivision of producer service activities and the depth of expertise they require probably favour the continued displacement of NPEM activities by bought-in services. Again, however, many important strategic functions are likely to be retained by manufacturers, if only to enable them effectively to evaluate outside services. Paradoxically, this in itself may occupy a growing share of manufacturers' non-production employment in the future.

More note also needs to be taken of market trends in blue collar service work. A high proportion of such functions in manufacturing has always been subcontracted out to specialist distribution, transportation, and maintenance and repair companies, often in nearby areas. It is certainly an important basis for sustaining small firms in many regions. Such producer services are particularly susceptible to the policies of large firms over the 'in-house' provision of these functions.

6. In considering the geographical patterns of changes in NPEM, organizational structures and the impacts on them of technological changes are of critical importance. There is clear evidence that the increasing external ownership of local and regional manufacturing, leading to the internalization of many service functions within large companies, has undermined the local producer service support base. Crum and Gudgin's evidence, however, indicates the reality is more varied than this generalized evidence might suggest. While it seems unlikely that the past concentration of high level manufacturing functions in the South East will be reversed, there is some indication that other functions may be dispersing away from such a centralized pattern of activity. The scale of headquarter staffing may be reduced to cut overhead costs, and some firms may also seek to move away from high cost locations in the South East. The share of non-production jobs in branch plants may well grow in response to these trends, as well as to declining employment in production itself. Even so, the employment effects of any such locational changes will, of course, continue to be overshadowed in many areas by the continuing closure and contraction of manufacturing plants.

Another consequence, however, may be a better market for independent producer services in areas that are able to retain a healthy manufacturing base, even though manufacturing employment may be falling. These markets are not likely to be in the highest level white collar functions, but may well strengthen demand, for example for office services, legal advice, production planning expertise, and sales and advertising activities, and for the already relatively decentralized blue collar maintenance, security, and distribution functions.

The functions of all service activity must be judged in relation to the contribution it makes, through the expertise it offers, to the operation and effectiveness of other economic activities. The failure to recognize this, and the consequent tendency to view services as separate from other functions, particularly those associated with production and international trade, underlie the current widespread misunderstanding about the functions of services and the future of service employment.

Non-production workers in manufacturing (like similar supporting activities within large service firms) offer 'captive' services to the primary activity of their company. In principle they are inter-changeable with the independent producer service sector, whose role is therefore analogous. A better understanding of trends in NPEM is therefore important, not only because of the importance of what it does for the success of production, but also because it affects the demand for producer service work in ways that are likely to be significant nationally and in different parts of the country.

5.3. Physical Distribution

Physical distribution (PD) is the collective term for the range of activities involved in the movement of goods from point of production to final point of sale. Until recently, these activities, in particular transport and storage, were managed separately by most manufacturing firms and considered to be of minor importance relative to other functions such as production, marketing, and sales. Over the past twenty years, however, many firms have begun to integrate the management and costing of these activities and raise the status of PD within managerial circles. This case study will assess the importance of PD to the national economy, outline the factors that influence the total demand for distribution services and examine the division of reponsibility for these services between producers, distributors, and outside contractors. Later sections will concentrate on the spatial distribution of demand for PD and the impact of new technology on the nature and location of these services.

Studies of the British distributive system are at present seriously constrained by a lack of data, both on 'own account' operations and those of outside contractors (also known as 'third party', 'hire and reward', and 'specialist' operators). Much more information is available on freight transport than on storage. Unlike the US Census of Transportation, the British Department of Transport's surveys of the transport industry ignore ancillary storage. This case study is based upon the limited amounts of information available in official publications and data collected in a series of small scale studies of different aspects of the distributive system.

Physical distribution as a producer service

The problem of differentiating producer from consumer services is particularly acute in the case of PD. Distribution channels extend from factories to shops or, in some cases, direct to the home, and it is difficult to decide which sections of these channels should be regarded as providing a service to the producer and which to the consumer. In his functional classification of services Key (1985) creates a separate category for distributive services, in recognition of the fact that they contribute to both intermediate and final demand.

Responsibility for transporting goods to the customer and storing them *en route* is shared between manufacturers, wholesalers, and retailers in proportions that vary between trades. Although wholesalers and retailers perform a service for manufacturers in bringing their products closer to the consumer, they are not contracted as such by the manufacturer and not paid a fee for their work. The relationship between manufacturers and wholesale and retail distributors is essentially a market relationship involving the transfer of ownership and risk. This should be contrasted with the services provided by 'third-party' transport, storage, and distribution contractors, which do not assume ownership of the goods they handle and are employed by manufacturers on a 'hire and reward' basis. If producer services were to be defined as those services *purchased* by manufacturers then the work of wholesalers and retailers would be excluded and, within the context of PD, attention would be confined to specialist contractors.

There are good reasons, however, for broadening the definition of producer services to include the logistical activities of wholesalers and retailers. First, much of the PD work carried out by these agencies, comprising storage, breaking-of-bulk, load consolidation, and local delivery, closely resembles that done by manufacturers and distribution contractors. In some trades, most of this work is undertaken by wholesalers and retailers. Second, manufacturers can influence the allocation of their output between, on the one hand, wholesalers and retailers and, on the other, distributive channels more directly under their control, by varying trading terms, minimum drop sizes, and service levels. Although manufacturers do not pay wholesalers and retailers as such for their services, the cost of distributing goods via these agencies can be calculated and compared with the costs of operating an 'own-account' distribution system or employing contractors. In the light of such comparisons, manufacturers try to optimize the allocation of their product flow between the different distributive channels (Buxton, 1975). Third, given the traditional definition of consumer services as being those provided mainly in response to final demand or meeting public needs directly, it would seem that the work done by wholesalers and retailers 'upstream' of the shop is more of a producer than a consumer service.

Greenfield (1966), Marquand (1979), and Hubbard and Nutter (1982) include the wholesaling and dealing MLHs in their definition of producer services but not retail distribution. This is understandable because official statistics on retail distribution do not distinguish those activities based at retailers' warehouses from shop-based activities. Evidence from the grocery trade suggests that retailers can vary enormously in the extent to which they assume wholesale functions making it difficult to generalize about their logistical commitments (McKinnon, 1985a). It would be wrong, however, to ignore the PD activities of the larger retail organizations simply because of the inadequacy of official statistics. Indeed, in the present context, it is especially important that account be taken of retailers' involvement in distribution 'upstream' of the shop as they contract out much of their transport and storage to the same agencies as manufacturers.

Figure 5.5 presents a rough classification of the PD services that firms can currently purchase from outside contractors. These services are grouped under the major functional headings of transport, storage, and information processing, and arranged in ascending order of client commitment. Most can be purchased separately or as part of an integrated distribution package. Individual contractors vary enormously in the range of PD services they provide. The largest firm in the sector, the National Freight Consortium (NFC), can, through its numerous subsidiaries, offer most of the services listed in Fig. 5.5. At the other extreme, most of the 30,000 or so small haulage firms with fewer than five vehicles merely provide a basic road transport service. Between these extremes lie a wide assortment of contractors, differing in their service offerings, the types of product they handle and the geographical extent of their operations. The diversification of contract services in recent years has made it increasingly difficult to classify firms into neat functional categories. This is well illustrated by the following statement by the Chairman of the Transport Development

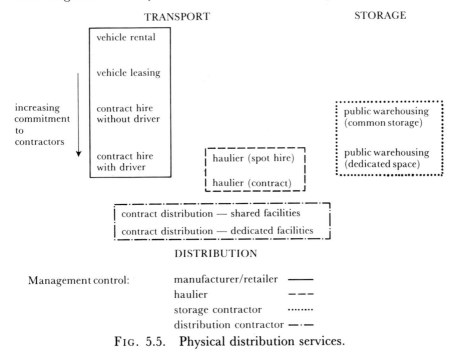

FIG. 5.5.   Physical distribution services.

Group, which owns around fifty haulage, storage, and distribution firms in the UK:

storage and distribution patterns are changing rapidly to meet the needs of manufacturers and major retailers. In reporting on the performance of the Group companies it is no longer easy to classify them under the simple headings of warehousing companies, cold stores or road haulage businesses and analyse their results accordingly.

Road hauliers build warehouses to act as distribution centres, cold storage companies operate fleets of refrigerated vehicles, warehousekeepers find they have to provide temperature or humidity controlled storage. There are no longer clear functional demarcation lines. Furthermore, as the individual Group trading companies grow in size and seek to develop in line with the requirements of their major customers, the geographical limits of their activities spread and overlap. (Transport Development Group, Annual Report 1985, p. 5)

To complicate matters further some firms engaging in contract distribution themselves hire vehicles, thereby establishing linkages within the sector.

It has been predicted that in the near future some distribution contractors may also be prepared to assume ownership of the goods they store, relieving clients of the high financial cost of stockholding and exerting tighter control over stock levels (*Financial Times*, 5th December, 1986). This would blur the distinction between these contractors and wholesalers though, unlike the latter, the contractors would eschew the risk-bearing functions of buying and selling. Their status would, therefore, remain that of a 'facilitating intermediary' (Kotler, 1967), rather than a full trading partner in the marketing channel.

There has been a tendency in recent years to broaden the definition of 'wholesaling' to include the localized storage, break-bulk, consolidation, and delivery operations of manufacturers, retailers, and contractors. Rajan and Pearson (1986), for example, refer to 'in-house wholesaling' and to firms externalizing the wholesale function, using the term 'wholesaling' as a synonym for physical distribution. Wholesaling, however, is more than simply a PD function as it also entails heavy involvement in the purchasing, marketing, and sale of goods. There is a danger that if the PD activities of other agencies are subsumed under the general heading of wholesaling, important differences between these activities and the traditional work of the wholesaler will be obscured. In the grocery trade, for example, distribution contractors and multiple retailers have been expanding their PD operations, while the proportion of business handled by wholesalers has been declining.

Expenditure on physical distribution

The only wide-ranging assessment of Britain's annual expenditure on 'logistics' was made by Childerley (1980). She employed Bowersox's broad definition of logistics which embraces, '. . . all of those activities involved in physically moving raw materials, in-process inventory and finished goods inventory from point of origin to point of use or consumption' (Bowersox, 1969*a*), and calculated that, thus defined, logistics accounted for 22.6% of Britain's GDP in 1976. This estimate, however, included the cost of holding stock and handling goods in the retail outlet, which would normally be regarded as a consumer service. If one removes these cost elements from the calculation, the total cost of logistics in 1976 falls to about 16% of GDP. A survey in 1985 of the distribution costs of a small sample of British firms found that, on average, these costs accounted for 8.4% of total sales revenue (Institute of Physical Distribution Management, 1986). Table 5.18 shows how these costs were divided between transport, storage, stockholding, and administration. Expenditure on PD, therefore, represents a significant proportion of sales revenue, but it can also be argued that to obtain a more realistic measure of its importance to individual firms, distribution expenditure should be expressed as a percentage of net value added or profit margins (Westwood, 1981).

PD costs have also been increasing at a faster rate than retail prices. Between 1978 and 1984 the retail price index rose by 87.4% while average distribution costs increased by 120% (Centre for Physical Distribution Management, 1984). Over this period the main cost components in PD, such as vehicle operating costs, interest payments, and equipment charges, were all subject to strong inflationary pressures. In many industries distribution costs have risen relative to production costs.

Table 5.18.   Breakdown of Physical Distribution Costs

	%age of total distribution costs	%age of total sales revenue
Transport	45.2	3.8
Storage	29.8	2.5
Administration	13.1	1.1
Inventory	11.9	1.0
TOTAL	100	8.4

Source: Institute of Physical Distribution Management (1986).

As the proportion of GDP associated with consumer services increases and that attributable to the production and consumption of material goods declines, one might expect relative expenditure on PD to diminish. In practice, however, there is no fixed relationship between the PD 'workload' and the material output of the economy. This relationship can be strongly influenced by the following factors:

1. The *spatial organization of production and distribution* affects the distance goods are transported, the volume of goods in storage, and the efficiency of materials handling operations. Between 1967/8 and 1984, the average length of haul for freight consignments increased by over 50% (Department of Transport, 1985), mainly as a result of the spatial concentration of production and stockholding, but also because of the expansion of market areas and, to a much smaller extent, the dispersal of industrial capacity to more peripheral locations (McKinnon, 1983a). The amount of freight movement, measured in tonne-kilometres, has, therefore, risen relative to the volume of goods produced and consumed. Increases in the demand for freight transport must, however, be set against the savings in storage and materials handling accruing from the centralization of inventories.

2. The *quality of the distribution service* (measured in terms of order lead times, reliability, product availability, and security). Improving the quality of distribution generally requires additional resources but is often justified by the extra sales it can generate (Christopher, Schary and Skjött-Larsen, 1979). To be able to deliver orders more rapidly to customers, for example, a manufacturer may have to hold larger stocks and/or be prepared to run vehicles at a lower level of utilization.

3. The *manner in which products are marketed* can strongly influence the way in which they are physically distributed. Recent trends in marketing, such as the proliferation of product lines, increasing reliance on temporary promotional campaigns, and shortening product life cycles, have tended to impose additional demands on firms' PD operations.

4. The *division of responsibility for physical distribution* among manufacturers, wholesalers, and retailers can also affect the total level of distribution activity. Multiple retailers, for example, by centralizing stocks and consolidating deliveries can increase the efficiency with which finished goods are distributed to shops (McKinnon, 1986a). In most trades, multiples have increased their market share, while assuming greater responsibility for distribution 'upstream' of the shop. This has relieved manufacturers and wholesalers of some of their logistical responsibilities and, by streamlining channels of

distribution, is likely to have reduced PD costs for the products that multiples handle. In many cases, however, the distribution systems of manufacturers and wholesalers have not contracted in line with the diversion of traffic to channels controlled by multiple retailers and, as a consequence, have experienced a decline in productivity.

The level of PD activity, as conventionally defined, has also been reduced by the transfer of responsibility for transport and storage to small independent retailers and consumers. The former now collect many of their supplies from cash and carry warehouses, while the latter are today prepared to travel longer distances to purchase goods less frequently and in greater bulk. As small retailers and shoppers transport goods in their own cars and as the latter hold larger stocks in their own homes, their increased involvement in PD is not reflected in freight transport and stockholding statistics.

5. The *distribution of imported goods* creates a demand for PD services which partly compensates for the drop in demand for such services by British manufacturers whose share of the home market is declining. As imported consumer goods arrive in a finished state, however, their logistical demands are much lower than those of products manufactured in the UK which are also stored and transported in raw and semi-finished states.

The contribution of physical distribution to the competitiveness of manufacturing industry

The cost and quality of PD can influence industrial competitiveness at home and abroad in various ways. The direct cost of distributing goods to customers will be reflected in prices and thereby affect the level of demand. This cost must always be related to the level of service provided. Research on service levels has suggested that industrial and commercial customers often attach more importance to the speed and reliability of deliveries than to marginal variations in price levels (Schary, 1983). Christopher (1981) has argued that the substantial growth of imports into the UK can be partly attributed to British manufacturers' failure to deliver goods on time to domestic customers. The need for fast and efficient distribution to the domestic market is particularly strong in the UK as the structure of its distributive system facilitates the inflow of imported goods. In the UK, corporate retail chains hold a significantly larger share of total retail sales than in other European countries (Table 5.19) and, within many trades, small numbers of large firms dominate the market. In many sectors of the consumer goods market where imports have achieved high penetration, such as those of clothing, footwear, electrical goods, and photographic equipment,

Table 5.19.   Percentages of Total Retail Sales Held by Different Types of Organization in Seven European Countries, 1979[a]

	Corporate chains[b]	Independents and contractual chains[c]	Cooperatives
UK	47.8	44.8	7.4
Germany	34.0	62.6	3.4
France	30.4	66.6	3.0
Netherlands	26.4	73.1	0.5
Denmark	23.0	63.0	14.0
Belgium	18.5	80.8	0.7
Italy	7.0	92.0	1.0

[a] Britain changed its classificatory scheme for retail organizations in 1980 and this prevents a strict comparison of its retail structure with those of other European countries in more recent years.

[b] Corporate chains include multiples, department, and variety store chains, and mail order.

[c] Contractual chains comprise independents affiliated to voluntary groups, retailer cooperatives, and franchises.

Source: Institute of Retail Studies, University of Stirling.

the ten largest retailers account for over 40% of total sales (Business Statistics Office, 1985). Large multiples have also assumed much of the responsibility for intermediate storage and shop delivery that in other countries is vested in separate wholesale firms. By channelling their goods through the centralized distribution systems of these multiples, foreign manufacturers can, with comparative ease, gain wide access to the British market. Foreign manufacturers also benefit from the highly competitive market in the UK for contract distribution (McKinnon, 1986*b*). The relentless increase in import penetration in recent years has demonstrated that greater proximity to customers offers many British manufacturers little advantage in their home market. In the fashion, clothing, and footwear trades, where the large retail chains are today ordering smaller quantities more frequently and demanding more rapid delivery, domestic manufacturers have a clear logistical advantage over distant over-seas suppliers (*Financial Times*, 5th February 1986). In many other trades, however, where product life-cycles are longer, foreign manufacturers can easily match the order lead times of domestic producers.

British manufacturers have been criticized for the slow and unreliable delivery of goods to foreign customers. A study of firms marketing British goods in other European countries conducted by the Council of British Chambers of Commerce in Continental

Europe in 1979 identified poor delivery as the main factor limiting their sales of these products (Christopher, 1981). The widespread practice in British industry of selling goods to foreign customers on a free-on-board basis and leaving the customer to arrange transport usually deprives British freight forwarders and carriers of business, represents a loss of foreign exchange, and prevents the exporting firm from using PD positively as a tool of international marketing (*Focus on Physical Distribution Management*, 1984).

The quality of the distribution service can also indirectly influence costs through its effect on inventory levels. Slow and unreliable distribution requires higher stock levels which absorb larger amounts of working capital and are more costly to finance. British stock levels are significantly higher than those of most other developed economies and most of this excess stock is held in the manufacturing sector (Ray, 1981). This is considered to be both a cause and a symptom of Britain's poor industrial performance (Waters, 1984). British manufacturing industry has been slow to introduce the new 'just-in-time' systems of inventory management, pioneered in Japan and now widely adopted by North American firms. Such systems allow firms to make substantial reductions in stock levels by delaying the replenishment of supplies until they are actually required (Christopher, 1986).

It appears, therefore, that the poor performance of British manufacturing industry is partly attributable to shortcomings in the systems of stockholding and freight movement.

Externalization of the physical distribution function

Freight transport

The division of road freight tonnage between 'own account' and 'hire and reward' operators can be ascertained from the Department of Transport's Annual Road Goods Survey. For many years this survey indicated that responsibility for road freight transport (measured in tonnes lifted) was fairly evenly divided between the two types of operator. Between 1984 and 1985, however, the proportion of freight tonnage carried by haulage contractors rose from 51% to 55%, confirming widespread anecdotal evidence that firms are increasingly externalizing the transport function (Department of Transport, 1986). Individual manufacturers, nevertheless, vary enormously in their use of road hauliers (or British Rail) for trunk movements. Some have a policy of contracting out all their haulage; others use their own vehicles to varying degrees. It is common for manufacturers to use their 'own account' vehicles for shorter hauls, larger consignments and journeys on which they can obtain a return load (Ministry of Transport, 1970). Attempts to model the division of traffic between 'own account' and 'third party' operations on the basis of these and other variables using discriminant analysis have, however, yielded disappointing results (Bayliss and Edwards, 1970). More recent research has established that the choice of transport mode can only be understood within the context of firms' wider production and distribution strategies (Pike, 1982; European Conference of Ministers of Transport, 1985). It has been argued, though, that many firms do not adequately cost their 'in-house' transport operation or monitor its performance (Kelly, 1978). This suggests that, in many cases, the allocation of freight traffic to haulage contractors is not decided on the basis of a full and rational appraisal of the alternative modes.

Storage

There are no statistics available on the division of responsibility for storage between 'own account' and contract operations. The compilation of such statistics would be fraught with difficulty, particularly as there is no generally accepted standard unit of storage. The *National Expenditure Blue Book* presents information on the book value of stocks owned by various types of organization, but, as storage contractors do not assume ownership of goods they handle, no indication is given of the value of stocks held in their warehouses. Measures of the amount of goods in storage at any given time would also have to be supplemented by measures of the rate of stock turnover as it is the inward and outward movement of stock that generates most of the work in storage premises. It follows that expenditure on storage and associated materials handling is probably the best measure. However, available statistics on manufacturers' expenditure on storage do not distinguish between 'in-house' and contract operations.

Manufacturers' stocks can be divided into three categories: raw materials, work-in-progress, and finished goods. Work-in-progress is traditionally the largest category, accounting in 1984 for roughly 39% of the book value of manufacturers' stocks (Central Statistical Office, 1985). This type of stock is by definition intrinsic to the production process and is, therefore, almost invariably stored by the manufacturer on the factory site. Production schedules also require manufacturers to hold certain amounts of raw material and finished goods beside the factory. Ackerman and LaLonde (1980) have estimated that on average 30–5% of factory space is used for the storage of raw materials and finished goods. The remaining stocks are less tied to the production site and more suitable for contracting out to warehousing agencies. Manufacturers can have various motives for employing these contractors. Firms experiencing wide fluctuations in demand can improve the productivity of their 'in-house' operation by assigning a stable base load to their own storage facilities and contracting out the storage of peak volumes. The use of outside warehousing firms can also be a temporary contingency measure when unanticipated variations in the level of supply or demand cause stock volumes to exceed the capacity of 'in-house' storage facilities. Manufacturers often contract out the storage of slow-moving product lines that spend a relatively long time in storage, preferring to use their own storage premises for products that turn over more rapidly and use the available space more intensively. It is still common for firms importing goods to channel them through contract warehouses in the vicinity of ports and airports, though unitization of international freight in containers, road trailers, and rail wagons has greatly reduced the demand for warehouse space around seaports.

Integrated distribution

Over the past fifteen years, the nature of the services offered by contractors has changed markedly. Firms providing a haulage or storage service on its own have declined in importance, while there has been a large increase in the number and size of distribution contractors offering a complete distribution package, mainly for finished products and comprising storage, transport, break-bulk, and consolidation services, order processing, and even telephone sales. The substantial growth of the market for integrated distribution services can be attributed to a series of demand and supply factors.

On the demand side, it partly reflects a growing acceptance of the fact that by integrating the various PD functions it is possible both to cut costs and to enhance the quality of service. Contracting out a range of inter-related PD functions to the same firm also relieves management of the need to co-ordinate the operations of a number of separate storage and haulage agencies.

On the supply side, the low profitability of general road haulage (Harvey, 1984) has caused many of the larger firms to diversify into storage, break-bulk operations, and more specialist forms of haulage in an effort to 'trade up' into more profitable services (Firth, 1976). Similarly, many warehousing firms whose business was in the past confined to storage have been able to generate new and more profitable trade by developing distribution services. In 1983, for example, 48% of warehouses operated by members of the National Association of Warehouse Keepers offered distribution as well as storage services. Many contractors aim to provide clients with a comprehensive distribution operation on a dedicated basis, thereby securing business in the longer term and 'isolating' themselves from over-capacity in the general storage and haulage markets (Warner, 1986).

A recent survey of 82 manufacturers and retailers in the food, drink, confectionery, household goods, and pharmaceuticals trades has given some indication of the relative use of contractors in the distribution of finished goods (*The Grocer*, 19th July, 1986). This has shown that only 12% of manufacturers and 23% of retailers rely totally on their in-house distribution operations (Table 5.20). The majority of the firms surveyed used contractors to supplement their 'own account' operations. In the field of PD, much of the demand for contractors arises from spatial and temporal variations in the volume of throughput. The high cost of accommodating marginal flows in 'own account' systems can generally by undercut by the rates charged by contractors. Contractors are able to offer these favourable rates by balancing customers' requirements through time and consolidating traffic volumes in areas of low demand. However, contractors are not always cast in this subordinate role. A substantial proportion of the manufacturers surveyed entrust them with their entire distribution operation. Overall, the manufacturers exhibited a stronger dependence on contractors than retailers, appearing more willing to relinquish all responsibility for PD to contractors.

Over the past decade, manufacturers and retailers have been externalizing an increasing proportion of their PD work. Evidence of this trend can be found in the input–output data summarized in Table 3.3, which shows that between 1968 and 1979 manufacturers

Table 5.20. Relative Dependence on Distribution Contractors

	Manufacturers %	Multiple retailers %
Total dependence on own account	12	23
Total dependence on contractors	39	15
Mixed own account/contractor	49	54
All goods direct from supplier	—	8

Note: Based on a sample of 82 firms in the grocery, confectionery, drink, pharmaceutical, and household goods trades. (Results of market research undertaken by Kae Developments Ltd., for Lowfield Distribution Ltd.)

Source: The Grocer, 19th July 1986.

significantly increased their relative expenditure on specialist transport and distribution services. There is also much anecdotal evidence in the trade press to suggest that this externalization process pervades many industrial sectors and is well advanced.

Factors promoting the growth of contract distribution

Economic and technological processes

In the recent period of high interest rates and low financial liquidity many manufacturers and retailers have externalized their PD to convert it from a capital to a current cost element on the balance sheet. This has also enabled them to divert their financial and management resources away from what is commonly perceived as an ancillary function towards their main activity (Latta, 1977). PD has become more capital-intensive as a result of computerization and the development of highly mechanized storage and handling systems. Many firms have felt unable or unwilling to commit the necessary resources to their in-house systems to keep up with this new technology (Hawkins, 1976). The gradual phasing out of capital investment allowances since 1984 has reinforced the trend away from 'own-account' operations, discouraging manufacturers and retailers from making further investment in distribution facilities and strengthening the relative economic advantage of contract services.

Some of the larger contractors, such as BRS and Systemline, now offer to buy out a firm's 'in-house' distribution system and thereafter operate it for them on an exclusive basis. In October 1986, for example, the computer firm, ICL, transferred ownership and management of its entire transport operation to BRS. Such deals facilitate the change-over to a contract system and can inject much needed capital into the client firm's business.

Sharp increases in the cost of PD (Centre for Physical Distribution Management, 1984) and the growing realization of the high cost of delivering small orders (McConkey, 1979) have also prompted firms to reassess the relative merits of 'own account' operations. By grouping many firm's traffic, contractors generally achieve higher levels of depot and vehicle utilization, making them better able to withstand cost increases.

Uncertainties about the operating environment

In the 1970s, many manufacturers and retailers were deterred from investing in distribution facilities by uncertainties about future increases in fuel prices, environmental controls on lorry movement,

EEC legislation on drivers' hours and vehicle specifications, and the reliability of new storage and handling systems. It was often considered more prudent to let contractors shoulder the risks associated with these developments.

The use of contractors has also enabled firms to reduce the risk of their distribution operations being disrupted by industrial action. Some firms, such as Sainsburys (Barber and Payne, 1976), require contractors to provide a parallel distribution service, while others use the threat of contracting out more distribution work as a bargaining lever in trade union negotiations.

Structural change in the distributive trades

The development of superstores, retail warehouses, and hyper-markets, the growth of multiple retailing, and the increasing tendency for multiples to channel their supplies through central warehouses has increased the proportion of manufacturers' finished output being distributed directly from the factory. This has led to a reduction in the volume of business handled by manufacturers' shop delivery systems. Manufacturers have responded to this situation in two ways. Many have scaled down their 'own account' operations and diverted an increasing proportion of their traffic to contractors. Others have tried to compensate for the loss of throughput by taking advantage of the freedom granted to 'own account' operators by the 1968 Transport Act and carrying traffic for other firms on a 'hire and reward' basis. This helps them to spread the high overhead costs of their delivery system. Across industry as a whole, there is very limited sharing of 'own account' facilities (Cooper, 1978); however some firms, such as Imperial Foods, United Biscuits, and Tate and Lyle, have been so successful in securing 'third party' traffic that they have made their distribution operation into a separate profit centre or even a subsidiary.

There have been some instances of multiple retailers exercising their bargaining power to induce manufacturers more directly into making greater use of contractors. They have instructed manufac-turers to channel their supplies through 'nominated carriers' rather than deliver them directly to branch stores. This offers a means of consolidating incoming orders and relieving 'backdoor congestion' at retail outlets.

Increased import penetration

Foreign manufacturers generally have a greater propensity to employ contractors than domestic manufacturers. A recent survey of

55 foreign manufacturers marketing consumer durable products in the UK found that all but two of these firms made substantial use of British PD contractors, while over 70% of these firms' total sales volume in the UK was delivered to wholesale and retail customers by British contractors (McKinnon, 1986*b*). This heavy reliance on contractors can be attributed to several factors. Many foreign firms do not generate sufficient sales in the UK to mount a cost-effective 'own-account' distribution operation. There is also an unwillingness on the part of many multinationals to invest heavily in distribution facilities and a desire to take advantage of the greater flexibility offered by contract operations. Some foreign subsidiaries are also influenced by the prevailing distribution practices in their country of origin, where the use of contractors is often the norm.

Employment in physical distribution

In contrast to manufacturing, PD has maintained roughly its share of total employment, though this is not revealed by analyses of employment creation conducted at the level of the SIC, partly because this classification groups freight handling with other activities that have experienced a sharp decline in employment and partly because it gives little indication of employment in 'own account' distribution operations.

Firms providing PD services are to be found in the 1968 SICs of transport and communications and distributive trades. The former experienced an overall decline in employment between 1959 and 1982 of 21%, most of which was attributable to employment losses of 32% in road passenger transport, 64% in railways, and 66% in ports/inland waterways. It is not possible to estimate how much of the employment reduction in railways was due to the contraction of their freight operations. The substantial reduction in employment in seaports has been caused primarily by the adoption of new systems of modal interchange involving the use of containers and roll-on and roll-off ferries, and the realignment of Britain's trade away from deep sea routes to near and short sea links with Europe. In contrast to these MLHs experiencing heavy job losses, those representing road-based transport and distribution operations together increased their employment by 62% over the period 1959–82. The numbers employed in general haulage fluctuated between 200,000 and 260,000, while the miscellaneous transport services and storage category, including the new generation of specialist distribution companies, increased its employment steadily from 66,000 to 189,000.

Similarly, in the case of the distributive trades SIC, an overall decline in employment of 3.5% between 1959 and 1982 concealed an employment growth of 3.6% in wholesaling and dealing activities. The average figure for the SIC as a whole was depressed by a decline in retail employment of 6.5%. This employment estimate for retail firms is also likely to mask a shift in employment from retail outlets, where productivity has been raised by the adoption of self-service techniques and improved goods reception facilities, to the storage, handling, and delivery of supplies 'upstream' of the shop.

It is interesting to note that wholesaling and dealing showed net increases in employment between 1959 and 1982, despite the fact that in many market sectors, such as those of food, drink, clothing, footwear, and electrical goods (NEDO, 1985), an increasing proportion of business has been bypassing the wholesaler, to be transferred directly from producer to retailer. Furthermore, the rapid growth of the cash and carry mode of wholesaling during the 1960s and 1970s has significantly increased its labour productivity by shedding responsibility for the picking and delivery of orders onto trade customers. In the food and drink trades, where competition from multiple retailers has been most intense and the development of cash and carries most extensive, wholesale employment in fact declined by 6% between 1970 and 1982. This employment loss was more than offset, however, by a sharp increase in the number employed in firms dealing in machinery and industrial materials (other than fuels, building materials, and agricultural produce), and a smaller gain in the other wholesaling category.

The seven MLHs that are most closely associated with PD increased their employment by 16% between 1959 and 1982 (Table 5.21) while manufacturing employment delined by 25% and total employment by 5%. Such a comparison may be misleading, however, as some of the growth of employment in haulage, wholesaling, and dealing firms may have resulted from PD work being transferred to these agencies from manufacturers and retailers. Rajan and Pearson (1986) estimate that between 1979 and 1985 approximately 100,000 jobs were 'redistributed' from other industries to the wholesale sector, which in their definition includes distribution contractors. As employees engaged in PD tasks within manufacturing firms are usually included in the corresponding production SIC, some of the decline in manufacturing employment may have been due to the externalization of PD services. To obtain a more complete picture of employment in PD it is necessary, therefore, to quantify employment in the 'own account' sector.

In assessing total employment in 'logistics', Childerley (1980)

Table 5.21. Employment Change in Major Distributive MLHS, 1959–1982

	1959	1982[a]	% change
Road haulage contracting for general hire and reward	187	191	+12.2
Other road haulage		19	
Miscellaneous transport services and storage	66	189	+186.4
Wholesale distribution of food and drink		229	
Wholesale distribution of petroleum	538	32	−2.6
Other wholesaling		263	
Dealing in coal, oil, builders' materials, grain, and agricultural supplies	169	132	−21.9
Dealing in other industrial materials and machinery	124	205	+65.3
TOTAL	1084	1260	+16.2

[a] Estimates.

Source: Census of Employment.

assumed that 20% of employees in 'manufacturing and production industries' were engaged in logistical work. Occupational data collected in the 1981 Census of Population shows a much smaller proportion of manufacturing employees working in transport, storage, and materials handling, suggesting that Childerley based her calculations on a very wide definition of logistics. The 1981 Census of Population indicates that approximately 1.9% of manufacturing employees were directly involved in transport and 2.7% in storage and materials handling, though these proportions varied markedly between industrial sectors. When compared with figures of 2.0% and 3.0% respectively in 1971 (Crum and Gudgin, 1977), it seems that PD's share of total manufacturing jobs has declined only slightly. This evidence appears to conflict with the input–output data presented in Table 3.3. Two reasons can be offered for this apparent anomaly. First, the occupational classification used in the Census of Population changed between 1971 and 1981, and this may distort the comparison of manufacturing employment profiles in the two years. Second, it is necessary to take account of differences in the rates of productivity improvement between PD and the other activities manufacturers perform. It is possible, for example, that productivity has risen faster in production than in PD. Productivity gains might then be responsible for a larger proportion of job losses in production than in PD. Under these circumstances one would expect PD to increase its share of total manufacturing employment.

The fact that its share has slightly diminished would then suggest that firms are externalizing more PD work. It is unfortunately not possible to test this hypothesis empirically.

It appears that the aggregate reduction in PD employment in 'own account' operations, railways and ports more than offset the increase in employment in haulage/distribution contracting, whole-saling, and dealing. On balance, employment in PD has declined slightly more than total employment, but to a much lesser extent than employment in manufacturing. The available evidence also indicates that there has been a net transfer of PD employment from manufacturing concerns to outside contractors, wholesalers, and multiple retailers. The unavoidable exclusion of multiple retailers' PD activities from the calculation probably causes some over-estimation of the net employment loss in PD across the economy as a whole.

Although PD has approximately maintained its share of total employment, it is often argued that it creates only low skilled, blue collar jobs. However, surveys of employment in warehouses, which are the main centres for PD operations, indicate that the quality of employment is higher than is often imagined. A survey of 266 warehouses in the East Midlands, for example, found that on average only 46% of warehouse employees were directly engaged in lorry driving or materials handling (McKinnon and Pratt, 1984). The remaining staff had clerical, managerial, sales, or other non-manual duties. The 1981 Census of Population revealed that only about a quarter of those working for wholesaling and dealing firms were employed in transport and materials handling. The employment categories associated with PD, therefore, include a large element of white collar work.

Spatial distribution of demand for PD services

1. *Bulk storage*. The greatest demand for bulk storage services is in the vicinity of production premises and the ports. Most of the warehouses accommodating manufacturers' bulk stocks of raw materials and finished goods are production-oriented (Bowersox, 1969*b*). Raw materials must be readily available for injection into the production process, while bulk supplies of finished goods are best stored centrally at or near the factory prior to distribution. Warehouses that draw bulk stock from more than one factory and serve as 'mixing points' can occupy intermediate locations between factories and distribution depots. There are also concentrations of bulk storage space around the ports, though, as indicated earlier, these have dimished over the past twenty years as a consequence of containerization and the development of roll-on–roll-off services.

2. *Trunk Haulage.* Manufacturers tend to employ outside hauliers more for long distance, bulk movements than for shorter hauls and smaller consignments (Bayliss and Edwards, 1970; Ministry of Transport, 1970). In 1984, the average length of haul for hauliers was 84 km. as opposed to 52 km. for 'own account' operators (Department of Transport, 1985), while in 1977 hauliers' vehicles lifted an average of 5,700 tonnes per annum by comparison with 1,990 tonnes per annum on 'own account' vehicles (Department of Transport, 1978). Most long distance movements begin or end at a factory, making factories a major focus of demand for trunk haulage services. Very little is known, however, about the factors influencing manufacturers' choice of hauliers and the geography of this selection process. The relationship between the industrial demand for trunk haulage services in an area and its manufacturing base will be determined partly by the nature of this selection process, but also by the propensity of local manufacturers to contract out their haulage operation. It is likely that both these factors will be affected by the nature and organizational structure of local manufacturing industry, though there are no empirical data available with which to test this hypothesis.

3. *Local Distribution.* According to Bowersox's classification, local distribution services, comprising storage, breaking of bulk (and/or consolidation), and short distance deliveries are 'market-oriented' and are, therefore, widely dispersed. Manufacturers differ markedly in the number of local distribution depots through which they channel their output. The national distribution of perishable foodstuffs might require a minimum of around 20 local distribution points, fast-moving convenience products 8–10 and slower moving consumer durables 1–3.

Numerous factors influence the spatial structure of manufacturers' distribution systems. Considerable importance is attached to the trade-off between storage/stockholding costs, which increase as systems become more decentralized, and delivery costs, which follow the opposite trend (Fig. 5.6) (Waller, 1983). The actual configuration of the two cost curves varies with product type, choice of handling system and the number, sizes, and spatial distribution of customers. Total distribution costs, however, are often relatively insensitive to marginal variations in depot numbers. Cadbury–Schweppes, for example, when redesigning its distribution system in the early 1970s, found that total distribution costs were only 0.2% higher in a ten depot system than in one comprising only seven depots (Beattie, 1973). In distribution planning, cost minimization is generally constrained by the requirement, usually stipulated by marketing and sales departments, that customers' orders be delivered within a given time. This 'service level' requirement can

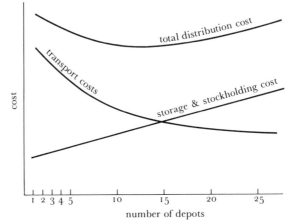

Fig. 5.6.   Relationship between distribution costs and depot numbers.

determine the maximum size of depot hinterlands and hence the number of depots necessary to supply the national market.

While some firms, such as Brooke-Bond–Oxo (Barnett, 1978), have developed completely new distribution systems from scratch, it is more common for systems to evolve gradually through a series of marginal changes in depot numbers and locations, prompted by such things as company mergers, the opening of new motorway links, and the expiry of a depot lease. There are numerous instances of competing manufacturers in the same industry decentralizing their distribution operations to widely varying extents. Little attempt has so far been made to explore the reasons for such variations, though it is likely that they partly reflect differences in marketing strategy, the spatial distribution of production, and historical circumstances specific to individual firms.

Despite the variations in depot numbers there is considerable agreement among manufacturers on what are the main strategic locations from which to supply the national market and on the order in which these locations should be incorporated into their distribution systems (Sussams, 1969). A survey of the distribution systems of 29 food manufacturers revealed that roughly two thirds of their stockholding depots were within 20 miles of nine cities: London, Bristol, Glasgow, Birmingham, Manchester, Newcastle, Leeds, Nottingham, and Southampton (McKinnon, 1983*b*). Particularly high concentrations of distribution depots have also developed in towns such as Warrington, Swindon, and Rochdale, which have been promoted as major centres for distribution largely on the basis of motorway accessibility. As depot numbers vary widely, it is difficult to make a direct comparison of manufacturers' choices of depot locations. The available evidence suggests, however, that there is a good deal of regularity in the sequence in which depots are 'added' to national distribution systems as the degree of stock dispersal increases. Firms centralizing their operations tend to do so at a location in the Midlands or Home Counties. Those distributing from two depots would be likely to locate them round Manchester and London. Further locations are subsequently added to this two-depot system in the order indicated in Table 5.22 (Sussams, 1969; Stoker 1978; McKinnon, 1985*b*). Various factors, such as factory location and the pattern of sales, may cause a particular manufacturer's depot locations to deviate from these generalized sequences.

Manufacturers also differ in the extent to which they employ contractors to handle local distribution. It is quite common for manufacturers to serve areas of high demand from their own depots and use contractors in more peripheral areas where throughput volumes fall below the minimum required for a viable 'in-house' operation. Heavy use is, nevertheless, made of contractors in more central locations, as demonstrated by the fact that half the depots operated by the large specialist distributors of food products are located in or around London, Birmingham, Bristol, and Manchester (Institute of Grocery Distribution, 1984). Many of these depots are used by manufacturers and multiple retailers contracting out a large proportion of their local distribution work. Little research has been done on manufacturers' choice of distribution contractors, though it appears that, in searching for suitable contract depots, manufacturers adhere to the same sequence of depot locations as exhibited by their 'in-house' operations.

The spatial structure of contractors' distribution systems reflects the types of product handled. Firms providing a national distribution service for groceries, for example, generally require 8–11 depots to meet manufacturers shop delivery requirements, whereas for firms

Table 5.22. Generalized Sequences of Depot Locations

Sussams (1969)	Stoker (1978)	McKinnon (1985*b*)
1. Birmingham	London	—
2. London	Manchester	London
3. Manchester	Birmingham	North West
4. Glasgow	Glasgow	Glasgow
5. Bristol	Bristol	Bristol
6. Newcastle	Newcastle	Newcastle
7. Southampton	Southampton	East Anglia
8. Leeds	Hull	West Midlands

handling clothing and electrical products 3–6 depots can suffice. The situation is complicated, however, by contractors operating some depots exclusively for individual clients or channelling flows of different types of product through the same depot.

Over the past twenty years, manufacturers have substantially reduced the number of depots through which they distribute their products to minimize stock levels and take advantage of economies of scale in warehousing (McKinnon, 1981). According to the 'square root law of inventory', the spatial concentration of stocks permits a large reduction in the total amount of stock that must be held to provide a given level of service (Maister, 1976). Newson (1978), for example, reports the case of a British office equipment supplier that achieved a 40% reduction in inventory investment by closing twelve regional depots and centralizing stock in a single location. High real interest rates over the past seven years have exerted a strong pressure on firms to cut the financial costs of stockholding and increased the cost advantages of centralizing stocks. Major improvements to the road network, the use of heavier vehicles and the increased consolidation of deliveries have enabled manufacturers to concentrate their stocks in fewer, larger depots and supply customers over longer distances from these more centralized facilities. This has increased the concentration of warehouse capacity around the main strategic centres listed above. In some cases manufacturers have absorbed within the hinterlands of their own depots peripheral areas previously served by contractors. A more common occurrence, however, has been manufacturers centralizing their stockholding to such an extent that direct deliveries to more peripheral areas become uneconomic. Many manufacturers have overcome this problem by separating storage and break-bulk operations, centralizing the former, while dispersing the latter to numerous transshipment points around the country. Much of the localized break-bulk and delivery work is contracted out, as these services are often provided most efficiently and expeditely on a groupage basis. The centralization of stockholding has, therefore, promoted an increased and more dispersed use of contractors in a break-bulk–local delivery role.

Market services

The demand for 'contract' local distribution services in an area also depends on the level of manufacturers' sales to wholesalers and retailers. It has been shown in the case of grocery distribution, for example, that wholesalers and multiple retailers play a more prominent role in PD in some areas than in others (*Nielsen Researcher*, 1974).

1. *Wholesaling and Dealing*. Geographical studies of wholesaling have been severely constrained in the UK by a lack of data. The only spatially disaggregated statistics available are those collected in the 1951 Census of Distribution. These showed that the number of wholesale establishments, wholesale turnover and employment all correlated closely, at a regional level, with population (Edwards, 1982). Wholesaling and dealing functions have tended to be concentrated at the upper levels of the urban hierarchy, though changes in their location quotients between 1971 and 1981 (Table 4.11) suggest that they have been decentralizing from the major conurbations to lower-order towns. The structure and spatial organization of the wholesale trades are, nevertheless, extremely complex. Wholesalers are not simply intermediaries between manufacturers and retailers, as conventional models of the distributive system tend to portray them (Moir, 1984). Indeed in 1974, only 57% of their purchases were from UK producers and 37% of their sales were to retailers (Business Statistics Office, 1979). In the case of dealers, just over half the industrial goods they handled were obtained from manufacturers. Wholesalers and dealers organize the exchange of goods at all levels of the systems of material procurement, production, and distribution. Some sections of the wholesale trade, such as those dealing in clothing and hardware, have a hierarchical structure with some goods passing through several wholesalers *en route* to the retailer or final consumer. In other trades, such as those of grocery products and books, wholesalers typically occupy a single tier between producers and retailers.

What little spatial theory has been developed on wholesaling derives from central place theory and suggests that higher-order wholesalers are concentrated in major urban areas and around the main producers of the goods in which they deal (Rabiega and Lamoureux, 1973). Wholesalers at lower levels in the distributive channel are more widely dispersed and serve smaller areas. Wholesaling, particularly of finished goods, has been subject to considerable rationalization over the past decade, with the concentration of wholesale operations in fewer, larger depots in higher-order settlements and their decentralization to the urban periphery (Dawson, 1979). Between 1981 and 1984, the number of wholesale grocery depots (excluding 'cash and carries') declined from 409 to 270 while their average size increased from 30,292 sq. ft. to 48,000 sq. ft. (Moir, 1984).

2. *Multiple Retailers*. Over the past 25 years, multiple retailers have greatly increased their control over physical distribution, both

through direct involvement in intermediate storage and shop delivery and by employing contractors to store, consolidate, and deliver their supplies. The numbers and locations of multiple retailers' warehouses are dictated largely by the size and geographical extent of their chains and the nature of the products they sell. Broadly speaking multiples centralize their distribution operations to a greater extent than wholesalers and manufacturers in the same trade. They are able to do so partly because they serve smaller numbers of larger outlets, but also because their direct consolidated deliveries have a longer range than multiple drop deliveries from manufacturers' and wholesalers' depots. As in the case of manufacturers, multiples selling similar products and in direct competition can differ markedly in the way they organize their physical distribution.

Retail chains vary enormously in their relative dependence on central warehouses under their control. In the grocery trade, for example, some firms, such as Safeway and Sainsbury, direct the vast majority of their supplies through such warehouses, while others, most notably Asda, require most of their suppliers to deliver orders directly to branch stores (Robson, 1985). Even firms that exert similar levels of control over the inflow of supplies can differ in the number of warehouses they employ. Of the 'mixed retail businesses', British Home Stores, operates a highly centralized system based on a single warehouse at Atherstone, whereas Marks and Spencer and Littlewoods channel their supplies through several regional depots. Some firms, such as Boots and Currys, supplement central warehouses with a series of satellite trans-shipment depots. It is very difficult, therefore, to generalize about the nature and extent of multiple retailers' involvement in physical distribution 'upstream' of the shop (McKinnon, 1986*a*). The spatial distribution of warehouses, operated by multiples and by contractors exclusively on their behalf, nevertheless shows a pronounced clustering around the major conurbations of Greater Manchester, West Yorkshire, West Midlands, and London and along the motorway axes of the M4, M1, and M6. There has also been a general increase over the past fifteen years in multiple retailers' use of distribution contractors, partly to support the geographical extension of retail chains and the expansion of their product ranges, but also in response to similar pressures to those already examined in the case of manufacturers.

Effects of infrastructural and technological change

The effects of these changes on PD can be examined under three headings.

1. *Freight Transport.* The substantial improvements that have been made to the road network and goods vehicle performance over the past 20 years have permitted the centralization of stockholding and expansion of depot hinterlands (Corcoran, Hitchcock, and McMahon, 1980). This has had the effect of concentrating the demand for PD services and warehouse-based employment in more central locations. The resulting increase in average journey length is unlikely in itself to have created much additional employment in freight transport because the acceleration of freight movement has enabled drivers to travel longer distances during their daily shifts. Some of the benefit of transport improvement has been offset by the introduction of tighter environmental controls on the routing and scheduling of delivery vehicles. The reduction, between 1979 and 1981, in the maximum permitted daily driving time for lorry drivers from 10 to 8 hours appears not to have reduced the productivity of road transport (Newton, 1985). This productivity has, on the other hand, been considerably enhanced by the adoption of new handling systems and by the gradual replacement of multiple drop rounds with direct consolidated deliveries, both of which have promoted the centralization of PD operations. Sharp increases in the cost of new, higher performance vehicles may have encouraged some manufacturers to contract out more of their transport or enter into vehicle leasing arrangements. On the whole, however, technical improvements in freight transport appear to have had little impact on the balance between 'own account' and 'contract' operations.

2. *Storage and Materials Handling.* There have been sweeping improvements in materials handling technology over the past twenty years, greatly facilitating the movement, stacking, sorting, and retrieval of stocks in warehouses. There has been comparatively little development, however, of fully automated warehouses in the UK. It was estimated in 1982 that there were around 110 warehouses with automated storage/retrieval systems (AS/RS) in the UK, and most of these were operated by manufacturers and multiple retailers (Williams, 1982). The very slow rate of development of these systems was attributed in the past to their high capital cost, unreliability, and long commissioning times. A survey in 1982 found that firms were no longer so concerned about reliability and commissioning times, but they still regarded AS/RS as very expensive, inflexible, and, in many cases, unsuited to their product ranges, order picking requirements, and depot sizes. The National Materials Handling Centre has forecast that the future development of AS/RS in the UK will be slow (Williams, 1982).

There has been much wider application of smaller scale technical improvements in stock handling, involving the use of conveyor systems, guided track vehicles, and mechanical stacker cranes (Rushton, 1984). This apparatus is much cheaper and can be installed incrementally, used more flexibly, and accommodated in warehouses of standard construction. Investment in such equipment is only justified, however, where there is a need for rapid sorting and throughput of stock and a wide product range. Much of this equipment is found in multiple retailers' distribution centres, warehouses in which manufacturers store components, and in the depots of parcel carriers.

As a general rule the more highly mechanized the handling system the more closely it must be tailored to the products and sorting requirements of individual firms, reducing the likelihood of the storage/distribution operation being contracted out. Some PD contractors have, however, installed specialist equipment in depots dedicated to the distribution of a particular firm's products, where this client has been prepared to enter into a long term contract. More generally, the increased use of mechanical handling (and computing) equipment is making the distribution function more capital intensive and raising the viability threshold for 'own account' operations. It is likely, therefore, to encourage a greater use of contractors, particularly by smaller firms.

The main spatial consequence of the increased mechanization of warehousing has been a further concentration of warehousing capacity. As there are economies of scale in the installation and operation of many of the new handling systems, firms have a strong incentive to centralize their stockholding and sorting operations in fewer locations. This has been a major factor in the development of 'hub' systems by parcels carriers in which automated sorting is centralized at a single location (Scott and Cooper, 1985).

Improvements in materials handling technology are both reducing warehouse employment and altering its occupational structure. Manual portering jobs, formerly done by warehousemen, are declining. However, as indicated earlier, these represent on average less than a third of total warehouse employment. Some of these jobs are being replaced by lighter, more technically demanding jobs in the operation, checking, and maintenance of handling equipment. It should also be noted that the installation of more advanced handling systems is often motivated much more by a desire to accelerate the throughput of stock than to reduce staffing levels.

3. *Information Processing.* Many aspects of PD have benefited from the increased use of computers. The computerization of stock control has permitted a reduction in stock levels and the associated paper work reducing the demand for materials handling and clerical staff (NEDO, 1982). Many of the new developments in computerized

stock monitoring have been pioneered by multiple retailers. They are responsible for the spread of portable data entry terminals (PDET) and electronic point of sale (EPOS) equipment, which, when linked to a central computer, permits the continuous monitoring of stock in shops, and quickly relays this information to the warehouse. This rapid transmission of stock data enables firms to reduce the amounts of stock they need to hold, particularly in their shops. The scale of this stock reduction depends on the speed at which the supply system can respond. The best results are achieved when supplies are drawn from a small number of warehouses, thus giving retailers an additional incentive to centralize their stockholding. Some of the contractors employed by multiple retailers have been linked into their computerized stock monitoring and order processing networks. David Quarmby, Sainsbury's distribution director, sees the application of new computing and communications systems creating a major opportunity for distribution contractors. He argues that:

In order to achieve the real benefits in total distribution systems, from suppliers' factory right to the shelf in the branch, the required investment in software, and in the management effort to market and implement it is enormous. There is, I believe, a potential for the larger distribution companies to develop, market and operate total branch ordering/stock control/depot replenishment systems, either for smaller suppliers and/or smaller retailers or groups. (Quarmby, 1985)

In marketing their PD services to manufacturers and retailers, several contractors already place great emphasis on the highly computerized nature of their operations.

Conclusion

The level of PD activity is not simply a function of manufacturing output, nor is its spatial distribution closely tied to that of production. Over the past 30 years total employment in PD appears to have fallen, but by a much smaller amount than manufacturing. Manufacturers have been relinquishing responsibility for PD to outside contractors, which they hire directly, and to retail and wholesale customers. Having assumed much of the reponsibility for intermediate storage and shop delivery, multiple retailers have contracted out an increasing proportion of this work to specialist distribution firms. Contractors have been quick to exploit the rapidly increasing demand for integrated distribution services by diversifying their operations and entering into long term contracts

with manufacturers and multiple retailers. Many have used technical innovation as a means of prising traffic away from 'in-house'
systems and to strengthen their competitive position *vis-à-vis* other
contractors. According to a recent survey by the Institute of
Manpower Studies there is likely to be further widespread application of new technology in storage, packaging, and distribution in the
next few years (Rajan and Pearson, 1986).

As many of the pressures on manufacturers and retailers to
contract out their physical distribution are likely to remain strong,
one can anticipate a further expansion of specialist distribution
firms, particularly those offering a comprehensive range of services.
A Delphi forecasting exercise undertaken by the Cranfield School of
Management (1984) found universal agreement among four panels
of experts that contract distribution would continue to grow. It was
predicted that the proportion of large and medium sized firms
employing dedicated distribution contractors would reach 75%
between 1994 and 2002.

The extensive growth of contract distribution will significantly
affect the future level and spatial distribution of employment in PD,
the competitiveness of British manufacturing industry and the
structure of the wholesale and retail trades. More detailed investigation of these effects will require much more data on the demand for
and supply of distribution services than is currently available.

5.4. The Financial Sector: Employment, Location, and Technological Change

The technical debate

No analysis of producer services would be complete without an assessment of the impact of technological change because the application of computer-based technology has the capacity to alter the nature of producer services, their role in the economy, and also the location of their employment.

It is uncommon to find blithe optimism in academic circles concerning the impact of technology on services, but there are differences in emphasis. One theme of work argues that the production, manipulation, and communication of information will play an increasingly critical role in the economy. This work looks beyond the present fragmented introduction of information technology (IT) to integrated office systems, local area networks, and the development of a high quality telecommunications infrastructure. It suggests that, by reducing the cost and improving the availability of information, IT will lead to a considerable growth in demand for exisiting and new types of information service (OECD, 1981). In so far as employment is concerned, while the potential negative impacts of IT are not discounted, the emphasis is on the adaptive efforts required to maximize the benefits of IT, and the communications infrastructure is argued to mould this adaptive response since its uneven quality will offer windows of opportunity to firms in some areas to develop a technical leadership in new services (Gillespie *et al.*, 1985).

It is possible to take a less sanguine view of developments in IT. Information provision and processing is not central to all services, nor are the outputs of many intangible services solely information. Producer services provide a range of service commodities and to characterize their development as a response to a demand for information trivializes the very significant changes at work in the markets for producer services; and may in turn lead to an over-emphasis on the communications infrastructure which supports them. A critical feature of producer services is that they have created jobs during a period of contracting manufacturing employment, and the impact of IT on the labour process in services could have important implications for this employment creation in the future.

This case study also avoids the pitfalls associated with the assessment of IT's impact using macroeconomic projections of the relationship between output and employment which may not take account of the extent to which the application of IT will break historical trends. On the other hand, too many studies have focused on the potential of the technology and given insufficient consideration to the economic and organizational circumstances in which it operates. It is argued here that a case study of the impact of IT on employment in one producer service is an appropriate means of study because it will examine the impact of the technology in a specific market, institutional, and workplace context.

Employment and technological change in finance

Chapter 3 has shown that during the last twenty-five years the financial sector has been an important source of employment growth in producer services. The sector has also been at the forefront in the use of IT. To a large extent this can be explained in terms of the opportunity and capacity to use the technology, as well as the market demands on financial organizations to adopt the equipment (Stoneman, 1976). Financial activities process vast quantities of routine information which is well suited to computer applications. Generally firms have easy access to investment funds. Many financial markets also have an oligopolistic market structure where firms command a sufficient market share to ensure a degree of stability in business volume and justify investment. Firms tend to compete on the basis of technological innovation and improvements in the quality of their service (Barras and Swann, 1984*b*).

There is considerable interest in the impact of IT on employment in financial services. Case studies have examined the use of IT in individual industries, organizations, and offices, but it is very difficult to see how these results 'add up'. A common approach to estimating the employment impact of the technology in macroeconomic projections is to estimate the relationship between output growth and employment, and to project the latter forward minus labour productivity improvements associated with the use of IT. However, this is an artificial division because the growth in business witnessed by most of the financial sector has been sustained by the use of IT which has allowed new products such as credit cards to be developed which would be too expensive to support in their present form using manual methods of administration. In such a situation any labour saving associated with IT's use in the data processing of credit card transactions is purely hypothetical because business growth is likely to have been slower without the technology.

A further point, leading on from this, is that technology does not have an independent impact on employment. For example, the market context in which the technology is used is related to its ultimate impact. In a growing market IT is likely to be used to cope with an increase in demand, deliver new products, or improve the quality of service. On the other hand, where business growth is sluggish IT is more likely to be introduced to improve efficiency, reduce unit costs, and implement staff savings. Technology, then, is a vehicle through which companies respond to differing economic circumstances.

Understanding the impact of technology on the location of financial employment is constrained by a lack of secondary source information and by the diversity and complexity of the sector. The financial sector is taken here to include insurance, banking, and bill discounting, as well as other financial institutions in which building societies are prominent. Such financial institutions provide a plethora of services. Some act as intermediaries in the financial system as well as providers of industrial finance, and as such they are deeply integrated into the activities of the City of London. Not surprisingly therefore, the principal clearing banks, financial intermediaries, and insurance companies are largely based in London and the South East. The financial sector in Scotland and Northern Ireland does have some independence, for example each region has its own organization of local clearing banks and some smaller insurance companies are headquartered there. Nevertheless, both financial sectors are closely linked to the rest of the UK and service organizations based in the south have substantial share holdings in regionally based companies.

On the other hand, in parts of the financial sector providing retail services, large organizations have extensive branch networks closely tied to the location of population. In addition, organizations such as the building societies which have until recently operated largely as self-contained deposit-taking and lending institutions in the personal sector have remained locationally independent of the other financial institutions.

This diversity and complexity creates formidable problems when attempting to provide a coherent overview of the financial sector and this is reflected in the somewhat complicated pattern of locational change described later in the case study. The approach adopted here is to combine material in specialist journals with trade union reports, academic publications on the financial sector, and information collected during interviews with professional associations in an attempt to identify a number of broad themes with regard to the impact of technology on the financial sector.

Market changes

IT has been introduced into the financial sector in the context of a growth in business. Nevertheless, traditional markets particularly in insurance have during the last ten years grown slowly or declined, and new expanding markets throughout the sector are characterized by keen competition. Competition has been encouraged by deregulation, government pressure, and responsive diversification by financial organizations into new business related markets. Increasingly, though, financial institutions are also facing competition from new entrants into the sector.

The expansion of the banking institutions can be clearly seen in the growth of the assets of the London and Scottish clearing banks from £56 million in 1975 to £270 million in 1984, half of which were controlled in 1984 by the top banks, Barclays and the National Westmister. In spite of recent losses through intensive price competition and worsening operating ratios, the members of the Insurance Association and Lloyds experienced an average growth of business of 10% p.a. (in current prices) between 1972 and 1982. In the building society movement assets have risen from £18 million in 1973 to £86 million in 1983 and the number of shareholders from 14 million to 37 million.

In recent years deregulation has encouraged business growth. The abolition of exchange controls in 1979 created new investment opportunities and was followed by the abolition of domestic credit controls in 1980 and the abandonment of official regulation of consumer investment credit in 1982. More recently the so-called 'Big Bang' in the City has initiated a restructuring of the London securities market. Legislation to allow building societies greater freedom has also been enacted, and they are to be allowed to become more involved in activities such as consumer banking and estate agency. Internationally, the European Commission is attempting to remove the barriers preventing the transnational transaction of insurance business, and in the US steps are being taken to deregulate financial markets.

As business has grown and markets have become freer, the cartels in financial markets have declined, competition has intensified, traditional demarcation lines between organizations have been broken down, and new entrants into financial markets have appeared. The result has been increasing concentration and interpenetration in the financial sector. Mergers and amalgamations have taken place in the banking sector. This process began at the end of the 1960s when a spate of mergers produced the present 'Big Four' clearing banks. The clearing banks have also acquired hire purchase, leasing, and finance companies. New services such as factoring, leasing, merchant banking, and business advice first developed by the clearing banks in the 1960s have been developed into key sources of business. Life assurance companies have also merged and the number of building societies has fallen from 726 in 1960 to 206 in 1983 largely due to acquisition.

The foreign banks are continuing to increase their presence and activities in the UK. Whereas in 1960 there were 103 foreign banks in London, by 1986 there were about 400 directly represented (see Section 5.1), all but one of the top 100 international banks being represented. Although primarily interested in the international money markets, their participation in corporate business and in the retail market through money shops is growing. In turn, the demands of corporate customers are acting as a general spur to competition because, due to technological developments, they are increasingly able to manage their financial transactions themselves, and by shopping around for business they are encouraging the banks to offer new and more customized services.

During the last ten years the building societies have continued to erode the retail deposit base of the clearing banks and are now beginning to seek wholesale as well as retail funds. They have established links with banks and credit card companies, built up networks of automatic telling machines (ATMs), and become involved in home banking and electronic fund transfer at the point of sale (EFTPOS). With their more specialized product range and (until recently) favourable tax treatment they have provided effective competition for other deposit taking institutions.

The larger composite insurers have expanded into merchant banking, investment management, and property development. The TSB has diversified to provide a range of personal banking services. The same is also true of the National Girobank. Finally, retail stores such as Marks and Spencer and Debenhams have moved into the credit card and personal financial business.

Technology, organization, and location

The market context described above has had a marked influence on the introduction of IT into the financial sector. A growth in business has brought with it rising operating costs especially in retail business. For example, the growth in the number of small accounts in the clearing banks has increased the number of small transactions which are relatively expensive to handle. Inflation has also resulted in frequent changes in the amount of regular financial transactions and the administrative costs of this have been increased by the move towards monthly rather than annual payments. Staff costs form the main element of firm operating costs, being between 60 and 75% in retail banking (Revell, 1980; 1983) and it is likely that they are of a similar order in insurance companies (Barras and Swann, 1983).

In an increasingly competitive market firms have sought to stem increasing operating costs via the containment of staff numbers. A large number of staff in the financial sector are tied up in servicing retail business, so this has implied a reorganization of the branch network in the major firms. IT has been introduced to facilitate this reorganization, but it has also contributed to the change itself.

In the early 1960s the administration of claims and policies in large insurance companies and of customer accounts in the main clearing banks was automated using a small number of large mainframe computers. The emphasis was on setting up new data-processing sites to cope with the growth in business. The early introduction of technology was very much in sympathy with the existing organization of the financial institutions which in general were tightly controlled from head office. Thus, a central computer department was usually set up as a headquarters' function which was located at a new site with a mainframe computer. This processing centre substituted for branch personnel so the reorganization implied depended on the location of the computer centre relative to the branch network.

During the 1970s automation spread throughout the financial sector. Firms have sought to achieve a competitive lead by early adoption of IT, which in turn facilitates the development of new or improved services and reduced costs. However, vanguard users of technology tend to suffer problems in introducing new equipment and their specialized systems can be overtaken by industry standards set up by later users. Late adapters may also be able to leapfrog a generation of systems, but in turn expose themselves to the danger of being a vanguard user. Thus, individual companies tend to progress at differing rates through a cycle of innovation (Barras and Swann, 1983).

In the 1970s interactive terminals linked to the central mainframe were established in branch offices and this extended data capture and processing closer to the point of each transaction, thus reducing the double handling of paper. In retail banking and building society offices IT became more prominent in the 'front office' with ATMs and counter terminals becoming widespread. In the last decade the international transmission of financial messages and electronic same-day-clearing systems have also been introduced. Throughout the sector mini- and micro-computers have been used to maintain records and word processing systems have been widely installed, as well as specialist data capture technology (e.g. optical card readers).

Remote banking by terminal from the home has been slow to take off in the UK. Although both the Midland and Barclays have tested homebanking systems, the major banks are reluctant to invest, given that they already possess nationwide branch networks. For the Bank of Scotland, however, which launched the first nationwide home-banking service in January 1985 the aim is to develop new business in areas where it does not have an established branch network. So in this case homebanking may, by avoiding the need to develop a system of branches, reduce barriers to entry in retail banking. However, the evidence suggests that the take-up of homebanking by the general public will be slow and corporate users and mail order customers will be the first to use the technology.

EFTPOS has given a boost in the UK by the announcement in 1985 that the English and Scottish Clearing Banks and the Retail Consortium have reached agreement in principle on a nationwide system. However, key questions, notably how retailers and banks divide up the costs of running the system, have not been fully resolved. Thus, notwithstanding the number of recent experiments (including the Anglia Building Society, Clydesdale Bank, and Barclays) it is anticipated that the take up to EFTPOS will be slow in the immediate future.

The reorganization associated with the 1970s and 1980s phase of automation in financial institutions has been considerable. Recent developments in technology have been introduced in a more competitive market and in some instances with a slower growth in business, so the emphasis has shifted from the setting up of new sites towards the reorganization of existing offices and the rationalization of branch networks. This is not of course general across all of the sector. The smaller specialist insurers, the building societies, and smaller banks are continuing to build up their branch networks.

IT now allows a more decentralized mode of operation. It is financially and technically possible to break up computer centres and establish a number of mini-computers rather than a mainframe. While this may imply greater initial expenditure, overloading on a central mainframe is avoided, technical problems on any one machine become less important, the information system is less prone to stoppage due to industrial action, and the future integration of data processing and text production functions at a local level becomes a real possibility. However, even distributed processing still requires some centralization of data processing at the local level to achieve economies of scale.

It is difficult to disentangle the impact of such technology on organizations from changes taking place for other reasons. Nevertheless, it is clear that financial institutions are under contradictory pressures. The diversification and acquisition strategies of the major organizations in the sector in response to market pressures have required reorganization. The increasingly complex and unwieldy central organization of many companies has been replaced by a more decentralized mode of operation. Within the branch networks of these organizations their retail business still requires personal contact and a widely distributed set of branches. However, new business markets with irregular demand, and often served by intermediaries require a central location.

These tendencies have been reinforced by technological changes. In the larger clearing banks and insurance companies there appears to have been a parallel process of concentration and dispersal in part as a result of technology. There has been some devolution of functions from headquarters to main branches and regional offices as part of a strategy to create profit centres and to make organizations more responsive to variations in demand. This has been more pronounced in banking and in insurance an initial tendency to centralize has only recently been reversed. But this decentralization process has been accompanied by a concentration of activities at an intraregional level associated with a general rationalization of branch employment. Until the early 1970s each branch provided a full range of financial services, but there have been attempts (not all successful) to group smaller branches around larger ones. Smaller branches provide a limited range of personal services, while the main branches provide a full range of personal services as well as serving corporate clients. Along with this trend has gone another tendency to move clerical functions into separate accommodation, thus releasing the more expensive space for customer related activities. Finally, as administration has been concentrated the levels in the corporate hierarchy have been reduced, and sub-branches, small offices and branches with overlapping market areas, often in small towns, have been closed or downgraded.

These dominant features of the financial sector are complicated by a number of other developments which make the overall locational pattern rather diverse. For example, new, often foreign-based, entrants into the insurance and banking sectors have differing methods of working which reduce the need for an extensive retail branch network. Foreign banks dealing in the Euro-dollar market and co-ordinating their European zone activities from the UK or life insurance companies relying on brokers, mail order, or a small sales force for business have established their main activities close to the capital, extensive automation has been introduced, processing centres have been decentralized, and a limited number of branch offices in the main conurbations set up.

In the declining segments of the insurance business, such as industrial life, technological changes have been introduced in association with a major rationalization of sales forces and large offices in the conurbations. In contrast, smaller offices outside the conurbations have remained relatively untouched because of physical limits to the market areas which can be served by sales staff (Morris, 1984).

The dispersed pattern of employment in the building society movement, the sustained growth of that sector, and the extension of many societies' branch networks have contributed to a dispersal of employment at the regional scale. Here IT was introduced relatively recently and its impact so far has been muted. Since societies have a relatively poorly developed regional structure, central processing has been concentrated at head office and intelligent terminals located in branches. Until recently such reorganization as there has been in the sector has resulted from the merger of largely local societies. This has had little negative impact on the branch network since partners usually have complementary locations. Where rationalization has occurred it is frequently in the branch offices of the societies outside the host region. After mergers both head offices are retained, though one is gradually downgraded (perhaps associated with the introduction of new technology) and there is a tendency for head office locations to move up the urban hierarchy (Morris, 1984). It remains to be seen whether larger mergers such as that between the Nationwide and the Anglia will change this pattern.

Employment

The traditional view of services as labour intensive forms of economic activity where self employment, personal relationships, and individual initiative are important do not apply to much of the financial services. Large organizations have dominated in most markets for some years. The segmentation of internal labour markets, the concentration of female employees into lower grade clerical work, bureaucratization of activities, the routinization of many jobs, methods of job evaluation, and work organization were all well-established features of office work in financial services prior to the last twenty years of automation.

Studies of the financial sector indicate that important changes have taken place in the employment provided by such services, as technology was introduced. Cross-sectional studies of the introduction of centrally organized batch-operated data processing suggest it has extended the breakdown of individual tasks and the technical de-skilling of clerical work (Cromton and Jones, 1984). The concentration of clerical work in data processing 'factories' has also done much to facilitate the industrialization of service work. In contrast, though, there are examples of interactive data processing enriching work by removing the need for boring or mundane tasks and by permitting the individual to perform a range of tasks and customer services rather than simply data input or processing (Rajan, 1985). High quality technical systems analysis, and programming jobs have also been created by the technology, and managerial staff who deal with technology are being reskilled. However, these benefits tend to be felt predominantly by male employees. By reducing the job specific skills involved in clerical work and transferring supervisory functions to the information system, career hierarchies for clerical staff can be disrupted. This is tending to reinforce the effect of dual recruitment policies which separate career staff who must obtain pre- and post-entry qualifications from non-career, largely female clerical workers (Werneke, 1983).

However, an analysis of the employment record of the financial sector suggests that so far, while some job displacement has occurred associated with the introduction of IT, actual redundancies have been limited. Table 5.23 summarizes a number of recent employment forecasts produced for the financial sector. Interpretation is restricted by definitional and temporal variation in the forecasts. Nevertheless, the table highlights the divergence of opinion concerning the prospects for employment growth. In general, sectoral forecasts, which project historical relationships between output and employment, tend to be more optimistic concerning employment growth than case studies of users of IT. The former can be inaccurate because the introduction of IT into the financial sector is changing output–employment relationships, while the latter tend to be unduly pessimistic because they overemphasize the impact of technology and place insufficient emphasis on the counterbalancing effect of business growth. Comparing projections with recent trends suggests that employment growth lies somewhere between the extremes of both sets of projections.

The diversity in the projections in Table 5.23 also reflects different views of the trajectory of technological innovation in the financial sector. One view based on experience in manufacturing and agriculture argues that the development of new technologies in the financial and other service industries will follow a version of the 'product cycle' where new services, and in turn employment, are generated during the early stages of the innovation cycle but, as these services mature, the immense labour saving potential of IT as

Table 5.23.   Employment Forecasts in Financial Services

Forecaster	Type of service	Projected employment	
		Percentage	Period
Sectoral forecasts			
Robertson, Briggs, and Goodchild (1982)	Insurance, banking, finance, and business services	+7 to +36	1978–85
Warwick (1985)	Insurance and professional services	+12	1984–90
Rajan (1984)	Insurance, banking, and building societies	−4 to +1	1982–7
Banking			
Pactel (1980)	Clearing banks	−10	1980–90
Palmer (1980)	European banks	−5 to −20	1980–90
Kirchener and Hewlett (1983)	London clearing banks	−5 to −10	1983–90
Shaw and Coulbeck (1983)	European banks	−12	1981–90
Gaskin (1980)	Scottish banks	+15	1979–84
Robertson, Briggs, and Goodchild (1982)	Banking and business services	+8 to +51	1979–85
Rajan (1984)	Commercial Merchant and Trustee savings banks	+5 to +10	1983–7
Insurance			
Sleigh *et al.* (1959)	Insurance	−15	1979–85
Gaskin (1980)	Scottish insurance	No change	1979–84
Robertson, Briggs, and Goodchild (1982)	Insurance, finance, and property	+5 to +12	1978–85
Rajan (1984)	Insurance	−12 to −18	1983–7
Building Societies			
Rajan (1984)		+10 to +15	1983–7

Source: Adapted from Rajan (1984).

a process innovation takes over and the net effect of technological change is to encourage job loss (Rajan, 1984). However, others argue that as new technology is transmitted from manufacture to application in a service industry a 'reverse product cycle' occurs whereby the first applications of the new technology improve the efficiency of existing services. The next stage is to improve their quality and finally the technology is used as a vehicle for developing new services. In terms of jobs the transition is from job loss to employment creation (Barras, 1985).

The current situation with regard to the application of IT in the financial sector is quite fluid, but it would appear that, given the possible productivity improvements available through its use, an increase in business growth on the scale implied by a 'reverse product cycle' view is going to be necessary to sustain the recent employment growth in financial services. It is possible that this could take place through the development of new services such as homebanking. However, this innovation has been slow to take off and a necessary precondition for widespread adoption of new services may be a comprehensive, cheap and high-quality communication infrastructure, and this is only likely to be provided incrementally. Nevertheless, Barras and Swann (1984*b*), argue that major attempts to maximize the productivity improvements available through the use of IT only occur periodically when external pressures enforce restructuring. It is possible therefore, that other factors which have ameliorated the impact of IT, namely the concern in financial institutions to project a paternalistic image and the reluctance of managements to embrace major organizational changes, could cushion the employment impact of IT until new services take off.

General conclusions

While during the 1960s and 1970s insurance, banking, and finance were major sources of employment growth, this looks less certain in the future. The deregulation of the financial sector and the subsequent increase in competition is certainly encouraging business growth. (Rajan, 1987). But widespread automation implies that a considerable growth in demand will be needed for employment to continue to grow rapidly. There is also a widespread belief that considerable additional output can be produced by existing employees.

There is some evidence that occupational structures are being modified as IT is introduced. Automation is routinizing some existing data processing tasks, and reducing the need for female clerical workers as well as some middle management staff. At the same time the development of new and existing products, which is intimately tied to technological changes, is continuing to encourage the expansion of employment though this is skewed towards specialist, highly skilled, largely male managerial staff.

Thus far automation would appear to have modified the existing pattern of reorganization in insurance, banking, and finance. In an increasingly competitive market firms have sought to reduce labour costs via the use of IT. The routinization and automation of tasks have facilitated their relocation and the decentralization of activities away from London. Relocation has occurred to small labour markets, largely in the south of the country, with access to supplies of clerical labour, but in areas sufficiently close to the capital to attract senior personnel. Such relocation has reduced operating costs and improved control of clerical labour. At the same time the capital has benefited from a significant growth in international financial business, encouraged by technological progress, and this has sustained its financial employment.

Provincial metropolitan areas have been subject to conflicting trends (Morris, 1984). There has been a concentration of activities there in insurance and banking associated with the reorganization of branch networks. New organizations building up limited branch networks have also expanded in some conurbations. On the other hand, building society mergers have reduced branch offices in major centres. Not all conurbations have been affected equally by these various changes. Conurbations in Yorkshire and Humberside have benefited from the concentration there of the expanding Halifax and Yorkshire Bank. Scottish cities have benefited from the expansion south of the Bank of Scotland in a way that maximizes the benefits to the home region. However, the North West and West Midlands have suffered due to the rationalization strategies adopted by insurance organizations headquartered there in the face of declining markets. Finally, regions such as the North and Wales are served by regional offices elsewhere. The North West and Manchester in particular is used as a regional centre to serve Wales and the North.

For the future, changes in the occupational structure of the financial institutions imply that senior management functions are likely to exert an increasing influence on the location of the sector. The need for clerical labour which lay behind the relocation of data processing activities is not so strong. Reorganization within existing sites appears likely with employment change reflecting the balance between *in situ* changes brought about by technology and the transfer of work between offices. In such a context it seems unlikely that employment in small town locations outside the South East which have been developed as data processing centres will expand, and the attachment of the financial sector to professional labour in the south may be increased. Such a trend is likely to be intensified if the current growth in demand for corporate and personal business from that location continues. On the other hand the growth of international financial business in the capital may decline. The UK based international institutions are locating some of their existing co-ordinating activities closer to the source of their business, and international business is becoming increasingly competitive.

5.5. Business Service Offices: The Influence of Service Organization on Location

This section is based on case studies of the advertising, accountancy, marketing, market research, computer services, and management consultancy industries. These services (with the exception of accountancy) unlike those in the financial sector have little consumer business. As a consequence organizations tend to be much smaller, less locationally ubiquitous, and dependent on a smaller number of clients.

Business service offices are not all identified separately in service employment statistics. Table 5.24, therefore, presents the distribution of offices in the management consultancy, accountancy, market research, marketing, advertising, and computer services. It is based on a number of data sources primarily provided by professional associations (see Appendix 2). Some sources are lists of the organizations which are members of an association, others are a list of firms where employees who are members of an association are employed, others are lists compiled by directory organizations such as Kelly's and some are the result of surveys of individual firms. Care should be used in generalizing too readily on the basis of the results because Table 5.24 is likely to be biased towards larger firms.

Nevertheless, the table indicates as expected the concentration of business services in London and the South East, though interestingly the degree of concentration differs considerably. All services, apart from accountancy, are more represented in the South East than expected on the basis of total employment, though market-related services such as marketing and market research are most concentrated with more than 84% of national offices in the South East. These two services also have more than 50% of their total offices in Greater London. Virtually all provincial regions have fewer offices than expected on the basis of employment for every service apart from accountancy and to a lesser extent management consultancy. The main provincial centres for business services are the North West, West Midlands, Yorkshire and Humberside, and Scotland. Within these and other regions offices concentrate in the major urban centres. For example, Birmingham accounts for 66.2% of advertising agents and 75% of management consultants in the West Midlands region, Manchester and Liverpool for 83.6% of advertising agents and 53.9% of management consultants in the North West, and Glasgow and Edinburgh for 85.5% of advertising agents and 64.1% of management consultants in Scotland.

There is also tentative evidence to suggest that there are qualitative differences in the services offered in different parts of the

Table 5.24. Percentage Distribution of Business Service Offices, 1980–1

	Management consultants	Accountancy	Market research	Marketing	Advertising	Computer services
Greater London	23.0	14.2	62.7	59.4	44.7	31.9
South East	25.9	15.7	21.9	25.5	18.9	24.1
East Anglia	1.6	4.0	1.0	0.4	1.6	2.1
South West	5.9	9.4	2.0	2.2	4.4	5.8
East Midlands	3.2	6.6	0	1.1	3.7	3.4
West Midlands	9.4	8.3	3.9	3.6	5.8	8.0
North West	11.5	12.8	2.0	2.5	8.8	9.3
Yorks & Humberside	4.6	11.1	2.3	1.1	4.4	5.5.
Northern	2.1	3.5	1.3	0.4	1.4	2.4
Scotland	9.1	9.2	1.3	1.1	4.7	4.9
Wales	1.3	3.4	0.7	0.4	0.8	1.8
N. Ireland	2.4	1.7	1.0	2.5	0.8	0.7
N	374	649	306	278	1402	1490

Source: Department of Trade and Industry, *Accountancy Age*, *Campaign*, *Computer Users' Year Book*, Computer Services Association, Institute of Chartered Accountants, Association of Chartered Accountants, Market Research Society, *Advertisers Annual*, Management Consultants Association, Institute of Management Consultants.

country. In marketing the main activities of firms in the provinces are more likely to be selling, distribution, and conference organization. While these services are provided in the South East, research and consultancy are also frequently offered. In computer services software and consultancy activities are slightly more concentrated in the South East in contrast to data processing which is more prevalent in the provinces. This could indicate that more sophisticated services are located close to the capital, and that firms in the South East offer a wider range of services.

Though it is often assumed that business service industries are dominated by small, independent single-site companies Table 5.25 suggests that this is an over-simplification. It follows that an analysis of the organization of business service firms can add to an understanding of their location. Table 5.25 compares offices in the South East of England with offices in other regions on the basis of their corporate status. A very coarse measure is used, that is, whether offices are single-site firms, a main or subordinate office in a multi-site firm. The measure does not distinguish between independent limited companies, subsidiaries, or partnership arrangements. Further, the subordinate office category does not differentiate between branches and offices staffed by the regional partners of a nationally organized partnership.

Nevertheless, Table 5.25 does suggest that there are differences in organizational structure between the South East and provincial areas. Though single-site firms are usually the largest single category in the office sector in both areas, such firms are considerably more important in the South East where 79.2% of management consultants and 87.9% of advertising offices are single-site firms, compared to 48.7% and 68% of offices respectively in the provinces. Provincial areas have larger proportions of subordinate offices in multi-site firms in all services, while in contrast the South East has more main offices. These differences are most marked in management consultancy where 13.1% of offices in the South East are main offices and 7.7% subordinates, while in the provinces 3.1% are main offices and 48.2% subordinates.

Interestingly within provincial regions the distribution of single- and multi-site companies are different, with the former strongly represented outside the main conurbations while particularly branch offices are more likely to be in the main centres. For example, in advertising in the West Midlands 46.6% of single-site companies are located in Birmingham compared to 87.5% of offices in multi-site firms. In the North West 78.3% of single-site companies are located in Manchester and Liverpool compared to 97% of multi-site firms.

Table 5.25.   Organizational Structure in Business Service Offices

Status	All firms 1980–1 (%)								Large firms 1979/81 (%)					
	South East				Provinces				South East			Provinces		
	MC	M & MR	Adv.	Comp.	MC	M & MR	Adv.	Comp.	Acc.	Adv.	Comp.	Acc.	Adv.	Comp.
Multi site firm														
Main office	13.1	4.7	7.1	10.8	3.1	0.8	6.5	5.6	26.8	41.9	17.5	3.7	6.3	15.1
Subordinate office	7.7	3.5	5.0	18.7	48.2	5.6	25.5	49.8	67.0	51.1	17.5	93.0	85.7	72.7
Single site firm	79.2	91.8	87.9	70.5	48.7	93.9	68.0	44.6	6.2	7.0	64.9	3.3	7.9	12.1

N = Management Consultants (574), Marketing and Market Research (584), Advertising (1402), Computer Services (1490).
N = Accountancy (649), Advertising (106), Computer Services (90).
MC = Management Consultants
M & MR = Marketing and Market Research
Adv. = Advertising
Comp. = Computer Services
Acc. = Accountancy
Source: Marshall (1987).

There is, then, in the large conurbations a corporate hierarchy centred on London, with the exception of marketing and market research where single-site firms are the overwhelming majority of firms. However, for market research, information available from the Market Research Society suggests that 39.5% of all firms are subsidiary companies. So even here corporate organization may be important.

These data give no indication of the relative size of firms. Table 5.25 therefore also singles out the location of the larger organizations in the accountancy, advertising, and computer consultancy services. As expected most of the larger organizations are multi-site and the contrasts between the provinces and the South East in terms of the distribution of sites within these companies are more pronounced. In advertising 41.9% of offices in the South East are main offices in multi-site companies, compared to 6.3% in the provinces, while in accountancy 93% of offices in the provinces are subordinates compared to 67% in the South East. The computer consultancy service differs somewhat from this pattern. While the provinces are dominated by subordinate offices (72.2% of all offices), there is a larger representation of single-site companies in the South East than is the case for the other services.

This evidence from directory sources is supported for provincial conurbations by a study of business services in Birmingham, Leeds, and Manchester. Here 33.4% of offices and 52.2% of employment were found in 1980 to be in firms with an ultimate head office outside the local Economic Planning Region.[5] These firms were largely controlled from a Greater London head office. National service organizations had expanded more rapidly than local companies during the 1970s and it is likely that as the demand for services has increased national business service firms have been taking a larger market share (Marshall, 1982*b*). The following sections attempt to explain this expansion of the corporate sector in provincial areas of the UK.

Accountancy: the growth of service organization

Developments in accountancy seem closest to the traditional view of the business service sector in that the location of accountants is mainly a response to clients' demands, and linkages with sectors such as manufacturing have produced spatial changes. There are differences, however, stemming from the fact that the accountancy

---

[5] The services studied included accountants, advertising agents, computer services, management consultants, consultant engineers, architects, solicitors, insurance brokers, and finance companies.

profession has responded to changes in the location of service demand, not simply by relocation or industrial movement but through acquisition and merger activity. Thus, the organization of accountancy practices together with market demands produce locational outcomes.

In the 1940s accountancy was largely characterized by small single-site partnerships, dealing with personal business, and auditing small private company accounts. The last forty years have witnessed a growth in accountancy business, stemming from the increased disclosure of company accounts, and new legislation concerning accounting and financial practices (Briston, 1979). This has been associated with both merger and organic growth. In 1958 the largest 20 accounting organizations controlled 32% of the audits listed in the Stock Exchange Year Book, by 1979 they accounted for approximately 76% (Briston and Kedslie, 1984). The pressures encouraging organizational change have been partly internal to the service industry, such as a search for new markets and economies of scale, but more important has been the changing demands of client companies (see Section 5.1).

Large multi-product, multi-divisional, and geographically dispersed organizations have special accountancy requirements. Their complex internal management procedures and financial structures require, for example, advice on the computer programming of accounts, budgetary systems, and costing procedures, and all such services must be provided on a national or even international basis to match the location of the client firm. Therefore, in response to the growth of large manufacturing and service organizations, accountancy practices have diversified in terms of the service they provide and the locations they serve. Acquisition has been the preferred means of access to regional markets, because it provides companies with a ready-made organization in new markets. Such acquisition in accountancy has been encouraged because medium-sized accountancy practices are favourably disposed towards incorporation in larger organizations because elsewhere in the economy acquisition has resulted in the attrition of their corporate clients when accounts are transferred to the parent firm's accountant after the merger (Jones, 1981).

Changes in organizational structure have been promoted by the growth in the size of accountancy firms. A corporate hierarchy has replaced the relatively simple traditional accountancy organization. There is no one single dominant structure in accountancy firms, and it is likely that changes will occur if practices become incorporated in the future. Currently a common form of organization is for regional partnerships to be responsible for a local system of branch offices, and a national committee with representation from all the regions plans corporate strategy (see Section 5.1). It is possible that this decentralized partnership organization is one reason why employment is relatively dispersed in accountancy. Nevertheless, where demand tends to be insufficient in any one region to justify a full range of accounting services, activities such as insolvency, management consultancy, and general management support functions are provided by a national office (Jones, 1981).

The national office tends to be located close to London for reasons of convenience of travel, but also because corporate accounting activities are usually co-ordinated for multi-site client organizations by their head office located in the South East of the country. This implies that the growth of national accountancy organizations may have reduced autonomy in some provincial offices, and innovation in service provision may be removed from the provinces to national offices. On the other hand, provincial offices have gained in terms of

Table 5.26. Auditors Ranked by Total Fee Income

	Value (£000s)	No. of Clients	Rank (by No. of clients)
London area			
Ernst and Whinney	19,028	143	4
Deloitte, Haskins and Sells	16,454	165	2
Coopers and Lybrand	15,629	117	5
Price Waterhouse	15,166	210	1
Peat Marwick Mitchell	9,881	161	3
KMG Thompson McLintock	8,351	70	9
Touche Ross	7,174	104	6
Arthur Anderson	4,315	97	8
Arthur Young	4,314	100	7
West Midlands			
Coopers and Lybrand	3,931	83	2
Peat Marwick Mitchell	2,570	133	1
Ernst and Whinney	2,021	43	6
Arthur Anderson	2,017	38	8
Price Waterhouse	1,334	72	4
Deloitte, Haskins and Sells	1,323	83	2
Touche Ross	1,030	51	5
KMG Thompson McLintock	711	40	7
Moore Stephens	505	30	9

Source: Audit Guide Ltd. (1985).

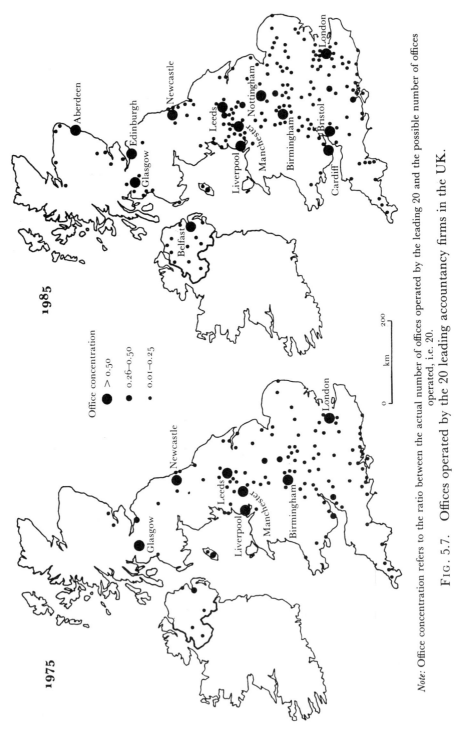

Note: Office concentration refers to the ratio between the actual number of offices operated by the leading 20 and the possible number of offices operated, i.e. 20.

Fig. 5.7.   Offices operated by the 20 leading accountancy firms in the UK.

access to new markets because the accountancy profession is becoming increasingly polarized with a large number of small practices serving private individuals and local business, and a smaller number of large practices serving national and international corporate clients.

The growth of the leading acountancy firms in terms of fee income, chargeable hours, and employment has fuelled locational change. Between 1975 and 1985 the number of offices operated by the 20 leading accountancy firms increased by 63% to 492 offices. This growth has reinforced the concentration of large firms within leading centres, but has also seen them penetrate previously unserved areas (Table 5.26 and Fig. 5.7). Office growth has been concentrated in the South East, Scotland, the South West, and East Anglia. All other regions suffered a relative decline in their share of total offices. Office growth appears to be driven by four strongly interrelated forces. First, the expansion of offices in major centres is a result of firms attempting to construct comprehensive national office networks in order to ensure market share. Second, offices have been established in localities that have experienced industrial growth (for example, Aberdeen, Thames Valley, Cambridgeshire). Third, the invasion of the traditional small business market of the medium-sized accountancy firms by large accountancy groups has seen them open offices in increasingly smaller towns, in many cases where they have no existing clients. Finally, the increasing importance attached to public-sector work has encouraged office openings near centres of local government, particularly in some major cities. The spatial restructuring of office networks has been one of increasing orientation to perceived market opportunities.

Computer services: the development of a new service industry

The computer service industry is recognizable as a 'typical' service industry in that firms are small, and few organizations have a substantial market share. While the industry is small—approximately 70,000 employees (Miles, 1985)—it has been characterized by considerable growth. Official statistics for 1971–80 suggest that in constant prices billings rose at an annual average rate of 14% and employment at about 7% (Green, 1981). Though the industry has undergone considerable recent change in association with developments in technology, it remains a product of the 1960s and 1970s, and the original organizational structure of the industry has had an important bearing on its development and spatial distribution.

The origins of the industry can be traced back to the setting up of companies as established computer users such as management consultants, accountants, and the banks diversified. More recently small independent firms have been established as 'spin-offs' from firms which have developed computer expertise. This has been facilitated by the development of professional services such as software products, consultancy, and advice, which have lowered the capital costs of entry into the industry. Finally, mainframe computer manufacturers and suppliers have increasingly provided mainten-ance, back-up, software, and consultancy services.

Not surprisingly, given the influence of organizations in other services on the computer industry, there are a significant number of subsidiary companies. Of 1,018 companies identified using industry sources in 1981, 33.7% were subsidiaries. These were predominantly larger organizations, with 66.7% of those firms with more than 100 employees being subsidiaries. However, few companies were multi-site, such companies accounting for a little under 13% of firms.

The location of the computer service industry reflects the strategy of service firms in serving particular markets, as well as the demand for computer services. During the early stages of the industry's development many subsidiaries set up on parent's premises or in close proximity to serve largely established markets and customers. As new independent companies were formed through 'spin-offs', there was no true location decision, the founders setting up close to where they resided (Green, 1982). Given the existing structure of tertiary activities this has encouraged computer services in the South East. Firm movement in the industry is constrained by the need to retain key personnel, though spatial decentralization from city centres has been possible to minimize costs.

In so far as locations in the provinces are concerned, companies have established branch offices as business there has expanded. The nature of the branch office is determined by the perceived market size. Organizations usually set up a small sales outlet initially, and if business expands a greater range of functions are established there. Branches are usually established in the North West as a central location to serve the North, and Manchester, the location of the National Computer Centre, is particularly attractive. For London-based firms some business in the provinces is more expensive to serve because of the costs associated with centrally located staff working on clients' premises for extended periods (Green, 1982). In part as a consequence, a local computer service sector has developed in provincial regions. The market for provincial firms can be limited to consumer business and local industry if they do not have the national network required to serve multi-site organizations, though some highly specialized firms are able to build up a national reputation.

Other services

There is only fragmentary evidence available for other service industries. The existing material reinforces the view expressed concerning the dichotomy in business service office industries between dominant and other firms. For example, in market research the top ten organizations accounted for half the recorded commercial research in Great Britain in 1980 (Simmons and Gordon, 1980). There appear to be three types of organization, larger multi-site generalist firms offering services from offices throughout the country and smaller specialist organizations offering a service (possibly nationally) from a limited number of offices. Both tend to be either limited liability companies or partnerships. In addition, private individuals offer their consultancy skills. As in other industries the larger firms tend to service major national and international clients and the smaller companies are tied to local clients, though there are *ad hoc* arrangements between larger and smaller suppliers, the former using the latter to provide specialist expertise on certain contracts (ECOTEC, 1985).

Organizational structures are surprisingly complex given the small size of many firms. For example, one well-known management consultancy is divided into separate business or profit centres and each of these is subdivided into individual divisions. These businesses operate throughout the UK in a matrix structure with shared regional offices under the supervision of a regional manager, and there are in addition a number of specialist subordinate branch offices. Not surprisingly, therefore, in such instances it is very difficult to produce simple generalizations concerning the influence of service organization on the location of business service activities.

Nevertheless, a number of companies in market research, advertising, and consultancy have expanded into regional markets in response to a growth business. Rather like the computer service the nature of branch offices is determined by the perceived market size. Branches are located in major provincial centres to serve more peripheral areas.

The market for office-based business services is more cyclical than the market for financial services (Bullmore and Waterson, 1983; Simmons and Gordon, 1980). Several of the larger national firms in advertising and management consultancy responded to a decline in business during the mid-1970s by specializing in a narrower range

of services and concentrating on serving larger clients. The specialization has reduced the need for a geographically dispersed network
of offices and staff in provincial areas. As a consequence there have
been closures in smaller urban centres, and a concentration of
specialist teams of staff in centres higher up the urban hierarchy.
This tendency towards concentration is limited, however, by a desire
to retain a presence in most regions and by the additional travel
costs resulting from concentration. In contrast, the tendency for
larger companies to move 'up market' has allowed smaller, often
regionally based, companies to expand into the gaps created at the
lower end of the market.

General conclusions

These case studies have supported the financial sector analysis
(Section 5.4) and highlight again the interdependence of service
industries. For example, accountancy practices are well established
in management consultancy and in advisory services related to
technology, and the larger management consultants provide
computer-related services. Firms have responded to the growth of
large client organizations and their changing demand for services by
diversifying in terms of the service provided and the locations
served. In some services such as accountancy, acquisition and
merger have been the preferred means of access to new markets
because they provide a ready-made organization. In contrast, in less
well established services such as advertising or management consultancy, firms have had to set up new branch offices or functions.
The end result, however, is similar in that, alongside the existing
stock of local companies, a corporate hierarchy has developed in
most provincial regions.

This corporate structure has influenced the expansion of employment in business service offices. It has encouraged employment
growth in a limited number of provincial urban centres, while
concentrating sophisticated services for which there are insufficient
demand in any one region, and general management support
functions, at a national office usually in the south. The existing
organization of service companies has also influenced the development and location of new service activities. The location of the
computer service industry, for example, owes something to the
influence and location of established computer users such as the
banks, accountancy, and management consultancy organizations.

Though it is not widely recognized or researched, multi-site
business service organizations in provincial areas, rather like their
manufacturing counterparts, internalize their purchases within their

own organization and outside the local areas. Thus, it is likely that the expansion of national service organizations into provincial areas has reduced the level of interdependence in the local service economy (Marshall, 1987). This could be a serious disadvantage given the evidence that the purchasing demands of service firms are an important source of growth in service demand in the UK (Section 3.4).

6

Understanding the Location of Producer Services

6.1. EXISTING APPROACHES

The case studies in the previous chapter have described the economic background to the diverse patterns of locational change in producer services described in Chapter 4. In this chapter we attempt to synthesize this material and to present a general framework within which the location of producer services can be understood.

It is sensible before we do this to comment on previous research. The purpose here is not to produce an extensive review of the literature but rather to comment on the types of explanation for spatial differentiation contained in existing studies, before we develop these through a deeper consideration of the market for producer services.

Existing work has tended to be fragmented in terms of the subject matter and spatial scale considered, and this has produced a partial and incomplete understanding of service location. An important tradition of work has been interested in producer services because of their perceived importance in the urban and regional growth process and because of the weak development of such activities in many provincial areas (Polese, 1982). This work has usually studied manufacturing demand for services and has often implicitly assumed that manufacturing is the dominant sector leading economically dependent services (Marshall, 1979). In a pioneering study of Hamilton metal industries, later extended to other towns in mid-Ontario, Bater and Walker (1971) and Walker and Bater (1976) show that while repair, maintenance, and transport services are predominantly purchased in the local area, more specialist and infrequently used information services are brought in from Toronto. The usual explanation for this pattern of purchases is that the concentration of ownership in manufacturing industry, and the location of the corporate administrative functions of large companies at head offices situated close to the capital city, combined with the 'internalization' of many of the service demands of subordinate establishments within their organization encourages imports of services into provincial areas and limits the development there of both 'in-house' and specialist suppliers (Goddard, 1979).

Many studies have concentrated on offices in manufacturing and services seeking to explain their concentration in major cities and subsequent decentralization to the suburbs and smaller towns. Early work described locational patterns and inferred underlying ag-glomeration economies to explain office concentrations in urban areas (Haig, 1927; Foley, 1956). Other work has analysed com-munications linkages between offices in an attempt to explain agglomerations usually in a static or a quasi-dynamic, cross-sectional framework (Gad, 1975; Goddard, 1975; Goddard and Morris, 1976; Tournquist, 1973). As research interest has grown, behavioural studies have focused on the way in which different decision-making processes within firms influence locational out-comes (Edwards, 1982), and other micro-economic approaches have drawn on the results of such empirical work to model the location of firms (O'Hara, 1977; Tauchen and Witte, 1983).

In general the location of offices is seen to result from their ability to pay for highly accessible but costly sites in the centre of cities. A spatial hierarchy evolves in which higher status office activities, which are most able to justify the cost of a central location, are concentrated in the centres of the largest cities, while lower order offices are more dispersed. This pattern of office activities is related to corporate structures, because the concentration of strategic activities, which need a wide range of contacts, at head office encourages their location in major cities with considerable contact potential. Recent decentralization is seen as a response to the increase in rents and related costs in city centres and especially London, encouraging less contact-intensive functions to relocate. Work on London suggests that savings in rents, rates, and salaries through office decentralization beyond 80 miles from the capital are outweighed by the increased communication costs (Alexander, 1979; Daniels, 1975; Goddard, 1975; Goddard and Pye, 1977).

In spite of their significance as support for manufacturing, there has been little work on the location of blue collar services. Some studies have provided indirect insights into distributive trades through an investigation of transport flows and retail outlets. It can be inferred from this work, and non-spatial studies of transport and distribution organizations, that there has been a considerable reorganization of distribution which has been associated with a decentralization of activities from city centres and a withdrawal of establishments from peripheral areas (McKinnon, 1985c).

6.2   MARKET CHANGES

The perspective adopted in this study which proceeds from con-sideration of the demand for various types of service and the role they play in facilitating all other economic activities suggests that study of their location requires a broader context than that provided by previous research. Based on the case study reviews it is clear that, though it may be difficult to quantify trends, there have been significant changes in the pattern of demand for producer services which have influenced their location. A number of factors have encouraged the growing demand for producer services.

1. The growth of large, complex and multi-locational organizations, frequently through acquisition, has enhanced the demand for services; new services are required and these must be provided by producer service firms on a national and even international basis.

2. The increasingly dynamic and complex context for business, including the growing complexity of legal and financial regulation, has also encouraged service demand. Also, as consumers become more sophisticated, markets fragment, and product differentiation reflects this. In turn a greater emphasis results on the marketing and selling functions. Technological changes are increasing the complexity of products and production, and the research intensity of production. Training and consultancy services are therefore required to meet the new organizational requirements of the technology.

3. There also appear to be structural changes underway in service markets. Contraction in the production sector has affected the demand for some physical distribution services. But well established professional services, such as branches of advertising and market research, also appear to have reached maturity, so that demand has been cyclical or grown slowly. Here low barriers to entry have allowed employees to set up small firms, adding to capacity in an already crowded market. Against this, however, must be set the fact that the demand for some accountancy, management consultancy, and financial services has actually been increased by recession. New services associated with information technology such as on-line data bases and information systems, value-added telecommunications, and data processing services, while they are small scale, have also been growing rapidly.

4. The balance between the 'internalization' and 'externalization' of service demand by non-specialist producers has also been changing. A number of considerations influence the decision by organizations whether to 'internalize' or 'externalize' service production. Factors of importance include: the element of confidentiality associated with the service, whether a service is strategic to the company's activities or simply routine, the amount of specialist knowledge required to carry out the service, the cost of alternative sources of supply, and the availability and quality of services outside the firm (Greenfield, 1966; Williamson, 1978). To

preserve commercial advantage, confidential or strategic service needs are likely to be met within the company. Where service needs are uncertain or changing 'internalization' again is likely to be preferred. However, where specialist skills are costly to acquire, outside service suppliers may be used. Finally, the amount of service 'internalization' within firms will be increased if the number, range, quality, and cost of outside service suppliers does not match the firms' requirements.

Organizations are likely to respond to these pressures in different ways. For example, a considerable volume of research in the organizational sciences has examined variations in service employment within firms particularly associated with differences in organizational size (Miles, 1985), and this has been applied to establishments in a geographical context by Marshall (1979; 1982a). Though differences in the unit of analysis (organizations versus establishments) cloud the analysis, small units appear to have few service needs, but favour 'in-house' service provision because of their small scale requirements, and for cost reasons (Sema Metra, 1986). For more sophisiticated services, however, small firms will not have an 'in-house' capacity and are likely to subcontract out (Marshall, 1982a). Larger units need a wider range of services than small units, but the scale of their requirements tends to allow the development of an 'in-house' service capacity. Economies of scale in service provision mean that notwithstanding this trend the share of support services in total employment declines with increasing size (Blau, 1972). Large units also tend to specialize and breakdown individual functions, and this can favour the 'externalization' of services. This has been interpreted by some as encouraging a decrease in the average size of establishment in manufacturing in Western Europe (Contini, 1984, quoted in Miles, 1985).

There is evidence that the subcontracting out of service demand by client companies is growing. In some instances legislative changes have been important. For example, in physical distribution, the 1968 Transport Act permitted firms to carry the traffic of other companies in their own vehicles and this has allowed large manufacturing firms and retailers to sell their distribution service to other organizations. Within the public sector expenditure controls and central government's preference for the private sector have encouraged the contracting out of cleaning, catering, and maintenance services. In part provoked by economic crisis, some larger manufacturing firms have also adopted more flexible methods of working involving subcontracting arrangements for more routine services. In contrast, particularly where the service component has become critical to production, manufacturing firms that have built up expertise in service activities are selling this on the open market (e.g. software sold by computer manufacturers, and engineering consultancy offered by motor vehicle firms). Information technology has enhanced this fluidity in the 'internalization' or 'externalization' of service production. On the one hand, computerization can make the 'in-house' production of services possible for the first time by reducing costs and enhancing 'in-house' capabilities. On the other, changes in equipment and the possible mismatch of organizational requirements and capabilities in a time of rapid change may encourage subcontracting (Miles, 1985).

5. In general, competition appears to be on the increase, though the extent and explanation for it varies between individual markets. There is a long history of government legislation and official pressure encouraging competition in financial services. This has been intensified by the recent moves to liberalize financial markets by removing the restrictions on firms trading in the City and allowing building societies to expand into personal financial services. Government has also reduced public sector control of telecommunications. A privatized British Telecom no longer has a monopoly of network provision or control of the attachments to the network and faces competition from rival telecommunications services.

Foreign based and especially North American competition is prominent in banking, finance, management consultancy, and advertising. The expansion of North American companies in the UK was originally encouraged by transnational investment elsewhere in the economy. More recently such foreign-based firms have expanded in the domestic market by offering novel as well as international services. The internationalization of production and financial markets has also encouraged UK firms to expand abroad, further opening up UK service activities to trends and developments in the international economy. At the same time the number of domestic competitors for producer services has increased. Mixed producer–consumer organizations are facing strong competition in their traditional consumer business (e.g. the banks competing with building societies) and, facilitated by computer-based technologies, firms in other industries have diversified into producer markets (e.g. retailers expanding into distribution, financial, and market research services).

6.3 CORPORATE REORGANIZATION

Clearly, small firms are significant in producer services, and this fact is probably not sufficiently recognized in the case studies since much of the data is provided by trade and professional associations which usually only contain the major firms. It is generally assumed that the level of concentration in services is lower than that in manufacturing but we have only fragmentary evidence for this (Aaronovitch and Sawyer, 1975; Bolton Report, 1971). In fact, service activities are very diverse in this respect with the financial sector displaying very high levels of concentration (Aaronovitch and Samson, 1985), and other sectors such as professional services being considerably more fragmented. There is often significant variation between markets within industries. For example, in physical distribution, high concentration characterizes long distance freight haulage and warehousing and small firms predominate in freight forwarding. Notwithstanding this variation there is some evidence of a modest growth in concentration both in the case studies and in related work (Howells and Green, 1985). Also, in many producer services, a small number of dominant organizations account for a major share of the business income of the industry.

Dominant organizations have responded to the market pressures described in the previous section by a parallel process of specialization and diversification. Firms tend to specialize to differentiate their product from others and to obtain a market niche. This process has been encouraged by a growing division of labour. During the recessionary 1970s, firms have tended to discard peripheral activities focusing instead on core functions (Sema Metra, 1986). Recent technological changes have also encouraged new areas of specialization such as on-line financial information services, electronic mail, and data base services, as well as reducing the barriers to entry associated with the purchase of capital equipment. This, together with corporate specialization, has created opportunities for small firm development and growth, frequently associated with the spin-off of key employees from the corporate sector, perhaps even encouraged by the dominant firms. It is these types of process which account for the dense networks of firm linkages which are a feature of service production in several service industries. Thus, much as in the manufacturing sector (Taylor and Thrift, 1983), high levels of new firm formation and the growth of small firms in producer services need to be understood in the context of the role such firms play in servicing the corporate sector, whether as subcontractors with a reservoir of spare capacity, as a source of innovation, or in providing a competitive sector in which the price of services may be kept down.

At the same time corporate diversification has assisted the interpenetration of producer service and related manufacturing and service markets. Producer service markets are attractive to outside firms because of their growth potential, and manufacturing and retail firms have diversified into the sector. Producer service firms themselves have attempted to restructure away from slowly growing or traditional services to more dynamic markets (e.g. the expansion of accountancy practices into the management consultancy sector). Some producer service organizations have attempted to develop a more complete service involving related consumer business (e.g. the expansion of the banks into estate agency). Other organizations have expanded from a narrow market base to provide a stronger mix of service products (e.g. the expansion of advertising firms into public relations and management consultancy, and of computer service firms into consultancy on related organizational work practices). The deregulation of the City has encouraged foreign and domestic firms to expand into jobbing and merchant banking activities.

Acquisition activity has been a popular form of diversification. Nevertheless, the internal development of an 'in-house' capacity in a new market is not unusual. A company department such as computer services may expand to sell the service on the open market and this may eventually result in a new division or even subsidiary organization being set up.

The increase in concentration and interpenetration in the producer service sector has created new and rather complex corporate structures. Any study of these shows just how simplistic are conventional 'hierarchical' views of corporate organization. In producer services complex partnership and associate company arrangements as well as regional-divisional-matrix structures have evolved, and these make it impossible to make simple generalizations on the basis of dominant types of organization.

Acquisition and diversification activities can create overlap in corporate structures and result in responsive reorganization. Expanding services are grafted on to existing organizations, often becoming the basis of a new division or subsidiary organization. Where organizations have become more complex, a decentralization of autonomy to regional or divisional profit centres can occur. Where organizations have become more specialized, local offices have been replaced by specialist teams in more central offices. Technological changes have enhanced these pressures for reorganization. In organizations with a substantial data processing support staff, the original tendency for information technology to encourage the concentration of data processing at a single computer centre is no longer so apparent. The economics of computer-related technology have changed; smaller more decentralized data processing units are possible and the technology has been integrated into a range of management functions. Nevertheless, distributed processing can still require some centralization at a local scale to use equipment efficiently and both centralization and decentralization tendencies are apparent within corporate structures associated with the introduction of information technology.

6.4. EMPLOYMENT, TECHNOLOGICAL CHANGE, AND THE LABOUR PROCESS

It is, however, inappropriate to concentrate in this description of the context for locational change solely on market demands and corporate restructuring. Our case studies suggest that there have been considerable changes in the character of employment in producer services, in part associated with an increase in capital intensity and the introduction of information technology. Pressures similar to those associated with reorganization and employment decline in manufacturing can be found in producer services. The growth in business in producer services has been associated with an increase in labour costs. This was combined during the 1960s and early 1970s with difficulties of access to clerical labour, especially close to London. During the later 1970s, as competition intensified, the pressure on firms to reduce labour costs has increased. Office technology, and the improvements in labour productivity which it offers, has been used as a 'solution' to these problems.

It is very difficult to be precise about the role of technology. We have only fragmentary case study evidence available and few longitudinal studies. In addition, technology is frequently introduced in association with a considerable reorganization and it is difficult to disentangle the impact of technology from the impact of other factors. In any case the impact of 'technology' on employment will depend on the market situation, the character of the firm into which it is introduced, the job task automated, as well as managerial philosophy and the ability of the workforce to influence changes.

The level of producer employment reflects the balance between job generation associated with the development of new service products which require specialist labour and expertise and the automation of service production which displaces less skilled service workers. In practice the two processes are interwoven. For example, process innovation is most frequent in large firms with capital resources and job losses are likely therefore to be most frequent here. On the other hand much service innovation in the form of new types of expertise is taking place in small specialist firms. An exchange of work, personnel, expertise, and capital between large and small firms is an important characteristic of the producer service sector in conditions of rapid technological innovation.

So far the extreme prognostications of job loss associated with the introduction of computer technology in producer services have not materialized. The labour saving potential of equipment such as word processors has not been maximized because the technology has been used to produce an improved product, or because the reorganization required to obtain productivity improvements has not always been carried out. Although this may mean that typists are not losing their jobs, rising productivity can imply that there are less producer service jobs available overall than might otherwise be the case.

While technology has reskilled some managerial and secretarial work, in data processing 'factories' it has continued the subdivision and routinization of clerical and junior administrative office tasks, and by disrupting some career hierarchies increased the segmentation of internal labour markets. This fragmentation of work may have in some instances facilitated the growth of part-time work. However, there are also other strong pressures encouraging part-time work, such as its lower cost and greater flexibility as far as employers are concerned. In many of the functions which involve data processing and customer contact, automation has also allowed employees to develop their customer contact and enriched rather than de-skilled their work. Nevertheless, the growth in part-time employment is part of an increasing casualization of female work in services. Female part-timers are concentrated in the lowest graded occupations, and together with the pressure of information technology on routine clerical functions this could bode ill for the prospects for female employment in the future, assuming that avenues for promotion through the internal labour market are not improved. However, much will depend on the way in which 'clerical factories' are modified by the introduction of new more flexible information systems and the capacity of female employees to shape the changes which occur in their work. Disadvantages attached to female employment could also be reduced by fairer treatment of part-time workers. However, occupational segregation suggests that gender divisions will remain significant in the producer service workforce.

There is, though, as the financial case study implied, a considerable divergence of opinion concerning the long term impact of technology. Given the potential of computer-based technology to automate routine tasks, several authors point to the long term negative impact of information technology on employment in services (Jenkins and Sherman, 1979). On the other hand, others predict information technology will permit quality improvements in existing services and new service innovations which will generate demand and employment (Gershuny and Miles, 1983; Barras, 1985). It is worth bearing in mind however, that the latter optimistic view is dependent upon a cheap, sophisticated, and widely available communications infrastructure.

6.5.   SPATIAL IMPLICATIONS

It is clear that the observed concentration of producer services in the UK near the capital, with a decentralization of employment from London and major cities, and slower growth in northern areas, cannot be understood simply as a response of service activities to changes in the cost of sites or variations in communication costs. Nor is manufacturing demand the sole influence on service supply.

A parallel corporate hierarchy apparently exists in large organizations in manufacturing and producer services. National headquarters and many administrative research and technical functions are located in the south and east of the country and branch offices carry out production activities or serve local markets elsewhere. It is tempting to argue that the growing concentration of ownership in both manufacturing and some producer services, together with the interdependence of large organizations in the two sectors, is therefore a sufficient explanation for the continued concentration of producer services in the Greater South East of the UK and the slow growth of producer services in the provinces. Indeed there is certainly some evidence for such processes at work, with the declining representation of central office employment in provincial conurbations during the 1970s possibly reflecting the effects of the takeover boom in the early 1970s on provincially headquartered enterprises (Howells and Green, 1985).

In fact, while corporate structures are important, such a direct association of corporate and urban systems over-simplifies the nature of corporate restructuring and market changes in producer services. Changes in business and consumer markets for services, the reorganization of supplying companies, and changes in the labour process are each bound up with locational changes. A growing market for services has also been characterized by structural change, periodic slumps in demand, and an intensification of competition. Locational changes have resulted as firms have responded by reducing costs, entering new markets, or generally reorganizing. Information technology has provided the means to reorganize for firms with considerable amounts of data processing. Variations in labour supply, in particular the greater availability outside the capital of clerical labour, and the need to be close to London to attract senior managerial staff, have favoured the Greater South East.

Since the mid-1970s there has been a considerable reorganization of producer service activity in larger firms, with a shift in emphasis from setting up in new locations to developing selected existing sites with appropriate skills or investment. There has also been a tendency for firms to serve peripheral markets with a depressed manufacturing sector from more central areas.

The large banking and insurance companies provide excellent examples of the way in which these processes can occur. The insurance service has witnessed some decentralization of employment from London, but both insurance and banking have increased their concentration in metropolitan areas. Any dispersal of employment from city centres has been retained within metropolitan hinterlands and this has been supported by some withdrawal of employment from rural areas. In these services a growing but increasingly competitive market has coincided with increasing data processing costs and this has encouraged re-organization using computer-based technology. The economics of information technology and the centralized organizational structure of the companies during the 1960s led to the setting up of a small number of data processing centres to carry out the administrative work of the branch network. The high cost of a location close to the capital and the greater availability of female clerical labour in small town locations, together with the requirement for skilled male senior managerial staff encouraged a location in smaller labour markets in the South East and in the secondary financial centre of the North West.

The diversification strategies of the main companies and the development of new services has produced increasingly unwieldy corporate structures, and as a consequence, a limited decentralization of autonomy and functions to regional offices usually located in metropolitan centres. More recently, as computer-based technology has facilitated distributed data processing, the technology has supported a reorganization of the branch network, in which some branches have been closed and others have had their functions reduced. Data processing has been concentrated in key area offices and subordinate branches have been grouped round larger general purpose offices which carry out personal and business-related activities. This restructuring has operated against smaller rural branches with a limited market which have been deemed less economic and these have been closed or downgraded.

The association between market changes, restructuring, and

location is less obvious for other producer services, partly because our information is less good and partly because the SIC groups a number of services together. Nevertheless, for business service offices and distributive trades we can identify similar processes at work to those in the finance sector. Here the dominant trend has been growth outside London to serve the expansion of business from clients who have decentralized their activities. In part this decentralization process has been the result of branch office openings but, in accountancy in particular, regional companies have merged with national concerns. Again, this decentralization has been uneven with regional offices in the hinterlands of major conurbations serving outlying areas. There is also some evidence for a concentration in such offices as organizations have specialized in serving larger customers. National offices with specialist teams have also been used to support provincial offices and this has limited the decentralization process. However, the negative impacts of such processes are ameliorated by a parallel growth of smaller firms, frequently in suburban and small town locations, which are integrated by service contracts with the larger firms.

In contrast, the growth of international trade in financial, engineering, oil, and consultancy services has encouraged the growth of producer services close to London. For example, UK-based financial multinationals run their foreign business out of London and a few provincial offices. The regional offices of foreign banks co-ordinating their European activities are strongly tied to the City of London. Also the expansion of financial conglomerates into the domestic market has been primarily through a few offices in the major cities, though data processing activities tend to be more decentralized. A more general study of the location of foreign multinational offices in the UK by Dunning and Norman (1983) further suggests that these firms, influenced by the location of domestic company headquarters, locate in prestige sites close to London but with good access to international airports. This trend has been in general supported by the expansion of new entrants and of smaller organizations in producer markets. Here the existing organization of service supply has influenced the growth of new activity by affecting the distribution of new start-ups. For example in computer services, new organizations are frequently subsidiaries of existing organizations, or 'spin-offs' from such companies, and this tends to favour a location in the Greater South East close to the parent company.

However, overlayed on top of these processes the more dispersed character of employment growth in some mixed producer–consumer services reflects the decentralization of population out of the major cities. For example, the shift towards out-of-town retailing must lie behind the decentralization of the distribution of food and drink. The growth of other financial institutions outside the major conurbations throughout much of the country owes much to the expansion of the building societies into the personal savings market formerly occupied by the banks. As such the expansion of building society employment can be seen as the mirror image of the restructuring of the activities of the banks in some of these areas. However, this force for decentralization is critically dependent on the way in which building societies, historically rather separate from other financial institutions and with simple organizational structures, become integrated into the wider financial community.

7

Policy Towards Services

7.1. INTRODUCTION

An important theme of the preceding chapters has been the existence of marked spatial variations in producer service activity. The implications of the concentration of producer service activities in London and the South East of the country for regional and urban development has also been discussed. Spatial variations in the availability of producer services affect industrial and occupational structures, employment opportunities, export potential, and possibly entrepreneurial activity. It has also been hypothesized (although definitive evidence is lacking) that there is a relationship between the location of producer services and firm performance, i.e. that a regional deficiency in research and development, finance, distribution, or business services, for example, is detrimental to industrial innovation, efficiency, and competitiveness. Recent advances in telecommunications may have the potential to reduce any information deficits of the peripheral regions but the centralizing implications of infrastructure development suggests that regional disparities may be widened rather than the reverse.

The response of economic and industrial policy to the growth of service activities has been limited. Confronted by conceptual difficulties in understanding the intangible nature of services, a perception of the service sector as being dependent on manufacturing, and statistical problems in identifying eligible services, policy-makers have largely ignored the potential contribution of the sector to economic development. Regional policy has been in existence for over half a century, yet only in the last twenty years has the government taken any cognizance of services in terms of practical measures. Specific incentives for service firms have been implemented for little more than a decade and have been very much secondary to manufacturing industry assistance.

Since the mid-1970s, responses to the problem of regional economic development have not been confined to regional policy. Alongside an increasingly varied range of central government support for employment, new technology, and small firms (apart form inner-city aid generally aspatial in character), a plethora of regional and local agencies have grown up to add new dimensions to the task of economic regeneration. Here too, though, the possible contribution of producer services appears to have been largely neglected.

Faced with increasingly limited prospects for job creation in manufacturing, development strategies at central, regional, and local levels have recently begun to incorporate new policy measures for services. However, such initiatives lack co-ordination and there is some disagreement about which sevices should be assisted and what the most appropriate measures are.

This chapter reviews these issues. It first examines the extent to which past and present regional policies in the UK have incorporated assistance for the producer service sector and sets such initiatives within the wider framework of central government industrial policy. It also considers the growing contribution of regional and local bodies to the task of economic regeneration and the emphasis they place on assistance towards service activities. To place UK experience in a broader context, developments in service policy elsewhere in the European Community (EC) are also discussed. The possible contribution of infrastructure policies to the development of services in the regions, both in this country and abroad, is also examined. Finally, the chapter discusses the overall role of services in regional development strategies and makes some policy proposals.

7.2.   BRITISH REGIONAL POLICY AND SERVICES

A specific policy for those regions of the country suffering excessive economic hardship was first introduced in Great Britain in 1934 in response to extreme unemployment in the depressed industrial areas. Although viewed initially as a temporary measure, regional policy was retained after 1945 (though fluctuating in importance) despite low nationwide unemployment, as a means of minimizing geographical variations in economic development. The policy, which was based on influencing the inter-regional movement of mobile manufacturing industry, was primarily implemented through the provision of factories, industrial estates, and later loans and grants in the Development Areas, and through floorspace controls in the congested areas, particularly the South East and Midlands. During the 1960s, a worsening regional problem produced a higher priority for regional policy. Stronger measures were introduced by the Local

Employment Acts and greater emphasis was put on regional economic planning and the role of infrastructure. The policy, however, continued to be essentially reactive and to stress the creation of manufacturing employment. The problem regions were redesignated frequently, focusing on the location of declining traditional production industries. In the early 1960s the first policy measures towards service activities were introduced—Office Development Permits and the formation of the Location of Office Bureau—although the initiatives were prompted as much by increasing congestion in central London as the needs of the regions for office employment (McCrone, 1968).

During the early 1970s, a slow-down in economic growth, an increase in unemployment, and a reduced supply of mobile industry brought a reassessment of the regional problem. Regional policy became viewed increasingly as peripheral to the objectives of national economic growth, particularly as the once prosperous areas began to suffer decline. The emphasis of assistance was switched from the redirection of mobile investment to stimulating indigenous regional development. Also, the task of dealing with regional problems became progressively decentralized through the setting-up of development agencies in 1975 and the emergence of local economic development initiatives. Although the first financial incentives specifically for service firms were introduced in 1973, the overwhelming part of selective (as well as automatic) regional assistance continued to be directed at manufacturing industry throughout the 1970s. In 1979 the new Conservative government began a sequence of cutbacks in the coverage of the Assisted Areas and in 1983–4 undertook a major revision of the package of regional incentives to produce the regional policy currently in operation. Regional policy is now justified on social rather than economic grounds and has job creation as a primary objective. Despite a reduction in the regional aid budget, the review gave certain services parity with manufacturing for automatic assistance for the first time.

Prior to 1984 though, regional policy measures directed at the service sector were essentially two-fold: controls on office development, and financial incentives for mobile service firms. In addition, related to mainstream policy, government implemented a large-scale dispersal of public sector office jobs to the regions. These measures are now examined in turn.

Office dispersal

Office development during the post-war period was initially concentrated in London, stimulated by the removal of building licences in 1954 and the subsequent improvements in the supply of building materials (Wright, 1967). While the population of central London was decreasing after 1950, employment was growing at the rate of about 15,000 jobs each year (0.5% p.a.) and almost 45 million sq. ft. of new office space was built up to 1958 (Aucott, 1960). Until 1964, the only controls on this office growth were local physical planning regulations. Successive planning initiatives such as the Barlow Report and the Greater London Plan failed to recognize the problems of unchecked office development in the capital, and focused their attention largely on the manufacturing sector. The 1951 Greater London Development Plan noted that congestion was growing yet allowed for an increase in the office development area of almost 20%. Modifications to this Plan in 1955 brought a degree of rezoning from office to residential use, a decrease in building plot ratios, and some planned decentralization towards the outskirts of the city. The government made appeals for private office movement but these were not backed up by controls or incentives and the dispersal of government jobs was handicapped by civil service resistance and administrative difficulties. In the late 1950s and early 1960s, the London County Council again successively reduced plot ratios, but by 1962–3 some 7.5 million sq. ft. of new office space was still being permitted each year in the London area (Manners, 1962).

The first significant central government response came in 1964 with the setting up of the Location of Offices Bureau (LOB) to encourage office movement out of London. However, the organization was equipped with only advisory powers. Controls were introduced in 1965 with the Office and Industry Development Act which brought in the system of Office Development Permits (ODPs). The Act which was introduced retrospectively to November 1964 applied initially to the London Metropolitan Region and the West Midlands conurbation and required all office developments of over 3,000 sq. ft. to apply for an ODP. Permits were only granted where it could be demonstrated that there was a need for a central area location, that no other suitable accommodation was available, and that the development was 'in the public interest'. In 1966 these controls were extended to the rest of the South East, the West Midlands, the East Midlands, and East Anglia regions, although the following year the exemption limit was raised for these 'new' areas from 3,000 to 10,000 sq. ft.

After 1969 the policy became more relaxed: the ODP controls were removed first from East Anglia and the rural parts of the Midlands, then the whole of the East and West Midlands and the exemption limit was raised universally to 10,000 sq. ft. The ODP award principles were also modified to replace the need for a central area location by the demonstration of 'efficiency gains'. In 1977, the streamlining of administration contained in the Control of Office Development Act lessened the effect of the controls still further because congestion in London was considered less of a problem. With the emphasis increasingly on inner city development, the Act also revised the remit of the LOB to encourage the siting of offices in provincial cities rather than decentralization from London *per se*. However, with the advent of a Conservative government in 1979, both the ODP system and the LOB were abolished.

Both the rationale and implementation of the office dispersal policy were not very successful. The statistical justification for the introduction of office controls has been shown to be inaccurate, since it was based on a considerable overestimate of the growth of office employment in the central area of London (Evans, 1967; Hall, 1969). There was still a good case for limiting or redirecting office development (Alexander, 1979), but the early operation of ODPs was partly offset by the backlog of planning applications already granted. It was estimated in 1965 that there was some 36 million sq. ft. of office floorspace in the pipeline in Greater London, with a further 9 million sq. ft. in the Metropolitan Region (Wright, 1967).

Nevertheless, the ODP controls did restrict the development of additional floorspace in central London. From 1965 to 1976, almost 28 million sq. ft. of office floorspace was prohibited in the central area by the ODP system, about 30% of the floorspace applied for (Alexander, 1979). Moreover, the development constraints encouraged a greater degree of renovation and a more efficient use of existing space. The creation of an artifical shortage of floorspace at a time of increasing demand, however, contributed to a considerable inflation of rents (DOE, 1976; Wettmann and Nicol, 1977). In addition, the arbitrary way in which controls were applied provided no guarantee that offices forced to relocate were best suited for dispersal (Alexander, 1979). The effect was to disadvantage those firms which needed a central area location and to damage London's position as a commercial and financial centre as multinational firms located in other major European cities where rents were considerably less expensive (Cowan, 1971; Rhodes and Kan, 1972; Daniels, 1982).

Of course the efforts of the LOB and the ODP system did encourage a greater consideration of office movement while the suburbanization of office employment was in progress. Between 1964 and 1977 some 145,000 private sector jobs were recorded as being diverted out of central london (LOB, 1975; Alexander, 1979); indeed, Hall (1972) suggests that the figure may have been as high as 250,000 jobs. Much of the movement, however, took place over relatively short distances, often within Greater London to other parts of the South East Region (Daniels, 1975). Although the prime purpose of the policy was not to bring office employment to the Assisted Areas, of the 70,000 jobs decentralized between 1963 and 1970, only about 1% actually moved to the Development Areas. Office centres on the periphery of London such as Croydon, Watford, and the London ring of New Towns were the chief beneficiaries of the movement (Daniels, 1976). Moves further afield tended to be too costly for smaller offices (which constituted the bulk of movers) while larger offices risked the loss of qualified staff (Daniels, 1975). Any movement beyond the South East Region was more likely to be to 'uncontrolled' centres such as Bristol and Basingstoke rather than further north.

Government office relocation

In tandem with the government's efforts to redistribute private sector office employment, attempts were made to decentralize public administration from London. Although measures to relocate government office work date back to 1941, the first major initiatives were undertaken in the early 1960s. Between 1963 and 1972 some 23,500 civil service jobs were dispersed from London. These attempts at redistribution were more beneficial for the Assisted Areas than the decentralization of private sector offices: although almost 30% of the public office jobs decentralized remained in the South East Region, over 50% were moved to the problem regions—notably Scotland, Wales, the North, and the North West. In addition, after 1965 new public sector offices were to be located outside London whenever possible.

However, most of the relocation undertaken generally involved clerical, non-headquarters jobs, and the continued proliferation of new offical bodies in central London undermined the results. In 1973 the Hardman Report cited the government's disinclination to disperse a substantial number of civil service jobs as being partly to blame for the lack of success of its office location policies. Consequently, in a new phase of the relocation policy, the government decided in July 1974 to relocate more than 31,000 civil service jobs outside London over a 10-year period. Some 90% of these jobs were to go to the Assisted Areas. Glasgow, Cardiff, Newport, Merseyside, and Teesside were the greatest beneficiaries. Among the major transfers, the headquarters of the Property Service Agency with 3,000 jobs went to Teesside; 4,500 jobs, including elements of the Ministry of Agriculture and the Home Office went to the North West Region, mostly to Merseyside; over 1,000 Defence, Overseas

Development Administration, and National Engineering Laboratory jobs were allocated to Glasgow; the Laboratory of the Government Chemist was moved to West Cumberland; and 500 DHSS posts were allocated to Newcastle.

This programme, under which the government undertook to relocate jobs to relatively few centres in the Assisted Areas, was originally due to run until 1985, but was subsequently extended to 1989. Although it still continues (in 1985–6 some 600 Ministry of Defence jobs were relocated in Glasgow), a reduction in the projected number of relocated jobs, cutbacks in public expenditure since 1979 and opposition from civil service unions have combined to reduce the scale and effects of the programme. Consequently, while almost 31,000 civil service posts were dispersed from London between 1963 and 1983, more than one third of civil service employment is still concentrated in the South East.

Incentives

In the light of criticisms of the effectiveness of controls on office location (Daniels 1969; Rhodes and Kan, 1971), in 1973 the government introduced special incentives to encourage the movement of offices to the Assisted Areas. Incentives had of course been (theoretically) available to services for some considerable time. The Local Employment Acts of 1961–6, for example, permitted the Board of Trade to provide premises for rent or sale for both manufacturing and service firms in the Development Areas. In addition, the Board could award building grants of 25% (subsequently increased to 35% and then, by 1971, 45%) as well as loans or grants to establish an enterprise in a Development Area. The application of these grants to the office sector, though, received relatively little publicity and they were rarely used to assist service firms (Wright, 1967; Rhodes and Kan, 1972).

The Service Industry Removal Grants introduced in 1973 were a more overt formulation of regional policy interest in the service sector. The scheme provided employee transfer grants of £800, as well as grants providing rent relief for up to five years or to facilitate the purchase of premises (HMSO, 1974). Aid was, however, restricted to mobile projects (those with a choice of location) and those which created employment opportunities (in practice, 10 jobs for transferred firms and 25 jobs for new start-ups in the Assisted Areas). Assistance for local services was specifically excluded. In the mid-1970s the Service Industry Removal Grants scheme was modified with an increase in transfer grants to £1,500 per job, and an extension of the rent relief grant to up to seven years (in the

Special Development Areas (SDAs)). In addition, a job creation grant was introduced providing £1,500 per job in the SDAs and £1,000 per job in the DAs (HMSO, 1977). To take account of rising industrial costs, the rates of award were increased again in 1979 under the renamed Office and Service Industries Scheme (OSIS) to make available job creation grants of up to £6,000 per job and employee removal grants of £1,500 per job for enterprises setting up or expanding in the Assisted Areas (HMSO, 1979).

The increased value of service grants was accompanied by changes in the eligibility criteria. Firms were now also required to demonstrate their export orientation i.e. that they served markets at least partly outside the area of location. Also, the assistance could no longer be combined with other aid under the 1972 Industry Act. The last revision to OSIS before its demise took place in 1981 with a final increase in the maximum levels for the job creation and employee removal grants to £8,000 and £2,000 respectively and the addition of a feasibility study grant to contribute to the costs of the assessment of an Assisted Area location. OSIS was discontinued in 1984 in the course of a major review of British regional policy. The job creation element of the scheme was incorporated into the more general Regional Selective Assistance but the employee transfer and feasiblity study grants were abolished.

The Service Industry Removal Grant scheme and OSIS are generally believed to have been introduced too late to affect significantly the movement and location of office activities. The 1960s and early 1970s was a relatively favourable period for decentralization as a growing service market combined with the restructuring of organizations in both the private and public sector using computer-based technology encouraged locational change (Marshall, 1985; Marshall, Damesick, and Wood, 1985). The potential, though, for a planned redirection of service employment to the Assisted Areas was missed through insufficient stimulus. Since then, the pressures for decentralization have diminished and the concentration of new IT services in London and the South East has increased.

With respect to the schemes themselves, the incentives were not well publicized, the number of applications and awards were relatively low and the assistance constituted only some 1% of regional aid in 1977 (Daniels, 1982). Between 1977 and 1983 there were on average only 79 awards per year involving about 3,600 jobs (Yuill and Allen, 1985). The employee removal and feasibility study elements of the scheme were deemed to be particularly unpopular. Part of the poor success has been attributed to the restrictive design of the scheme. Given that office mobility was declining in the mid-1970s and that the scale of assistance was insufficient to cover the 'disturbance' costs associated with office moves, the mobility criterion was particularly inhibiting (Marquand, 1979; RSA, 1983). Moreover, the job creation threshold of 10 or 25 jobs was a significant restriction given the small size of many offices (Marshall, 1981). Together with the exclusion of local services, such conditions rendered much of the service sector ineligible.

Current regional policy[1]

The election of a Conservative government in 1979 brought an immediate commitment to review the system of regional aid. Initially this was manifest in a series of spatial cutbacks in the extent of the Assisted Areas. However, in December 1983 a wide-ranging White Paper was put forward proposing, among other measures 'less discrimination against service industries . . . [although] it would not be appropriate for all services to qualify because many serve local markets and do not have a choice of location' (HMSO, 1983). Comment on the White Paper was invited by the government; on the services issue most responses were said to favour the government proposal to assist services, especially research and development, tourism, business and computer services, headquarters functions, and finance. Very few submissions, though, argued the case for local services (DTI, 1985). The consultation period was followed in November 1984 by the introduction of a revamped regional policy. The main features of the new system involved a new two-tier structure and a redrawn map of Assisted Areas, a new regional development grant scheme (RDG) placing a greater emphasis on job creation, a cutback in expenditure, and an extension of the eligibility of the service sector.

In the new policy, services qualified for the first time for automatic regional assistance. Hitherto, the automatic grant had been restricted mainly to manufacturing activities. Certain exceptions had existed like repair services, scientific research, or staff training, but only in so far as they were related to manufacturing activities. The eligibility provisions of the new RDG scheme were widened considerably to include a broad range of service activities (Table 7.1).

Under the RDG scheme, eligible firms are now entitled to receive either a capital grant or a job grant, whichever is more favourable to them. The capital grant pays 15% of eligible capital expenditure but is subject to a cost-per-job limit of £10,000. For labour intensive projects, the award may take the form of a job grant which is worth £3,000 for each new job created. Small firms (defined as employing

[1] As this book went to press the government announced several policy changes including the phasing out of automatic regional assistance.

Table 7.1. The Eligibility for Regional Policy Assistance of Producer
Services

Scheme	Service eligibility
Regional development grant	Data processing and software development
	Technical design, testing analysis, etc.
	Business services
	Management consultants
	Market research and public relations
	Exhibition contracting and organizing
	Industrial research and development services
	Administration, headquarters
	Advertising agencies
	Industrial photographic services
	Venture capital providers
	Credit card companies
	Export houses
	Repair (except for consumer goods and vehicle repair)
	Value added network services
	Cable television
	Mail order houses and similar service provided direct to the public e.g. football pools
	Freight forwarders
Regional selective assistance RSA grant Training in support of RSA Exchange risk cover	All producer services, unless more specific forms of assistance are available, e.g. for research and development projects
Government factories	All producer services, although eligibility is subject to job density minima per 1000 sq. ft. (apart from in Northern Ireland).

fewer than 200 people and thus of particular relevance to services)
are given preferential treatment in that they do not have to create
jobs, nor are they subject to the £10,000 cost-per-job limit, unless
project expenditure exceeds £500,000.

In selecting the services for assistance, the Department of Trade
and Industry reviewed the activities covered in the 1980 SIC based
on three main criteria. They were interested in sectors with a choice
of location, those which were of 'regional importance', and those
which would have little displacement effect, i.e. which do not replace

existing jobs. Given the mobility criterion, it would appear that the regional export-base approach still holds sway and there is little evidence of a recognition of the potential service contribution to *local* industry's performance. Also, the emphasis on capital expenditure and large-scale job creation of the RDG scheme indicates a policy discriminating more in favour of manufacturing industry. It is of course too early to assess the take-up of the new RDG by service firms. In the first year following the 1984 review, some £1.3 million of grant was offered to banking, finance, insurance, business services, and leasing firms, and £935,000 for industrial research and development projects—together accounting for one-third of new RDG approved expenditure. But since then the scale of assistance to services appears to have declined.

Alongside the automatically-awarded RDG, selective assistance to services continues to be important. OSIS has of course been discontinued but services now qualify under Section 7 of the Industrial Development Act. Under the Regional Selective Assistance (RSA) scheme, services that meet the normal criteria for assistance (viability, proof of need, efficiency, employment benefit, and own contribution to costs) are eligible, but service projects must also export beyond the local area. This reaffirms again the DTI's doubts concerning the contribution of local services to regional economic development.

7.3. INDUSTRIAL POLICY ASSISTANCE AND SERVICES

Regional aid is of course only one part of government *incentive* assistance to industry, which in turn is a major component of a broader set of industrial policy measures which also include nationalized industry support, merger and competition policy, employment measures, and innovation policy (Hood and Young, 1983). Since 1979 all of the industrial policy instruments have been subject to significant change reflecting the government's desire to reduce state intervention, increase the role of the private sector, and improve the 'business climate'.

Nationalized industries have been gradually privatized or prepared for sale to the private sector. Capital allowances have been progressively phased out in favour of a reduction in corporation tax. The trend in the development of labour market policy, marked by a growing involvement in training and job creation since the mid-1970s, has been accelerated. A 'new' innovation policy has emerged: the private sector participation of the British Technology Group (formerly the NEB and NEDC) has been wound down, spending on scientific and technological assistance increased, and more consideration given to supply side measures (co-ordination of public sector research, reform of intellectual property rights, collaborative ventures, and the improvement and exploitation of the supply of qualified manpower from the education system) (*The Economist*, 1984). Restrictive practices in the City of London have been reduced and competition in the financial sector has been enhanced. Policies have discriminated more positively in favour of small firms by encouraging entrepreneurial attitudes, reducing the legislative and administrative obstacles to new firm formation and expansion, and by improving the flow of finance and the provision of information and advice. Lastly, the targeting of some government assistance has become more closely defined. While regional aid has diminished, increasing expenditure has been devoted to ameliorate economic decline and environmental decay in the inner cities (Leach, 1985).

With respect to industrial incentives, there have been three major areas of change. First, regional and general industrial support has been cut back in favour of a diversion of resources to scientific and technological assistance, which has grown from less than £100 million in 1978–9 to over £500 million in 1985–6 (HMSO, 1985). The decline in regional aid spending, including Section 7 assistance, was referred to earlier; selective assistance under Section 8 of the 1982 Industrial Development Act (formerly 1972 Industry Act) has also been restructured to put a greater emphasis on new technology. The sectoral schemes—providing assistance to older industries—have virtually disappeared, and have been replaced by the umbrella 'Support for Innovation' programme (part financed under the Science and Technology Act) for firms introducing technologies such as office automation, computer-aided design, and robotics (HMSO, 1979; HMSO, 1985). Second, there has been a dramatic growth in schemes of assistance in the employment and training field, part inspired by the need to reduce unemployment figures and the desire to improve the supply of qualified industrial manpower. This has been most evident in the areas of youth employment, job sharing, and incentives for self-employment. Third, support for new firm formation and small businesses has been expanded, through the measures introduced under the Inner Urban Areas Act and through various finance-related schemes aimed at encouraging investment in small firms.

Apart from changes in *national* industrial policy, the last decade has also seen the growing participation of regional, local, and private organizations in the provision of finance for industry. Regional development agencies, local economic initiatives, industrial sector associations, and others have been formed to improve the responsiveness of the state to regional and local development problems. Their activities add a further level of complexity to the industrial policy assistance scene.

The degree to which producer services are assisted by these policy measures is difficult to assess. The following sections, however, attempt to review the treatment of producer services in selected policy areas—national government incentive policies, regional development agency assistance in Scotland and Northern Ireland, and local development assistance.

National government incentive policies

Any assessment of government incentive assistance for industry is immediately confronted by the variety and complexity of the support on offer. A breakdown of central government incentive assistance into the individual measures of policy delivery, for example, produces a list of almost 150 separate financial and fiscal incentives for industry. The aid spans a range of purposes: employment and training, research and development, new technology, new firm formation, and small business development, land reclamation, export promotion, marketing, environmental protection, and energy saving. The types of industrial incentives vary from grants and loans to equity finance and tax concessions; some are automatic, others selective and conditional (Bienkowski and Allen, 1985).

This assistance displays little coherence or co-ordination, un-surprising in view of the range of administering bodies involved. At national level, assistance is provided by the Departments of Trade and Industry, Environment, Employment, Transport and Energy, and by the Inland Revenue, the Manpower Services Commission, ICFC, the British Overseas Trade Board, the Export Credit Guarantee Department, and the Overseas Development Administration. Many incentives are financed through European Commission policies and involve the European Coal and Steel Community, European Regional Development Fund, European Social Fund, and the European Investment Bank.

In Tables 7.2–7.5 an attempt has been made to categorize the incentives provided by central government according to their relevance for producer services. It is a somewhat crude and arbitrary classification based simply on the industrial sector eligibility of the schemes, but also taking into account other characteristics such as the purpose of the incentives and any size restrictions for eligible firms or projects.

Table 7.2. National Government Assistance Specifically for Producer Services

Scheme	Administering department	Service eligibility
Support for software products	DTI/NCC	Software producers
COSIT: Computer training programme	MSC	Computer services
EC: Transnational consultancy	EC	Consultants
Support for microelectronics DLVC	DTI	Producers of distance learning video courses
ECGD: Service policies	ECGD	Service exporters

Administering departments

BOTB	British Overseas Trade Board
DE	Department of Employment
DED	Department of Economic Development, Northern Ireland
DEN	Department of Energy
DOE	Department of the Environment
DTI	Department of Trade and Industry
EC	European Commission
ECGD	Export Credit Guarantee Department
ECSC	European Coal and Steel Community
EIB	European Investment Bank
EITB	Engineering Industry Training Board
ERDF	European Regional Development Fund
ESF	European Social Fund
ICFC	Industrial Credit and Finance Corporation
IDB	Industrial Development Board, Northern Ireland
IR	Inland Revenue
LA	Local authorities
LEDU	Local Enterprise Development Unit, Northern Ireland
MSC	Manpower Services Commission
NCC	National Computing Centre
NI: DOE	Department of the Environment, Northern Ireland
ODA	Overseas Development Administration
SEPD	Scottish Economic Planning Department
WOID	Welsh Office Industry Department

Source: CSPP (1986).

As indicated in Table 7.2, few schemes are specifically designed for producer services. The exceptions are limited to the computer services field. The Support for Software Products scheme, for example, makes available grants to assist with the development and marketing costs of new or existing software by computer bureaux, software and system houses, and consultancies. Grants are also

Table 7.3. National Government Assistance with Restricted Eligibility for
Producer Services

Scheme	Administering department	Service eligibility
(a) General assistance		
Loan guarantee scheme	DE/ICFC	Excludes a range of financial educational, property, medical, and telecommunications services
(b) New technology		
Support for AMT	DTI	AMT support services
Feasibility studies: AMT	DTI	AMT support services
Feasibility studies: microelectronics	DTI	Microelectronics support services
Investment support for microelectronics	DTI	Microelectronics support services
Investment support for fibre optics	DTI	Fibre optics support services
Support for innovation	DTI	Innovation support services
Support for training in microelectronics	DTI/NCC	Microelectronics consultants
Computer skills grants	MSC	Excludes computer services
(c) Research and development		
Support for biotechnology investment	DTI	Biotechnology R and D services
Joint opto-electronics scheme	DTI	Opto-electronics R and D services
Alvey research programme	DTI	IT R and D services
Joint appraisal scheme	DTI	R and D services
Support for biotechnology advice	DTI	Biotechnology R and D services
European conference support	EC	R and D services/consultants
ESPRIT	EC	IT R and D services
European stimulation action	EC	R and D services
EC: Non-nuclear energy programme	EC	Energy R and D services
EC: Basic research in industrial technology	EC	Industrial technology R & D services
EC: Hydrocarbon projects	EC	Hydrocarbon R and D services

Table 7.3.   (Continued)

Scheme	Administering department	Service eligibility
EC: Metrology and reference materials	EC	Metrology R and D services
EC: Storage of radioactive waste	EC	Nuclear R and D services
EC: Radiation protection programme	EC	Nuclear R and D services
EC: Materials research programme	EC	Materials R and D services
EC: Reactor safety research programme	EC	Nuclear R and D services
EC: Environmental action programme	EC	Environmental R and D Services
EC: Energy demonstration projects	EC	Energy R and D services
EC: Decommissioning of nuclear installations	EC	Nuclear R and D services
EC: Hydrocarbon pollution control	EC	Hydrocarbon R and D services
EC: Biotechnology programme	EC	Biotechnology R and D services
EC: RACE	EC	Communications R and D Services
(d) Exporting		
Overseas project fund	DTI/BOTB	Consultancy services for major overseas capital projects
ECGD: External trade guarantees	ECGD	Goods trading services
ECGD: Term guarantees	ECGD	Goods trading services
(e) Employment		
Attachment training scheme	DED	Excludes the professions
ECSC loan	ECSC	Certain (unspecified) services ineligible
Training on employers premises scheme	DED	Only services already assisted by IDB or LEDU
Trainee manager development scheme	DED	
(f) Transport		
Rail freight facilities grant		Rail freight handling services

Table 7.3. *(Continued)*

Scheme	Administering department	Service eligibility
Water freight facilities grant	SDD/WOID	Water freight handling services
Port modernization grant	DED	Port operation services
(g) Energy		
Coal-firing scheme	DEN/DED	Excludes banking and insurance

For a list of abbreviations see Table 7.2.
Source: CSPP (1986).

available through the Computing Services Industry Training Programme to help computing service firms take on, train, and develop staff. Both the ECGD service policies and the EC Transnational Consultancy scheme are designed to encourage international trade in services, through insurance of service contracts and support for international co-operation between small and medium-sized technical and management consultancy firms respectively.

Beyond this limited set of service-specific schemes, producer service firms have access to a range of other assistance. Some of this is on a sectorally restricted basis (see Table 7.3) where either specific services are excluded (e.g. the Loan Guarantee Scheme) or they are only eligible in so far as they are directly associated with manufacturing projects, mostly in research and development or the application of new technology. In a number of cases, eligibility is theoretically possible but inappropriate in practice (see Table 7.4) given the target of the aid or the award conditions. National Selective Assistance (Section 8), for example, is directed almost exclusively at manufacturing and medium- to large-scale projects.

A significant number of incentives are not restricted to specific sectors (Table 7.5). Most of these are in the employment and training, export promotion and general business investment field. Some, such as the Open Tech Programme or the MSC's Access to New Information Technology scheme are of particular relevance to producer service firms. However, the nature of the requirements of other schemes may make them less applicable to services. Qualifying expenditure, for instance, frequently relates to capital expenditure, more relevant to manufacturing than some services. Given the small size of many services firms, especially in the IT field, even job-related assistance can, on occasion, be of limited applicability.

Table 7.4. National Government Assistance of Limited Applicability to Producer Services

Scheme	Administering Department	Service eligibility
(a) Employment and training		
Job training scheme	MSC	Excludes producer services
Teaching company scheme	DTI	Manufacturing only
Visiting engineers scheme	DTI	Engineering only
Training in high technology skills	EITB	Engineering only
Iron/steel employees benefit	DTI/ECSC	Iron and steel only
Skill training scheme	NI: DOE	Primarily engineering
EC: Development of the specialized information market	EC	Primarily engineering
(b) General investment/advisory assistance		
National selective assistance	DTI	Primarily manufacturing; medium to large size projects
BTAS: Manufacturing element	DTI	Primarily manufacturing advice
BTAS: Quality element	DTI	Primarily manufacturing advice
BTAS: Support for design	DTI	Primarily manufacturing support
Quality assurance support scheme	DTI	Primarily manufacturing support
Advisory service to industry	DED	Manufacturing only
Capital allowances on machinery and plant	IR	Relief for capital expenditure
(c) Exporting		
Store promotion scheme	BOTB	Goods promotion overseas
ECGD: Foreign currency cover	ECGD	Minimum contract value: £1m.
ECGD: Bank finance guarantees	ECGD	Minimum contract value: £1m.
ECGD: Guarantees for banks	ECGD	Minimum contract value: £250,000
ECGD: Specific guarantees	ECGD	Capital goods exporters

For a list of abbreviations see Table 7.2.

Source: CSPP (1986).

Table 7.5. Non-sectoral Government Assistance

Scheme	Administering department
(a) Employment and training	
Adaptations for the disabled	MSC/DED
Individual training with an employer	MSC
Community programme	MSC
Job introduction for the disabled	MSC/DED
Travel to interview scheme	MSC/DED
Job search scheme	MSC
Sheltered placement scheme	MSC
New workers scheme	MSC
Youth training scheme	MSC
Fares to work scheme	MSC/DED
Voluntary projects programme	MSC
Aids for disabled employees	MSC
Local training grants scheme	MSC
Training for enterprise scheme	MSC
Management extension programme	MSC/DED
Local consultancy grants scheme	MSC
Wider opportunities training programme	MSC
Job release scheme	DE/DED
Redundancy payments scheme	DE/DED
Job splitting scheme	DE/DED
Enterprise allowance	DE/DED
ESF: Training/resettlement	DE/DED/ESF
Youth training programme	DED
Action for community employment	DED
Community volunteering scheme	DED
Key worker grant scheme	DED
Consultant grant scheme	DED
Training grant scheme	DED

Table 7.5.   (*Continued*)

Scheme	Administering department
(b) Exports	
Export marketing research scheme	BOTB
Inward mission scheme	BOTB
Trade fairs overseas	BOTB
Outward missions scheme	BOTB
Overseas seminars & symposia	BOTB
Market prospects services	BOTB/IDB
Export representative services	BOTB/IDB
ECGD: Matching aid	ECGD
ECGD: overseas investment insurance	ECGD
Exchange risk guarantee scheme	DTI
Aid and trade provision	DTI/ODA/ECGD
(c) Land reclamation	
Derelict land reclamation grants	DOE/LA
Inner Urban Areas Act Section 2	DOE/LA
Inner Urban Areas Act Section 4, 5, 6	DOE/LA
Inner Urban Areas Act Section 9	DOE/LA
Inner Urban Areas Act Section 11	DOE/LA
(d) General investment (loans, grants, tax relief, equity participation, etc.)	
Business improvement services (Eng.)	DTI/ERDF
Better business services	SEPD/ERDF
Better technical services	SEPD/ERDF
Business improvement services (Wales)	WOID/ERDF
Urban development grant	DOE/LA
Urban development grant (N. Ireland)	NI: DOE
Inner Urban Areas Act Section 3	DOE/LA

Table 7.5. (*Continued*)

Scheme	Administering department
Enterprise zones	DOE/SEPD/ WOID/NI: DOE
Share option scheme	IR
Profit sharing schemes	IR
Approved share options scheme	IR
Business expansion scheme	IR
Enterprise agency tax relief	DTI/IR
EIB loans	EIB
(e) Energy	
Energy efficiency demonstration scheme	DEN
Energy efficiency survey scheme	DEN
Energy conservation scheme	DED
(f) New technology	
Access to new information technology	MSC

For list of abbreviations see Table 7.2.

Source: CSPP (1986).

Similarly, incentives such as the Business Expansion Scheme, the Venture Capital Scheme, or those under the 1978 and 1980 Finance Acts, all related to share ownership, may be less appropriate for a sector where equity funding is less common. Since these incentives form an important part of the government's attempts to overcome the problems of small firm access to finance, they exemplify the wider lack of recognition that the small business sector is mainly comprised of service firms.

Overall, given the confusing and uncoordinated array of government incentives, policy support for producer services appears limited. As with regional assistance, the primary targets of industrial support are manufacturing activites. It is only in areas associated with information technology, computing skills, research and development, and the application of manufacturing technology that producer services gain directly from incentive support. There is of course a degree of indirect benefit from some of this assistance in terms of the demand for producer services which it necessitates. At a general level, this takes the form of information and advisory services about the range and nature of government aid which is available (a growth area among consultants and financial institutions in recent years). More specifically, a number of schemes are intended to stimulate the use of consultancy services, not just in research and development and new technology but in the field of business development such as the business improvement service schemes financed by the European Regional Development Fund. Similar spin-offs are evident in the increased use of design, marketing, and information services. Nevertheless, such indirect benefits cannot disguise the paucity of direct support for producer services, especially appropriate support which takes cognizance of the particular characteristics of small firms, such as relatively low capital or labour requirements, shortage of working capital, or infrastructure needs.

The effect on regional development of industrial incentive policies can only be discussed speculatively. The confusion engendered by the range of schemes, purposes, and administering departments is increased by the uneven spatial coverage of some of the government incentive policies. The result is a map of assistance composed of numerous sets of often overlapping 'assisted areas'. In addition to the Development Areas and Intermediate Areas of regional policy, there are the eligible areas of ERDF funded policies and the 'Special Areas' (Partnership Areas, Improvement Areas, Development Districts, and Urban Development Grant/LEG-UP areas) designated under the Inner Urban Areas Act. Further, there are the designated coal and steel closure areas, enterprise zones, and freeports. (The areas of operation of the development agencies and councils—discussed below—complicate the map still further.) Unlike some other policy areas which have been co-ordinated, for example the centralized responsibility for job creation or the joint ministerial focus on inner city regeneration, a common approach to the problem of regional development has not been accorded great attention. Aside from the overlap of spatial polices, there is also the potential for contradiction between spatial and aspatial measures, particularly between regional and sectoral policies. Indeed, it has been suggested that, given the high proportion of applications and awards made in the South East region under sectoral schemes, these policies serve to foster regional imbalance in key areas. The relevance of these conflicts to services is again hard to guage since there is little data on the sectoral as well as spatial allocation of incentive assistance. Given the small business orientation of much inner city aid, many of the beneficiaries have been service firms;

likewise, some two-thirds of the occupants of enterprise zones are said to be services, although mostly warehousing and distribution activities creating relatively few jobs (BBC, 1986). On the other hand, the distribution of much of the service-specific aid for computing services referred to above shows a significant concentration in the South East. Since much scientific and technological assistance is similarly distributed, the indirect benefits to producer service firms may be equally biased.

Regional development agency assistance

The absence of a development strategy for producer services on the part of central government within a generally complex framework of industrial incentives prompts questions as to whether the same is true at regional and local levels. It is at the regional level that much academic work on the role of producer services and on the nature of manufacturing–service relationships has been undertaken. It might be anticipated, therefore, that regional and local agencies would have more extensive and sophisticated approaches to assisting the development of the producer services sector than at national level. However, it appears that despite an appreciation of the importance and potential contribution of these services, actual policy measures have only been introduced very recently. Like central government, the dominant concern has been the health of the manufacturing sector.

The decentralization of responsibility for industrial development to the regional level in 1975 was part of the then Labour government's new industrial strategy and a result of its political commitment to devolution. This involved the creation of the Scottish, Welsh, and Northern Ireland development agencies. Initially concerned with estate management functions, they have since acquired a more comprehensive set of development responsibilities. (They have minor counterparts in the form of development councils and related organizations in the English regions, although these have operated with very few resources and their future development is currently in a state of flux.) The following discussion examines the position of service support in development agencies in Northern Ireland and Scotland.

Northern Ireland

Economic development in Northern Ireland over the last 20 years has largely followed patterns in the rest of the UK with a decline in manufacturing employment and a growth in services, especially in the public sector, financial business, and consumer services. Northern Ireland shares with some of the peripheral British regions a shortfall in private sector employment—especially as compared with the South East. This is most notable in service industries serving intermediate rather than final demand and non-production employment in manufacturing industry. The deficiency has been attributed partly to the low indigenous demand for services in the region and a reliance on service imports. Official industrial development policy, however, has consistently been directed at the manufacturing sector (Harrison, 1985).

Industrial support in Northern Ireland is split between two bodies: the Industrial Development Board (IDB), which succeeded the former Northern Ireland Development Agency, and which deals with inward investment and the development of indigenous medium- and large-sized firms; and the Local Enterprise Development Unit (LEDU) which is responsible for supporting small firms (with fewer than 50 employees). The basic industrial development assistance is provided as in Britain through a combination of automatic aid (the Standard Capital Grant (SCG)) and selective, employment-related, assistance, with the latter being responsible for some two-thirds of total expenditure (compared to less than one-fifth in the case of RSA in Britain) (Yuill and Allen, 1985). The emphasis of both incentives has been directed almost exclusively at the manufacturing sector: services are not eligible under the SCG and very few service projects have qualified for selective support. Since 1981, official policy statements have given a greater recognition of the importance of the service sector, especially internationally mobile services, but this does not appear to have been translated into practical action. Promotional activities aimed at inward investment and indigenous development both seem to have continued to focus almost exclusively (apart from computer services) on manufacturing.

The 1985 review of the SCG scheme reaffirmed the exclusion of services from assistance (apart from leasing) despite calls for the support of indigenous service activity. The Northern Ireland Economic Council, for example, proposed that a range of producer services such as consultancy, financial, computer, and office services should be eligible for support (NIEC, 1982). The major objection to such a policy was maintained to be the physical separation of Northern Ireland from the mainland which acted as an obstacle to trade. Given the intangible nature of several services, however, this has little logic and is contradicted by the limited information available. It is suggested that there is in fact a significant potential for import substitution in advertising, computer services, management consultancy, market research, and research and development (Harrison, 1985; 1986).

With respect to the other incentives in the IDB's industrial aid package, there is an equal lack of support specifically for the producer services sector (Table 7.6) although much of the assistance is not activity-related. In 1985 the IDB in the Province published its medium-term strategy for 1985–90: again, although the tradable service sector was defined as a target sector for development support, there are few measures to implement the stated objectives (IDB, 1985).

Like the IDB, LEDU's activities in the small firms sector were confined to the manufacturing sector from the inception of the agency in 1971 up to 1980. Thereafter its remit was widened to include inner city development and aid for services. Since then service assistance has accounted for an increasing proportion of job promotions (721 out of 4,009 in 1984–5), although recently the absolute numbers have fallen back. The level of job creation, though, is relatively minor against the scale of the unemployment problem; also very few jobs are created per project. Finally, LEDU's

Table 7.6. Eligibility of Producer Services for IDB and LEDU Assistance

Scheme	Service eligibility
IDB/LEDU	
Management incentive scheme	Not activity-related
Corporation tax relief grant	Not activity-related
Market prospects service	Not activity-related
Better business services	Not activity-related
Innovation support services	Not activity-related
Industrial development assistance	Services with genuine choice of location
rent grants employment grants development grants development assistance	not activity related, but less appropriate for small firms
IDB	
Market research grant scheme	Not activity-related
Marketing development grant scheme	Internationally traded services only
Research and development grant	Primarily manufacturing firms with over 50 employees
LEDU	
Small firm grant	Not activity-related

activities are said to involve a high proportion of assistance directed at services serving local and sub-regional markets, and involving possibly significant displacements effects (Harrison, 1985).

Scotland

The growth of service employment in Scotland over the last decade has also been most significant in the public sector, especially in healthcare and social services. Private service employment, most notably in business services, wholesale distribution, banking, tele-communications, research and development, and insurance, is under-represented in the region (SDA, 1984). Although the deficiency in such services has been identified as a key factor in Scotland's poor overall employment performance, it is only recently that regional development strategies have taken account of the sector.

Industrial policy in Scotland is implemented by three main bodies: the Industry Department for Scotland, the Scottish Development Agency (SDA), and the Highlands and Islands Development Board (HIDB). The SDA, with expenditure of almost £70 million, has the primary responsibility to promote both domestic and foreign industrial investment, to invest in industry, and to co-ordinate urban development. Most of the SDA's resources are directed at land reclamation and environmental improvement, particularly in the context of the Agency's 'area development projects' such as GEAR involving the economic renewal of nine local areas of Glasgow. Industrial investment has been based primarily on a sectoral strategy whereby key sectors have been identified for support—food-processing, distribution, electronics, health care, and biotechnology.

Hitherto, support for services has not featured prominently in the SDA's policies. Most of the standard business development assistance which the Agency provides (Table 7.7), like that of its counterpart, the Highlands and Islands Development Board, is available to both manufacturing and services (with particular emphasis on small businesses) but it is unclear how much of this support has gone to service firms. The only directly relevant incentive scheme is the ERDF funded 'Better Business Services' programme which aims to improve the access of small firms to professional finance, marketing, and management services, as well as supporting the consultants or other organizations providing such services themselves. The scheme is available throughout the UK Assisted Areas (pre-November 1984) but there is an additional version of the assistance for non-Assisted Areas in Scotland operated by the SDA and HIDB.

Table 7.7. Eligibility of Producer Services for SDA and HIDB Assistance

Scheme	Service eligibility
SDA	
Training employment grant scheme	Not activity-related
Local enterprise grant—urban programme (LEG-UP)	Not activity-related
Small business finance	Not activity-related
Finance for industry	Not activity-related
Better business services	Not activity-related
'Pride'	Leisure/environmental improvement associated services
Finance for crafts	Crafts support
HIDB	
Industrial and commercial finance	Not activity-related
Relief/emergency assistance	Not activity-related
Special grants	Not activity-related
Removal grants	Not activity-related
Business services scheme	Not activity-related
Community co-operative assistance	Co-operatives only
Support for social projects	Social projects only

Of greater significance to services are probably the SDA's 'project investments' with developments such as exhibition and conference centres in Glasgow and Aberdeen, the provision of office accommodation, and tourist/leisure initiatives like the hosting of the 1988 National Garden Festival in Glasgow or the 'heritage centre' in Dundee. More importantly for the future, though, is the SDA's affirmation in 1985 that the encouragement of service sector activity is (along with technology, small firms, and area initiatives) a top corporate priority. Although policy formulation is still at an early stage, three specific projects already initiated in Glasgow are the attraction of more company headquarter activity to the city, the development of local business service skills, and increased promotion of tourism (SDA, 1985).

Local development assistance

During the late 1970s and early 1980s the nationwide character of industrial decline, high unemployment, and the limitations of central government regional assistance prompted interest on the part of local authorities and others in economic development. Local organizations were felt to be more in tune with local needs, employment prospects, and the opportunities for investment, with an ability to react more quickly to changing conditions. In addition, bodies such as local authorities already had some measures at their disposal through their role as planning authorities and their powers to provide infrastructure for industrial development and a limited degree of financial assistance (Mawson and Miller, 1983).

Local economic development initiatives take a variety of forms including local enterprise agencies and trusts, co-operatives, development companies, and local enterprise boards. Central government has also been involved: through the national network of Small Firms Service centres and the activities of CoSIRA (Council for Small Industries in Rural Areas), and it has adopted various measures to mobilize private sector resources for inner city development. It has a financial interest in the Urban Programme and has set up Enterprise Units in various DOE Regional Offices (to co-ordinate urban policy) as well as forming Urban Development Corporations (UDCs) in Merseyside and London, both of which cut across the preserve of local authorities.

It is difficult to assess the significance of this activity and to what extent it involves the producer services sector. Local authority economic development initiatives, for example, have often consisted mainly of industrial promotion and the co-ordination of local organizations such as chambers of commerce, trade unions, and financial institutions. Although the provision of premises, advisory services, and financial assistance has grown considerably since 1979, by 1985 it still involved a relatively limited amount of expenditure— some £100 million p.a., over half of which was spent by the former GLC and Metropolitan Counties (Coulson, 1985). The local authorities are of course closely associated with producer services both as *providers* (in education, transport, etc.) and as major *users* (especially computing, architectural, and legal services). However, many of their economic development services seem to be directed primarily at the manufacturing sector with few policy measures for services. The emphasis is very much on the provision of manufacturing premises, factory conversion, industrial estates, enterprise workshops, and nursery units, though there are exceptions. The West Yorkshire Enterprise Board, for instance, has a policy of identifying and backing both industrial and commercial investment opportunities and, alongside the development of products and production facilities, undertakes property development for service industries.

With regard to the agencies sponsored by central government, the situation appears to be similar. Among a wide range of measures undertaken by the Merseyside Task Force, only two are directly relevant for services. Four IT Centres have been set up to offer workshop training in the application of micro-electronics to industry, and two centres have been provided by local councils to undertake commercial service industry training. In the UDCs, development in the London Docklands has concentrated on infrastructure renewal, private housing development and the relocation of manufacturing jobs. Plans include extensive office development and leisure facilities, but have little relevance for the requirements of the local communities (Wood, 1984). Similarly, the Merseyside Development Corporation is engaged in a programme of advance office building to attract mobile office employment, though again this expected to create relatively few local jobs. Also, attempts to identify growing service industries have focused chiefly on tourism with initiatives such as museum developments and the 1984 Garden Festival (Hubbard and Nutter, 1982).

Overall, there are encouraging signs of a greater awareness of services among both regional and local agencies. To what extent these are a true recognition of the potential of producer services, rather than a search for alternatives to manufacturing, is hard to say. The sophistication of service initiatives is not great: office building and leisure-related service assistance predominates. There are few instances of business service skill training, for example. Policies are generally geared to achieving job creation, though here too there appear to be contradictions in serving local needs and appreciating the specific requirements of service firms. As Wood (1984) points out in the London context, a number of producer services (e.g. computing, development and testing, leasing, catering, repair and maintenance) have a considerable employment potential but the conditions to promote the development of such activities (such as suitable sites, accommodation, and facilities) have yet to be properly understood and provided.

7.4. EUROPEAN REGIONAL POLICIES AND SERVICES

As in the UK, the central government policies of European countries towards improving the regional distribution of service activity have consisted mainly of office development controls, public office relocation, and service incentives. Most of the initiatives have been peripheral to mainstream regional policy where the concern has been focused on assisting manufacturing industry.

Office relocation

With respect to office relocation, the main parallels are evident in France and The Netherlands. As in Great Britain, the pressures associated with the concentration of offices in a few urban areas, such as the Paris region in France, or the 'Randstad' in The Netherlands, became apparent during the late 1950s and early 1960s. Policies have consisted of private sector administrative and financial disincentives, complemented by state control over the location of public or para-public organizations.

In France, initial legislation was passed in 1969 to make the location of scientific, technical, commercial, and professional accommodation in Paris subject to authorization by a 'decentralization committee'. This was supplemented by a floorspace levy on office (and industrial) building construction related to distance leading to increased development in the outer Île de France region. Towards the end of the 1970s, the stringency and breadth of control was relaxed with a view to strengthening the competitiveness of Paris *vis-à-vis* other major European cities, allowing the modernization of offices and encouraging the development of small- and medium-sized firms. Greater success was achieved through the planned location of state-controlled bodies which has been an important regional development instrument for the tertiary sector. Although early efforts in the 1950s had little impact, subsequent policies led to considerable decentralization particularly in education, banking and administration.

In the academic sector, a number of the 'grandes écoles' were transferred from Paris to the provinces; while these are now well-established, transfers continue and new departments are sited whenever possible outside the capital. In the early 1970s negotiations with the main clearing banks were undertaken to encourage both representation in the provinces and to increase the level of responsibility of regional managers: the aim was to ensure that all decisions relating to firms in the regions should be taken by the regional branches of the banks concerned. Beginning with Lyon, this was ultimately extended to Bordeaux, Marseille, Nantes, Nancy, and Strasbourg. The regional element of the banking sector has been reinforced following nationalization of much of the banking sector and the decentralization of leading credit organizations. Finally, in administration, each ministry and national public organization has been required to submit proposals for relocation outside Paris, a policy which was reaffirmed in 1983. Currently, it is planned to transfer 15,000–20,000 public office jobs away from Paris; no new space can be allocated (with a few exceptions) within the Île de France (CSPP, 1985).

Office relocation policies in The Netherlands have been more limited (Grit and Korteweg, 1976). The first government proposals in the early 1960s were to encourage office movement from the main urban areas—Amsterdam, The Hague, Rotterdam, and Utrecht—beyond the outer city centre and suburban districts to the peripheral regions. By 1972, though, only a few thousand jobs had been moved. However, in the early 1970s the relocation of offices changed from being an urban policy objective to a regional (socio-economic) policy issue. As the importance of service sector jobs was appreciated, the regional imbalance in office employment became a priority of government policy, and in 1972 it was proposed to relocate over 14,000 government service jobs to the peripheral regions by the mid-1980s. The rise of nationwide economic difficulties and the need to stabilize employment in the urban areas, however, led to a reduction in the number of jobs moved. A reconsideration of policy emerged: relocation to only a few centres was replaced by a broader set of objectives including the establishment of new services in the peripheral regions, a wider spread of receiving centres, and emphasis on the relocation of fast-growing government services (De Smidt, 1985). Relatively little of this policy has, however, been implemented. The planned Phase II (1981–85) relocation scheme involved 5,500 jobs: by 1983 only 700 has been relocated.

Similar measures to those in Britain, France, or The Netherlands are to be found elsewhere in the Community, although much less as distinct instruments of regional development. In Germany, for example, the federal nature of the country and the even distribution of service employment has meant less pressure for the kind of decentralization in evidence elsewhere, although there are a few cases of public sector offices being sited to the benefit of the problem regions. In Italy, there is encouragement for the relocation of non-production employment in private manufacturing firms to the Mezzogiorno (the main problem region in the south of the country), but more service assistance is provided through the requirement that state-holding firms direct a minimum proportion of their service activity investment to the Mezzogiorno—some L1,017 milliard in 1983. Among the smaller countries, office relocation in a regional policy context has not been significant and may reflect a general lack of interest in the role of services in regional development.

Service incentives

The early 1970s saw a growing awareness in Europe of the deficit of service employment in the problem regions. This recognition prompted an increasing number of countries, led by Britain and France, to widen the eligibility of their regional incentive assistance to include a limited range of service activities. The aid, though, has remained largely restricted to those services considered to be mobile, export-oriented, and manufacturing-related (see Table 7.8). There are some examples of incentive schemes or special components of schemes specifically for services, as well as instances of preferential treatment provided for the service sector. The more common situation though is for parts of the service sector to qualify along with a series of other eligible sectors in regional aid packages and for qualification to be in practice difficult, and for assistance to be small or non-existent. In contradiction to the employment trends and industrial structure of all the Community countries, service incentive assistance is still considerably less than that available for manufacturing industry.

The only current service-specific aid scheme is the International Services Programme (ISP) in the Republic of Ireland. Operated by the Irish Industrial Development Authority, it provides an incentive package comprising any combination of capital grants, training grants, rent subsidies, and employment grants up to a maximum ceiling of 60% of eligible costs according to location (in practice,

Table 7.8. European Regional Incentive Policies and Producer Services

Country	Scheme	Service eligibility
Belgium	Interest rate Capital grant	Businesses involved in trade Management and technical consultancy, and R and D. Parts of the transport sector
Denmark	Company soft loan Investment grant	Parts of the transport sector only
France	PAT (Regional policy grant)	Research companies and certain tertiary sector activities are eligible in certain designated zones (including administration, management, engineering, design, survey, and data-processing activities).
	PRE (Regional employment grant)	Individual regional authorities are free to specify eligible activities. In practice, similar to those under the PAT scheme
	Local business tax concession	Services are eligible which are not dependent on local markets

Table 7.8.   (*Continued*)

Country	Scheme	Service eligibility
Germany	Investment allowance	Regionally-exporting services (e.g. mail order trading, headquarters functions, credit institutions); tourist activities
	Investment grant	Basically as the allowance. In addition a special investment grant is available in respect of high grade jobs.
	ERP regional loan	Non-regionally exporting activities with no primary effect
Greece	Investment grant/ Interest rate subsidy/ Increased depreciation allowance/Tax allowance	Within the transport sector, certain coastal shipping lines are eligible
Ireland	IDA (New industry grants)	Services do not normally qualify under this scheme, but are aided instead through IDA (ISP)
	IDA (International services programme)	Target services are: data processing; technical and consultancy services; headquarters, R and D centres; publishing; training services; software development; commercial lab.; health-care services; recording services; and international financial services
Italy	Capital grant ⎫ National fund soft loan ⎭	Managerial transfers to the South; certain consultancy, research, and repair and maintenance activities
	Social security concession	Commerce, R and D, certain data processing, repair activities
	Tax concession	Those of an 'industrial' character—certain data processing, R and D, repair and handicraft activities

Table 7.8.   (Continued)

Country	Scheme	Service eligibility
Luxemburg	Capital grant ⎫ Interest subsidy ⎬ Tax concession ⎭	Services activities may be aided by a CG/IS, but only where they make an active contribution to the development of the economy
	Equipment loan	Services are eligible only if artisan or commercial—and must involve investment of FLX 500,000
The Netherlands	IPR investment premium	Regionally-exporting services plus certain research departments if of importance to industrial activities
Portugal	Financial assistance ⎫ Tax concession ⎬	None
Spain	Regional investment grant ⎫ Priority in obtaining credit ⎬ Reduction in customs duties ⎭	Only service sector projects put forward by private firms in the fields of education and health

Source: Yuill and Allen (1986). See also for detailed description of regional policy schemes.

generally 50%). Although the incentives are available throughout the Republic, higher rates of award are granted in the 'Designated Areas'—mainly the northern and western parts of the country. Target services within the service sector have been selected on the basis of their tradability, job-creation potential and strategic importance for future economic and industrial development. These target areas consist of computer services, technical and consultancy services, commercial testing/research and development, administrative headquarters, publishing, international financial services, hospital management and healthcare, recording, and training services. The eligibility criteria require projects not only to prove additionality (i.e. need for incentive assistance) and commercial viability, but to be internationally exporting and to have a high technological or scientific content (CII, 1983).

The July 1984 White Paper on Industrial Policy noted that the ISP had hitherto proved to be disappointing because relatively few new jobs had been created. Along with other areas of incentive policy, assistance under the service programme is now assessed with respect to the maximization of value added to the Irish economy (for example through local purchasing or technology transfer) rather than solely in terms of job creation (SO, 1984).

Elsewhere in Europe, services are rather less targeted for specific aid. However, preferential treatment for service activities is evident among regional incentive policies in four ways—through favourable award rates, supplementary grants, advantageous eligibility conditions, and special budgetary allocations. Such conditions are exemplified in the case of the German 'special investment grant' and some of the French regional incentives—notably the PAT grant and the fiscal concessions.

In Germany, the regional aid package contains a 'spatial component' for the creation of high-grade service employment. The base regional incentives are similar to those in Britain—an automatic investment allowance (of up to 10% of eligible expenditure) which may be supplemented by a discretionary investment grant to provide up to 25% of expenditure depending on the location and type of project. To encourage the creation of high-grade (managerial, technical, or research) jobs in the German *Gemeinschaftsaufgabe* problem regions, an additional special investment grant is available. This provides between DM15,000 and DM25,000 for each job created; jobs being defined as those which have considerable autonomy in decision-making and supervision and involve a salary in excess of DM60,000 p.a. (Deutscher Bundestag, 1985).

In France, discrimination in favour of services (and research) in the PAT (*prime d'amenagement du territoire*, a capital grant tied to job creation) occurs in three ways. First, service projects are not subject to investment-related ceilings on the level of award (compared to a 25% limit for manufacturing projects); instead, only job-related ceilings of up to FF50,000 in designated centres apply. Second, where highly-qualified staff are required, the minimum job target for setting-up and takeover projects is reduced from 20 to 10. Third, spatial coverage of the assistance is far more extensive (than for manufacturing projects) and covers most of France apart from the Paris and Lyon areas. Unlike manufacturing projects, however, the maximum rate areas for eligible service activities are concentrated on designated service nuclei, of which there are 52 throughout the country. Favourable treatment for services, based on relaxed job target requirements, investment targets, and spatial restrictions is also accorded to services (and research) in France by a number of the fiscal concessions.

Apart from these incentives, the nature of service sector assistance in Europe generally allows (certain) services to qualify for regional aid schemes along with a range of other eligible activities. Such schemes usually determine service eligibility on the basis of certain criteria: the degree of export orientation, choice of location, net regional benefit, or association with manufacturing industry activities. The main regional incentives in Germany, Italy, and Belgium—very similar to those in Britain—all involve such indicators for assessing service firm qualification. A further common feature is the objection to assisting local services and the fear of thereby distorting competition. One notable exception is the West German ERP soft loan scheme. Provided throughout the German Assisted Areas and financed by former Marshall Fund aid, the loans are directed specifically at small and medium-sized firms. It is unusual in that it is only available for businesses which are non-regionally exporting and it aims to help maintain a healthy commercial sector in smaller towns and rural areas. Consequently, the scheme assists a very extensive range of local service activities such as wholesale and retail trades, transport and distribution, business service offices, and leisure activities.

Lastly, in reviewing the nature of regional service assistance in the Community, there are of course countries and incentive schemes where the eligibility of services is more notional than actual, or is even totally non-existent. In part this may be because of the nature of the scheme. For example, neither of the regional depreciation allowances in Germany and France are sectorally discriminatory but few services are, in practice, likely to undertake much investment of a qualifying character (i.e. new depreciable investment). However, in Denmark, Luxemburg, and Greece it is the objectives of regional policy, the award conditions, or the approval of applications which lead to the virtual exclusion of the sector. In all three countries regional assistance is very firmly targeted on manufacturing industry.

Overall, it appears that the orientation of regional incentive policies towards the service sector in Europe is limited, emphasizing the continuing manufacturing bias of problem region assistance. Three points in particular stand out. First, incentive assistance for the sector is selective. Aid is most frequently limited to industrial-related services such as repair and maintenance, research and development, training, or technical consultancy, although in some countries this eligibility has been extended to include a number of business services. However, eligibility restrictions are not necessarily overt; most incentives are general investment schemes and are capital-related, others have minimum project size requirements which discriminate against some services. Second, most countries are extremely wary of assisting local services. Eligible service projects have to demonstrate their mobility or 'regional benefit' in terms of their contribution to inter-regional exports, the creation of additional jobs, or import substitution.

Third, most service sector policies have not been popular. Although it is difficult to obtain precise data, the information available indicates the poor level of support and low take-up of schemes. In Germany for instance, the special investment grant for high-grade jobs created only a few hundred jobs during its first three years of operation. The ISP in Ireland assisted an average of 35 projects per year involving associated employment of 1,640 jobs p.a. In both The Netherlands and Germany, less than 8% of regional policy grant expenditure has been allocated to service projects.

7.5. TELECOMMUNICATIONS INFRASTRUCTURE

The establishment of a national and international telecommunications and information technology infrastructure is likely to have an important influence on the generation of new service activities (Section 5.4 discusses employment and IT). Governments in the EC have generally been slow to appreciate the importance of the technical changes involved and to develop appropriate policies.

The implications of developments in telecommunications for the assisted areas are mixed. The problem regions may be handicapped by a poor information environment; IT may act to compensate for or eliminate this disadvantage. Improved access to information can reduce costs, mitigate peripherality, and make the problem regions more attractive for industry. On the other hand, the problem regions are lagging considerably in the provision of telecommunications services. The location of new facilities and services is essentially demand-related which is leading to a concentration in the core regions. Without the ability to respond to the opportunities offered by IT, the assisted areas may lose out. The benefits of telecommunications developments may in any case be restricted to large firms and to the main urban centres (Goddard *et al.*, 1985).

There is, then, a danger that the expansion of IT may accentuate regional disparities. Regional dependency may be increased, existing businesses in the problem regions may not have access to advanced telecommunications facilities, and the peripheral areas may be less attractive for new investment. For producer services, the degree to which centralization or decentralization of activity occurs is likely to be varied. Trends will affect different sectors depending on the forms of corporate organization and the size structure of firms in each sector (see Section 5.4).

The impact of public policy on such developments depends both on the responsiveness to innovation on the part of regulatory authorities and the distribution of infrastructure provision. The role of the government in this process is critical given the scale of investment involved.

During the last five years the British government has attempted to change Britain's telecommunications industry from a state-run monopoly to a more competitive industry with the involvement of the private sector. British Telecom (BT), was first liberalized and then privatized in November 1984. To encourage competition and the provision of additional transmission services, Mercury Communications a privately-financed company licensed by the government was set up in 1983 primarily to serve the business sector. Both have been active in the fields of digital private circuits, optical fibre cable networks, microwave, and satellite transmission. Service provision is undertaken on a commercial basis with an emphasis on market segmentation and individual profit centres.

There are three points worth noting about these developments. First, one of the initial moves in the liberalization of BT was to allow the private sector freedom to use BT circuits to supply value-added network services—(VANS add genuine value to, and contain substantial elements additional to, the basic network). The development of VANS, which have hitherto been highly concentrated (75% located in the South East (DTI, 1985)) was encouraged in the problem regions by the 1984 regional policy review when they were one of the groups of services granted eligibility for RDGs. Second, in the area of tariffs, BT has revised its charge structure to the benefit of business users rather than consumers. Previously, cross-subsidization enabled the cost of certain services (notably local calls) to be subsidized to a greater extent out of the profits from long-distance and international calls. Now, to the advantage of business, especially in the more peripheral regions, tariffs have been restructured to more closely reflect the cost of providing the service. In addition, the costs of the busiest long-distance routes and international calls have also become cheaper.

The third point is less positive for the problem regions. Given the new commercial environment in which the telecommunications industry is operating, the emphasis in the provision of new services is on the business user and high usage links. The development of the Mercury service, for example, began with the City of London and is currently being expanded to a network linking Bristol, Birmingham, Liverpool, Leeds, and Manchester—essentially the central and southern parts of the country (Scotland will be included at a later date). Likewise, the initial development of BT's optical fibre network (1,250 km. in length at the end of 1985) is heavily biased towards the South East and almost totally excludes the North, South West, Scotland, Wales, and Northern Ireland.

Given the centrality of telecommunications to IT, it has been argued that the liberalization of telecommunications organizations can provide business with a competitive business advantage (especially internationally) through potentially lower costs and greater variety of services (Woolcock, 1985). On the other hand, the role of public bodies in this area is important. It may be that only government can undertake the massive public investment programmes necessary to improve the telecommunications infrastructure and enlarge service provision, which will in turn generate the impetus for widespread demand and service innovation (Barras, 1985). More immediately, it is government which has the ability to invest in and regulate the IT network infrastructure to the advantage of the whole country. To date, however, there has not been an overt regional development dimension to infrastructure provision.

The situation in the UK is in contrast to that in other European countries. The development of IT has been largely undertaken by state monopoly organizations throughout Europe and, while this *may* have reduced the pace of network and service provision, it has certainly enabled account to be taken of the objectives of regional policy. There has been a clear link between telematics and regional development policy in France since 1981 when the redressing of the communications imbalance (enjoyed by Paris at the expense of the regions) was made a national priority. Consequently, DATAR, the main regional planning body, has been closely involved in the regional development of information and communications technology through the setting-up of experimental projects (such as videotex services), business-oriented systems (e.g. video transmission), and the development of a 'communications pole' (bringing together a range of technologies) in the problem regions. The position in Germany is less advanced but the regional policy authority, the GA, is jointly assessing with the Federal German Post Office how the provision of new telematics services can take account of the problem regions. Within the GA's own policies and capabilities, further initiatives are also being explored as to how the use of the technologies can be facilitated. In 1985, for example, the scope of regional infrastructure assistance was widened to include facilities for 'communication technologies'.

7.6. CONCLUSION

The history of British regional policy indicates a consistent bias towards manufacturing industry. The first measures for the service sector were negative controls to redirect both private and public office employment to the provinces. Financial incentives for services were introduced late and have involved relatively few awards, little job creation and a small proportion of regional aid. The 1984 regional policy review has established a greater degree of parity for certain services which qualify for the first time for automatic assistance as well as selective support. Although the overall emphasis of the package may still be largely manufacturing-orientated, the RDG scheme contains the useful option of either capital or employment-related assistance. However, expenditure on regional policy is being reduced and there is less employment-related assistance available in the new RDG job grant than under the old OSIS. There is also evidence that it is taking time for decision-makers to adjust to the shift in emphasis that has occurred in policy towards services. In addition, the regional distribution of national policy assistance for services (although limited largely to the computing sector) runs counter to the efforts of regional policy.

The last decade has seen a growing involvement in local development by regional agencies and local authorities. They provide a range of financial assistance and other services, but both domestic and foreign promotional and investment activities are geared primarily towards the manufacturing sector. Service support tends to be limited to office development, leisure-based activities, and tourism, and even these ventures are of recent origin. However, there are some signs, in the case of the SDA for example, that a more concerted and sophisticated approach is being developed.

Internationally, regional policy bears many similarities to that in the UK. Confronted by real difficulties in assisting service firms, financial assistance is mainly manufacturing-orientated and services are eligible only if mobile and regionally-exporting. There are some interesting exceptions, notably the support for high-grade service employment in Germany, the programme for internationally-tradable services in Ireland, and the creation of service nuclei in France. However, most of the service initiatives have not had conspicuous success and the overall level of assistance to service activities is limited.

Given the generally negative conclusions of the foregoing review, what type of regional policy is appropriate for the encouragement of service activity and employment in the problem areas? The following discussion attempts to identify some of the key characteristics which such a policy could contain.

The first point is that any regional policy towards services cannot be divorced from *wider political, economic, and technological developments*. Such issues as the GATT discussions on the liberalization of trade in services, government expenditure on public sector services, investment and control of IT infrastructure, and the downward trend in the size and cost of computing hardware have important implications for future evolution and location of service activity. Further, government attitudes to industrial assistance, the scale of resources made available, and the integration of public policies will have a major influence on the effectiveness of any measures employed. Policy initiatives for services should have *realistic goals*. The scale of direct employment creation in the producer services sector in the near future is likely to be significant, but it certainly will not be of the magnitude of job loss in manufacturing industry, and policy should recognize this. Nevertheless, as earlier chapters have indicated, producer services have considerable significance as a determinant of regional economic performance and support for them can be justified on these grounds.

To be effective, service support also needs to funded with *adequate resources*. The take-up of OSIS, as noted earlier, was not great; much of this could be attributed to the relatively low rates of grant provided. The absence of a more generous approach towards support for services in the new regional policy will undoubtedly constrain its effectiveness.

Turning to the *form* of potential policy instruments, the design of financial incentives needs to proceed from the special characteristics and requirements of the different parts of the services sector, which has traditionally suffered by the application of regional incentives originally intended for manufacturing firms. First, the choice of incentive type should be wide. Capital investment, although much smaller in scale for services than among manufacturing firms, should still be available to encourage (with a low minimum expenditure threshold) investment in IT equipment. Since many services continue to be labour-intensive in spite of developments in technology, employment-related assistance remains important. The emphasis on jobs also needs to take account of the variable quality of some service employment some of which is relatively low-skilled and poorly paid (although experience with the German support for high-quality service employment is not good). Other services may have neither significant capital expenditure nor major employment requirements yet produce a high turnover and may find tax incentives more appropriate. Moreover, it has been suggested that a major source of service firm difficulties is a shortage of working capital: while cash-flow problems may be as severe as in manufacturing industry, there is frequently little security to guarantee bank loans, a deficiency which industrial assistance has so far failed to recognize.

The balance between automatic and selective assistance should continue to be carefully considered. Automatic assistance is most highly valued by firms for its predictability and visibility but, because of the uneven nature of employment growth in service industries, needs to be targeted on specific services. Also, since many sectors and firms contain a mixture of consumer and producer services, any policy package should have a significant selective and discriminatory component. However, neither form of support need imply an excessive concern with mobility or export criteria. Preceding chapters have indicated the importance of *in situ* change for employment growth (as well as the in-migration of mobile offices) and the contribution of non-exporting services to local development. Assisting local services should not be considered out of bounds. Services with a local market can add to employment if they substitute for imports or fill a gap in service provision. Although LEDU support in Northern Ireland is considered to have led to major job displacement, the ERP Loan scheme for non-regionally exporting services in the German problem regions has created considerable additional employment.

With respect to *policy delivery,* such incentives would require a decentralized system of administration and award decision-making. To avoid job displacement problems, the allocation of assistance needs to be based on both detailed awareness of the characteristics of the regional economy and case-by-case award assessment. Since the majority of service projects are likely to be small, however, administrative procedures need to be streamlined to avoid discouraging applications. Again, the German experience provides actual examples of such a system; under the ERP scheme application and initial claim processing is handled by local banks and credit institutes which act as guarantors for government loans.

Finally, any regional support needs to take account of the *inter-relationships between producer services and other industries* and to provide co-ordinated assistance. Such a policy should encourage the service demands of firms in the problem regions (like the ERDF funded 'business improvement schemes') as well as encouraging the suppliers of producer services. This assistance could be part of a policy aimed at developing the competitiveness of indigenous industry. Given the successful provision of financial asistance by local enterprise agencies in the UK and the contribution of the financial institutions to regional policy delivery in Europe, the role of the financial sector in regional economic development in the UK deserves closer scrutiny, and the current boundaries between the state and the financial sector careful consideration. In a broader context, regional policy itself needs to be integrated with other national industrial assistance policies to avoid its efforts being negated. Also, greater co-ordination is necessary between the activities of central government and those of regional development agencies and local authorities. While national policies may command the resources for major incentive expenditure there is an important role for other bodies in the relief of regional skill shortages and the provision of suitable local infrastructure, for example.

However, a financial aid policy for private services cannot be separated from policies towards the public sector or *infrastructure development*. The importance of public sector work and the important impact of decentralization makes the continued relocation of government work (particularly new services such as data bases) desirable. Yet to achieve a substantial diversion of employment requires comprehensive policies including areas such as office development, airports policy, and telecommunications investment. With respect to infrastructure, the discussion earlier emphasized how developments in the UK appear to be concerned primarily with providing services of a high level of sophistication for the majority of business users, on occasion to the disadvantage of the more peripheral regions. This contrasts significantly with developments in other Community countries where the regional imbalance in IT is seen as a national priority for action. For the future, the areas of concern for regional development policies and infrastructure are threefold: (1) the regional provision of networks and services; (2) the form of tariff structures and access costs; and (3) the reduction of barriers to usage and stimulation of demand among potential users. The alternative would appear, as with 'physical' infrastructure in the past, to link the major urban and industrial complexes to the further disadvantage of the peripheral regions.

8

Conclusions, Research Questions, and Priorities

8.1. THE NATURE OF THE SERVICE ECONOMY

The UK is clearly a service economy. Services account for well over half of employment and economic growth. In recognition of this, the research aims to bring the study of service location and producer services in particular out from the wings of economic analysis and closer to the centre stage.

The study emphasizes that the growth in service employment should not be accepted uncritically as evidence that the UK is a 'post-industrial' economy in which material needs are largely satisfied, and producer services are sustained by the growing demands of an efficient system of production for information, skills, and knowledge. We believe that such arguments greatly simplify the demand for producer services. Intangible services are expanding apace but this is only partly based on growing requirements for information. It has been argued that many other factors have encouraged the demand for producer services, including the increased research intensity of high technology manufacturing, an increasingly complex financial and legal environment, a growth of large firms, and increasingly sophisticated markets. But in a UK context, the multiplier effects of a growth in consumer demand and export income are especially important.

It is important to differentiate between producer services. The poor performance of manufacturing constrains the growth of non-production employment, and an expansion of physical distribution and business service offices is sustained by the 'externalization' of service activities by production and a growth in demand from other sectors. In contrast, the financial sector possesses in large part its own dynamic, based on export earnings, retail business, and a complex web of inter-dependencies. The result is a considerable flexibility in the response of the economy to a poor manufacturing performance. Nevertheless, a dynamic manufacturing sector is a prerequisite for strong, well balanced producer service employment growth. In the absence of a significant improvement in manufacturing performance in the UK, it is unlikely that a growth in consumer services and 'mixed' producer activities can sustain an expansion of service activity sufficient to make significant inroads in the current level of unemployment.

It is probable, though we are not able to fully substantiate this here, that the jobs lost in non-production activities in manufacturing are full-time workers, while much of the employment created in producer service industries is part-time. This has important implications for the quality of employment provided by producer services since part-time work can be associated with poor conditions of employment and lower salary levels. This does not suggest that part-time work is not worth having, rather it implies that female workers, who make up the bulk of part-time employment, are at a distinct disadvantage in producer service labour markets. In addition, there is no career ladder for women in many producer service enterprises and many companies have a dichotomized employment structure: possessing a layer of male professional posts and a majority of female clerical support staff with limited promotion prospects.

There is also a worrying trend towards a 'dual' economy in the UK, in which those areas in the south least affected by job loss in manufacturing also benefit from agglomerative tendencies in producer service activities. The location of corporate headquarters, divisional offices, and higher order specialist services have a crucial bearing on the distribution of services. These activities are attracted to centres of government and finance, international airports, major markets, and other specialist producer services. The growth of high income occupations in these services provides a market for a range of consumer services such as theatres, restaurants, and retail stores. In addition, the growth of large multi-site organizations, via franchising and direct ownership in consumer services, adds a further corporate administrative layer to the producer service agglomeration.

The growth of activities associated with the City of London and the expansion of international trade continues to support the concentration of producer services in southern Britain. In contrast, the centralization of ownership in manufacturing and service industry constrains the development of producer services in peripheral regions. Provincial markets once controlled by regional producer service companies have been lost to national service organizations. Regional companies can find it difficult to break into national markets where they do not have an extensive branch network. Recent trends towards the decentralization of producer services from major cities have favoured the Greater South East. The decline of manufacturing limits the growth of services in problem regions like the North, North West, Wales, and the West Midlands. There has been a tendency for firms to serve peripheral markets with a depressed manufacturing sector from more central areas. The expansion of new foreign and smaller companies in producer service markets has been influenced by the existing organization of service supply and this again favours the south.

A strong urban and regional policy towards producer services is likely to be critical if we are to combat these centralizing tendencies. However, current policies seem unlikely to be successful. While there are industry and technology policies supporting producer services, these are small scale and at best loosely co-ordinated with spatial policy and at worst actually contradict it. Regional policies have had only a marginal impact on service location, and while recent changes are in some respects an improvement, expenditure on regional policy is in decline. Some initiatives by local and regional authorities have been innovative, but these seem likely in the immediate future to be constrained by central government restrictions on the activities of local agencies and by real difficulties in adequately assisting producer services.

Notwithstanding these conclusions we have only partly answered many of the questions raised in Chapter 1, and the investigation concludes by indicating some directions for future research.

8.2. UNDERSTANDING THE DYNAMICS OF PRODUCER SERVICE GROWTH AND DECLINE

Our review of recent research has provided ample justification for the work presented in this volume. Service activities have generally been neglected in the past compared with manufacturing. Notwithstanding the evidence of a growth in interest in service activity, we have been disappointed by the extent to which studies have compartmentalized service activities. Too much research has examined services without either an appreciation of structural changes at work in the economy, or a wider consideration of the role of services in economic change. Few have appreciated the interdependence of public and private services or of manufacturing and service activities. Many studies have focused on only a fragment of the total service activity, such as offices or blue collar services and within these have usually concentrated on only senior management occupations, and then have attempted to generalize to the dynamics of service activity as a whole.

In contrast, other research has examined services almost solely in terms of their links with other activities such as consumption or manufacturing. The study of the linkages between manufacturing and service activities are typical. In general, a limited view has been taken of the role of services in production. When combined with a failure to deal adequately with the internal and external use of services by client companies, and real difficulties in measuring transactions, this has severely limited the value of the work. The business communications studies of the 1960s and early 1970s represent another example of a linkage approach, and here the importance of such contacts has been over-emphasized because insufficient attention has been paid to the workings of the company in which they take place and their role in its operations.

The availability of directories of company headquarters and main sites has also helped foster a naive view of service organization which assumes that an over-simplified classification of establishments (headquarters, division, branch) derived from manufacturing can be applied to service companies. This interest in corporate structures, when combined with a concern for the minutiae of corporate decision-making and senior management communications, has produced until recently an almost total neglect of possibly the most critical aspect of service activities; namely that they have provided jobs at a time of declining manufacturing employment.

In so far as studies of service activity have been incorporated into a wider analysis of economic development processes, this work has largely been preoccupied with the argument that areas, if they are to sustain economic growth, need to have a full range of higher-order office services. It is clearly inadequate, however, to argue that all areas should possess a complete range of office functions. Also proposed policy initiatives to develop high quality office activities appear unlikely to benefit, in the short term at least, the needy in Assisted Areas.

Given these inadequacies of earlier work this investigation has attempted to stand back from the fray of empirical enquiry and to reflect on the processes underlying the changing location of producer services in the UK. It has shown that a number of statistical and definitional problems restrict the use of official statistics in this work, and that these deficiencies in the treatment of services are becoming increasingly damaging with the emergence of a service-dominated economy. We therefore believe that *an improvement in the statistical data base is a fundamental requirement for progress in studies of service activities.* We need sources of input, output, and employment information at a national and local scale which have a more subtle appreciation of the heterogeneity and complex market relationships within service activities. Essentially, statistical data should also allow us to trace over time the changing interdependence of services and other activities, because it is only with such information that the national and local economic significance of service activities for both indigenous production and trade can be fully explored. In the present circumstances, however, any significant improvements in government statistical data are unlikely, and in some respects the quality and reliability of such information is deteriorating. So, although the recent availability of employment data for 1984 will allow further analysis of service location along the lines of Chapter 4, in the absence of a major improvement in official sources, we believe *future research should concentrate on survey work supplemented by the plentiful literature available from trade and professional associations, trade unions, consultancy organizations, and specialist publications on service industries.*

Our research has provided a framework within which such material on producer services can be integrated. The approach stresses that some long-standing notions concerning service activities need to be revised; namely that they are solely servicing local manufacturing or consumer demand. It also suggests that the reorganization that has taken place in many local economies during the last decade has been altogether more complex than is indicated by perspectives derived from corporate restructuring in large manufacturing companies. Changes in the location of service activities have been related to:

(1) structural changes in the demand for service products associated with an integration of service markets and an intensification of competition,

(2) a reorganization within service firms partly to supply new markets but also associated with technical changes, and

(3) subsequent changes in the labour process.

Our work on the growing internationalization of producer service markets and the importance of multinational service organizations in several service industries indicates that services can no longer be understood solely in a national context. The liberalization of trade in services could lead to important changes in the pattern of this international trade since it could more closely reflect variations in national competitiveness. Information technology by speeding up financial transactions and making new services internationally tradable will also have an important influence on trade.

International comparative research provides one important means of responding to this growing internationalization of service activities. However, such studies are important in their own right because, by examining services in differing institutional, economic, and cultural circumstances, they can shed further light on the dynamics of the growth in service activities. Research in some developed countries will also benefit from the better quality of the secondary source data available outside the UK.

While this study has provided a means of thinking about service location, it has only described economic processes and the way they affect places in a very general way. This suggests that the detailed monitoring of changes in service activity in local economies should be an important priority for future research. In our view such *locality studies* offer a valuable way forward in the absence of a comprehensive national data base.

On the other hand, the investigation of service markets in previous chapters has highlighted the deepening integration of producer services with other sectors of the economy. Studies of the location of service activity at any spatial scale cannot, therefore, be conducted in isolation from developments elsewhere in the economy. This implies that an investigation of localities will need to be combined with *market-based studies*.

Whatever particular lines of research into services are pursued in the future, a number of conclusions arise out of our analyses of structural changes in the markets for producer services which should guide future studies, and in turn such studies will shed further light on the operation of individual processes.

The changing demand for producer services

A primary aim for the future study of producer services should be to *identify their strategic economic role in relation to production, consumption, and to other producer services*. A fundamental weakness of past studies has been their use of a service classification which has assumed that they perform separate functions from production and consumption. Services have been treated like manufacturing, as if they performed particular technical transformations of their inputs to produce discrete products. In fact, for many their role is quite different; they supply expertise to enhance the value of all other sectors' outputs (including other services). Their economic contribution can therefore only be evaluated in relation to the improved performance they bestow on the operations of customers. This is why a *'market-based' classification*, sensitive to the integration of services with other economic functions *is a basic requirement for future research*. Such a classification should as a minimum distinguish between the 'in-house' and 'external' provision of services, between markets that are 'purely' producer-orientated and those where consumer functions are also performed and also between the market needs of the private and public service sectors.

This perspective was fundamental to the Producer Service Working Party's deliberations. The main research priorities emerging from it are therefore for the refinement of our understanding of the *changing structure of demand for white and blue collar services*. At present we have only a preliminary appreciation of the processes encouraging the growing demand for producer services. The use of services to satisfy the information requirements of firms and to sustain and utilize new technology are clearly only part of the story. For example, we know little about the precise impact on the growth of producer services of the recession in manufacturing, the attempts of successive governments to reduce public expenditure and the growth of services satisfying final demand. There is some evidence that there has been a reorganization of producer service activities carried out by manufacturing firms and the public sector, and subsequent changes in the demand for specialist suppliers. But our limited understanding of these changes demonstrates just how little we know about the process of 'internalization' and 'externalization' of producer service demand by client companies. We need to know more about how *'in-house–externalization' decisions are taken by different manufacturing, private, and public service firms (e.g. large or small, and in different areas and sectors) and ultimately in the household sector.* An understanding of such processes will be critical to a fuller appreciation of the changing demand for intermediate services.

Supply response

Notwithstanding the importance of understanding the demand side, there are clear differences in the response of firms to market changes. The concentration of ownership is increasing in many services, and we need to know more about *the spatial implications of the considerable reorganization which is taking place in dominant firms*. However, given the significance of small firms in services and their locational variability, care must be taken not to produce simply a large firm explanation for economic change, we need to know more about *the dynamics of the current growth of small firms in producer services*. Studies of this process clearly require an appreciation of the interdependence of the large and small firm sectors; the fact that large firm specialization produces market niches for small firm growth, and the way the growth of small service firms, particularly in high technology industries is frequently a spin-off from larger more established firms.

The role of producer services

We also need to know more about the *types of service input that are instrumental to economic activities* at various stages of production and in performing various consumption functions, and the contribution of services to the performance of customer organizations, both home-based and overseas.

This study has commented on the divergent views of the role played by services in the recent economic changes in the UK. More questions have been raised than have been answered in this regard. Nevertheless, the complex factors which mediate the relationship between service use and firm performance suggest that a case study approach would be most fruitful in this area. Also, future work clearly should be guided by the need to differentiate between types of service, and in particular between blue collar and white collar services and between financial and other activities within office services.

A key issue at the local scale is whether, and in what circumstances locally or non-locally-based services are more effective in sustaining other regional activities. Clearly, the answers are likely to differ between types of service and in relation to different aspects of a region's economic base. There is some evidence, for example, that the efficiency of local blue collar activities, such as transportation, trading, distribution, and communications services may be more critical to the operations of manufacturing firms than that of many high-level non-financial information-based services. On the other hand, of course, the presence of such high income and growth activities provides a more general stimulus to the economic health of local economies, through both the producer and consumer service demands they create. This does not mean, however, that such functions have to be orientated primarily towards serving local needs; the opposite is probably preferable. But clearly *the role of service activities in local economies needs to be examined further.*

The nature of producer service employment

Although tracing the 'structural' role of producer services in the operation of both national and local economies is fundamental to any research progress, a principal reason for current interest in the sector lies in the employment it may sustain in the future. A high priority therefore needs to be given to the *processes of employment change, in terms of the demand for male/female, skilled/unskilled, and full-time or part-time work.*

It is clear that there have been important changes in the character of producer service work in recent decades. The most obvious manifestation of this has been the growth in part-time work and female employment. In fact a worrying dualism is developing in the growth of producer service employment which could have important implications for locational studies. It is possible that we are witnessing a spatial and social polarization in labour markets with a concentration of highly skilled male employment in a limited number of areas and a more widely distributed growth in female and frequently part-time work of dubious character in many labour markets. This is an important area for further inquiry.

Studies of this subject should be undertaken in a manner that recognizes, (1) the potential and actual *impacts of technological change* on service functions, and (2) the displacement of functions between sectors, types of organization, and locations in parallel with (1).

Technological change and producer services

The impact of technological change on service activities is pervasive and it is likely to influence all of the considerations described above. Technological change has probably been instrumental in the structural changes at work in service markets, and it is also likely to have influenced the changing balance of 'internalization' and 'externalization' of service demand. An appreciation of the *impact of technology on the demand for services* will improve our understanding of the dynamics of service employment growth. The introduction of *information technology* will also have important *implications for the nature of service organization*. This is clearly another important area for research, and it is our view that the subject is best considered in the wider context of sectoral or area studies.

Service policy

Given the history of national, regional, and urban policy affecting services in the UK, the lack of evaluation of such initiatives is surprising. Notwithstanding the DTI evaluation of OSIS and the monitoring of the recently introduced regional policy there is considerable scope for *studies of the effectiveness of service policy*.

Ideally, service policy should be grounded in an understanding of the economics of service location. Further information is required on the character of service organizations which might facilitate policy delivery. The diversity of institutions and policies towards services also suggests that further attention might be devoted towards mechanisms to co-ordinate policy delivery. Here there may be insights to be gained from a careful consideration of the implementation of service-related policy outside the UK.

Finally, as this chapter has shown the study of the location of producer services has been a very salutary exercise, because it has taught us how much we simply do not know about service activities.

Nevertheless, interest in service activity is growing and its study is likely to dominate employment and regional research in the 1990s. It is to be hoped that this study will fuel such interest and guide further work, which will in turn enhance our understanding of service activities.

9

International Perspectives on Producer Services

The research in this volume is intended to further understanding of the location of producer service activites. Recurring themes have been the diversity of the producer service sector, its international character and deep integration with other economic activities, as well as the difficulties involved in describing its dynamics. It is appropriate, therefore, to complete this volume by presenting other international perspectives on the producer services. The four papers: (1) comment on the conclusions of this study of producer services, (2) discuss the relevance of the results for work in other countries, and (3) develop the analysis presented in previous chapters.

The authors raise a number of issues, some of which support our results. The inadequacy of the secondary source data on service activities seems to be a general problem in many countries. A further theme is the need to progress beyond national case studies to produce internationally comparable research. A prerequisite for this is agreement on an internationally acceptable definition of producer services. This is a subject of growing interest (Bailly, Maillet, and Coffey, 1987), but progress is difficult without an improvement in government statistical sources.

Peter Wood, one of the members of the PSWP, shows how in Canada where better data is available, a fuller understanding of the growth of producer services and their role in the economy can be obtained. William Beyers also highlights the need for secondary source data to be supplemented by field work if we are to further understanding of producer services.

A number of authors argue the importance of developing appropriate policy measures to influence the relatively centralized location of producer services. It is interesting to contrast the rather pessimistic policy conclusions of studies in the Republic of Ireland and the UK with those in America and continental Europe. Michael Bannon's conclusion that the centralization of government in the former countries is an important constraint on the development of services in their provincial regions seems very pertinent. It is also possible that the different perspectives reflect the divergent national responses to the recessions during the 1970s. For the future the trend towards de-regulation and liberalization of service markets in an attempt to promote international trade could have negative implications for those regions with a limited internationally tradable producer service sector.

Finally, Jim Lewis highlights one of the less developed areas in the analysis of producer services presented here; namely the significance of changes in the character of employment in producer services (involving not only the growth of part-time but also temporary contract labour) for an understanding of their role in the economy. It is hoped that employment issues will be a major subject for any further work.

9.1. The View from the United States
W. B. Beyers

This study based on the work of the Producer Services Working Party represents a great achievement by UK geographers, documenting many key aspects of the producer services component of the contemporary economy. It goes a long way towards redressing an imbalance in the research emphasis of industrial geographers in the UK, who have tended to study the manufacturing sector from many different perspectives, while generally ignoring the growing service sector. This situation is not unique to UK geographers; American industrial geographers have also tended to concentrate their efforts on manufacturing industry and its related corporate control, research, and development components. Hopefully this UK effort will stimulate similar studies in other national economies, as called for in the conclusions.

Although the research reported here contains a wealth of information about the producer services, it is almost entirely drawn from secondary sources. These sources have created many problems in the interpretation of the causes of services growth, and even more fundamentally, they have contributed to an inability to fully characterize the role of the services in contemporary UK economic development. Chapters 2 and 8 argue convincingly for changes in the way that government statistics are gathered and published, so that service activities can be identified in whatever industrial sector they originate. Present methods of reporting tend to underestimate the magnitude of service work in sectors industrially classified as non-producer services. Hence, internally-supplied producer services, such as accounting, legal, or computer technical support in industries such as retailing or steel making, are unmeasured. This issue goes beyond these services within non-service industries, as little is reported even in the service sectors themselves about the nature of service work.

This problem is also recognized within the United States by the Census Bureau, and proposals are being made to begin to document more accurately the nature of the work in various industries as a part of the periodic industrial censuses. Given the dominance of service employment growth in many advanced economies, the call for better measurement of this type of activity is to be expected from scholars, and needed by government and the private sector. At this juncture it seems safe to say we are not fully in a position to identify exactly *what* should be reported, although Chapter 8 makes a number of good specific suggestions. In order for international comparative research to be undertaken, a common measurement framework for service work processes should be used by various nations, which means that transnational discussions on measurement systems will need to occur.

Although better statistics from government agencies will help in the analysis of the geography of producer services, field research is also a necessity. The analysis of the UK illustrates this need, searching as it does in Chapter 3 for the causes of the growth of the producer services, but being unable to present direct evidence in the case studies provided in Chapter 5 on the processes identified earlier in the text. Field-based industry case studies would teach us more about the structure and dynamics of firms in these sectors, including information on the demand and supply of such services, the nature of work processes in service firms, the nature of technology used in these services and would help form a relevant public policy towards services.

Having been involved in field research recently on the producer services, it is my opinion that British geographers need to augment the list of research issues identified in the conclusions to Chapter 8. This opinion is mirrored in the writing of other scholars working on the development of the US economy, including Birch, Noyelle, and Stanback. Human capital has been found in the US to be an extremely important ingredient in the development of the producer services (and some components of the public sector), and hence human capital formation immediately looms as a research issue. In new and emerging types of service activity, linkages with institutions creating new knowledge and directly or indirectly extending production systems to use that new knowledge, either as an industrial–public sector input, or as a consumer service–good, have been found to be critically important. The UK study of producer services does not focus on this issue, and it is my opinion that British geographers need to take account of entrepreneurial activity in the producer services, the way training and retraining is provided and how it influences competitiveness, the way that the adoption of information processing and telecommunications equipment changes the nature of work in service firms (and how it influences competitiveness), and how industry–research community linkages affect businesses over time.

This question of human capital in the producer services has important development policy implications, at the subnational level as well as the international level. The case study in Section 5.1 illustrates well how critically important the accounting sector is in London's economic base—where the key market is outside Britain, and how the major British firms must be viewed as in global market competition with American and other foreign enterprises. Maintenance of London's competitive edge in this particular service no doubt requires constant adjustment of labour skills driven by technological and organizational changes in this industry's environment. The local educational system, plus public and private sector training activities (including 'in-house' training) will contribute to this adjustment process, and clearly an understanding of the changing nature of work in the producer services should have a feedback loop to the educational system aimed at enhancing national industrial competitiveness as well as worker satisfaction and welfare.

In other arenas geographers have been calling for studies of the nature of work, and particularly how changing organizational and technological structures influence people's income and life chances. This would also appear to be a necessary area of work in the producer services.

This book includes in its case studies a set of activities considered in most classifications to be producer services (such as management consultancy), but quite rightly wrestles with the classification of many other service activities because of their mixed consumer–industrial–government markets. This is another case where fieldwork will help us understand the organization of these industries. Let us consider for a moment a sector such as legal services. At present in the United States, the SIC has one industrial classification for all legal firms, even though it is clear that legal firms serve very different clienteles. We have not done enough work on the structure of this industry to know how to classify it into major subgroups. However, even if we did have such knowledge, it is likely that we would still find many firms with mixed consumer–industrial markets. At some time in the future, we may have to develop more complex taxonomies of the service sector than we have developed up to now. None of the present classification schemes work satisfactorily, and differences in the organization of industry between nations makes the problem more difficult. For example, in the US the health service sector is clearly profit-oriented, while in most European countries, it is partially a public sector function. The solution to these classification problems is likely to be difficult, but will only come about through field research. Some of this may be conducted by government agencies responsible for economic statistics, but geographers and other social scientists need to help undertake the basic research that will be needed along the way.

This volume provides the stimulus for many of the avenues of research needed to provide directions for policy-makers as well as academics. As a final footnote to this American perspective on a UK research effort, it seems to me that there is a greater distance between the academic research community and the government in the UK than in the United States. This may not be a problem, but it seems as though the type of partnership that has often occurred at the state or regional level in the US does not exist in the UK in the research and policy formulation process. The lack of political entities in England comparable to our states, engaging in healthy inter-regional competition for industry *and* of scholars in universities working on development issues, is striking to an outsider. This is an issue needing both research and perhaps changes in UK government if *regional* interests are to be served in the same way as in the US where state agencies aim to help achieve regional balance in development. At present in the UK, it does not appear as though there is any sustained trend towards diffusion in the development of the producer services economy outside the South East of England. On the other hand, in the US the pattern of growth appears much more decentralized. How to help more of the UK space economy share in the new service economy must be a top priority for UK policy-makers, and is a central issue implicit in this book. Now the challenge is how to realize this potential.

9.2. Some International Perspectives on Services and Development: The European Community

M. Bannon

The UK experience of a growth of service activities and an increasing importance of producer services forms part of a wider global transformation of economic and social systems towards what has been called the 'service economy' (Bell, 1974; Stanback *et al.*, 1981; Gershuny and Miles, 1983) or the 'information society' (Porat, 1977; Masuda, 1980; Bannon *et al.*, 1982). This transformation has resulted in major shifts in the nature of production, it has required fundamental changes in the nature and components of production processes, and it is giving rise to a new geography of economic activities both within countries and within larger trading blocks such as the European Community. While this transformation is affecting most aspects of economic and social activity, it is most easily recognized through the growth of service activities and the increasing importance of service occupations. Over the past quarter century, services have come to dominate the output and labour statistics of advanced economies and services now perform an increasingly important role in international trade (Daniels, 1985*b*).

However, the services' transformation is not confined to the advanced economies (Gemmell, 1982) but is affecting the structure of economic activity and the composition of labour in all countries. This is not to imply that the services' transformation is affecting all countries in a similar manner. It is now evident that the size of a country's service sector, its contribution to wealth creation, and its geographic distribution will be affected by a large variety of factors. To an extent the size of a country's service sector is a good indicator of that country's overall level of economic development and service industries spectrum (Sabolo, 1975). The composition of a country's service sector is also likely to change as a country proceeds along the path to development. Thus, 'old' low income services dominate in many of the less developed countries while high value 'new' and 'complementary' services characterize the more advanced economies. The growth of service industries within a country will also relate to the nature of that country's overall development policies, its ability to create wealth and, importantly, the country's ability to retain and reinvest the wealth created. In countries characterized by colonial forms of exploitation much of the wealth which might be used to support and foster indigenous services is leaked, often to the more developed countries.

The pattern of service industry development within each country will also vary in response to a wide variety of factors. The size of a country's territory and the distribution of its population will inevitably affect the pattern of development of services therein. Thus, Canadian and Dutch experiences are likely to be different. The emerging pattern of services is likely to be influenced by the urban system of any given country and the ease of inter-urban accessibility therein. Thus, the new geography of services in Germany may be very different from that in France, as will that of Switzerland (Racine and Cunha, 1986), and Sweden (Warneryd, 1984). But, in turn, this pattern of services as it relates to urbanization, may be greatly influenced by the cultural and historical development of political systems. There is a good deal of evidence to support the view that devolved political systems with strong regional or provincial authorities and administrations give rise to a more even pattern of urban development than is the case in many more centralized countries (Marquand, 1980). In this respect the UK experience may be contrasted with that of West Germany. There would appear to be little doubt that a decentralization of government functions can foster a corresponding decentralization of private sector firms as has taken place in Denmark (Illeris, 1987). On the other hand, the increasing concentration of administrative power within central government, as has happened in Ireland, can be shown to be a major cause of the rapid growth of service employment in the capital Dublin, to the virtual exclusion of other cities and regions (Bannon, 1985; 1987).

Thus, while the pressures leading towards a growth of services are universal, each country's response to those pressures will be influenced by the economic, social, and cultural traditions and circumstances of that society. In this regard the UK experience as documented in preceding chapters has many lessons for other countries. The report emphasizes the interdependence between the growth of services and a healthy industrial performance. The findings also document clearly the importance of producer services both within the service sector and in the goods producing sectors. There must be considerable concern at the realization that a variety of both international and domestic forces are favouring a concentration of services in the south of the country and constraining the development of services in peripheral regions. The UK findings highlight other issues of profound importance, most notably, the inadequacy of data and the lack of empirical evidence on many aspects of service development such as the extent of part-time working, the levels of remuneration, the role of female labour, the linkages between producer and other services, and the difficulties of formulating a meaningful regional services policy. These conclusions are important, if not downright alarming, for many other countries since the range, continuity, and quality of UK statisitics and research data is likely to be superior to that in many other countries. Also these same questions constitute the research group agenda for the European Community where it is now recognized that the Community requires a policy for services which will both foster the international competitiveness of the EEC and help minimize disparities in regional opportunity within its boundaries.

With international trade in services valued at $550,000,000 in 1980 (Daniels, 1985) and forecast to grow rapidly, the overriding concern for the European Community must be the promotion of policies which enable Europe to capture an increasing share of this trade, while also using new services to enhance its industrial innovativeness and its overall competitiveness. Such objectives call for accelerated policies aimed at restructuring the Community, removing internal barriers to free trade, fostering de-regulation and facilitating the easier movement of people, goods, and information (Sutherland, 1986). This, in turn, requires a Community policy for services, research and development, higher education, and innovation. But such policies could lead to a further reinforcement of the existing 'gradient from central to peripheral regions in the location of producer services' (Daniels, 1985). The international trade perspective, requiring a move towards free trade, would inevitably favour the core regions of the Community with their relatively high economic development potentials (Keeble, Owens, and Thompson, 1981) at least as locations for the development of producer services.

On the other hand, the Community and most of its member states are committed to regional policies designed to foster the more rapid development of peripheral countries or peripheral parts of countries. For the most part, such strategies, at least in regard to employment creation, are highly dependent upon the further expansion of their service sectors, particularly the development of traded services and the promotion of producer service functions, to aid local production and as a help to countries' balance of payments. For many of the peripheral countries of Europe a more active Community regional policy for services is required both to help solve their national problems and to reduce their internal regional variations in opportunity. Rather typical of such countries is the Republic of Ireland with its relatively low levels of development, a high dependence upon agriculture, rapidly increasing population, and scarce resources to deal with the many urgent but often conflicting needs. While Ireland's service sector employment increased by 41.4% between 1961 and 1981 and while the share of employment in services has risen from 41.5% in 1961 to 54.0% in 1985, Ireland's level of service development lags well behind much of Europe. In addition, given both the primacy of the urban system and the centralized nature of the political and administrative system (Bannon, 1983) it is hardly surprising that almost half of all service jobs are located in the Dublin region with other regions having a low level of service employment, predominantly in routine or public sector jobs.

An analysis of producer services in the Irish context shows that 70% of all services could be classed as 'marketed' services but that some 60% of the growth of such services since 1971 took place in the Dublin region (Dineen, 1985). Within marketed services 'producer services' represent, as in the UK, an important and expanding category. By 1981 Dineen estimated that some 108,000 persons were engaged in 'producer service' activities with almost three quarters located in the Dublin region. Studies by Bannon (1985) highlight the consequence for peripheral regions of such concentration; not only are peripheral regions deprived of jobs and corresponding incomes, but service and goods producing firms in the periphery must buy in services from Dublin. This represents a sizeable flow of capital from the periphery to Dublin, and it partly offsets the benefits of existing regional policies and reinforces the unequal development of regions and urban centres. These findings are in general similar to those reported above for the UK and can be compared with the findings of other studies in Valencia (Rura, 1986). These findings, however, do show considerable contrasts with the pattern of business service supply in regions of Denmark (Pedersen, 1986).

Thus, peripheral countries and more especially their less developed regions require an accelerated development of their service economies to meet their economic and social needs. Within the European Community this can happen only if the Community is prepared to intervene much more effectively using an enlarged regional fund to promote the development of producer service functions outside the core regions of the Community and its member states. On the other hand such regional intervention will be opposed by advocates of 'free trade' and international competition for services. The UK study demonstrates the inter-regional outcome of an almost free market situation in which domestic intervention measures have had only a limited impact on the location of producer services and where European level policies have been almost non-existent.

The UK results would appear to demonstrate in detail the general impression coming from many European countries to date. But despite the information gained from a number of empirical studies, our knowledge of the producer service functions throughout Europe is limited and fragmentary. The detailed UK study could usefully be used as a model to explore on the standardized basis the development of producer services within the Community as a whole. The aim of such a study should be to clarify the potential of these activities as creators of employment and wealth and to devise policies which can influence their locational development for the simultaneous improvement of the Community and its peripheral regions.

9.3. The Economic Role of Producer Services: Some Canadian Evidence
P. Wood

Classification and economic function

Difficulties in examining the role of services begin at the most basic level, with the classification of economic functions. In fact, during its deliberations the main task of the Producer Service Working Party often seemed to amount to little more than escaping the tyranny of the SIC. In practice, of course, any use of established data bases in the UK makes this impossible.

Many alternative classifications of services have been suggested but, as Walker (1985) has argued, most have been based on, or resulted in a 'theoretical muddle'. How can any categorization encapsulate the essential economic functions of services, rather than latching on to the more obvious attributes of some of them? Producer services, for example, are not just 'white collar', 'information processing', 'labour intensive' activities, dependent on skills embodied in workers rather than in machinery. They are not even confined to the private sector, and they are certainly not only 'ephemeral' in their economic contribution. Some have all these characteristics but others can always be found that display opposite features.

These classification problems reflect a wider confusion about the evolving economic role of services. Daniels (1985*b*), in the preface to his recent book, suggests that past neglect of the service sector can be explained more by the fact that it 'defies application of a principal theory, a particular analytical method, or a dominant mode of interpretation' than by any lack of empirical data. The classification issue links these possible explanations; poor theoretical understanding has bequeathed inadequate categories with which to order data. The analytical usefulness of such data has thereby been severely restricted. Studies of services have become trapped in a self-perpetuating circle of confusion about their economic significance. To break out, alternative approaches to data analysis are needed that properly reflect the operations of service functions, both in creating employment and in supporting the productivity of other primary, manufacturing, and service activities.

In this light, the SIC and similar classifications are misleading in the way they depict the functioning of the modern economy. Their organizing framework assumes that materials transformation is the dominant form of economic activity. Applied to employment data, such a framework has become less appropriate as labour effort has increasingly been transferred away from direct production functions, both within and between individual sectors. In monitoring other aspects of the economy, such as investment, or the value of inputs and outputs, it neglects the essential and growing significance of resources employed away from the factory floor, including outside the manufacturing firm, in support of productive efficiency. More generally, of course, the significance of economic transactions that are not materially-based is liable to be consistently misrepresented.

At best, therefore, conventional classifications have treated services as being of subsidiary significance. At worst, their implied view of the economy sees services as operating in the same manner as traditional manufacturing; performing specific technical transformations of inputs to create discrete products. Today, such a view is inadequate even when applied to manufacturing itself. It assumes that each activity can be effectively defined on the basis of its internal, technical characteristics, and can be studied *separately* from other forms of production or from consumption. In contrast, the 'service' role is best appreciated in terms of its *inter-relatedness* with other activities; of the ways in which it enhances the worth of other primary, manufacturing and service functions. Such a perspective incidentally also clarifies the technical role of materials transformation itself within the wider pattern of production. Modern needs are served by inherently complex sequences and *combinations* of goods processing and service expertise applied at various stages of production and circulation, from materials extraction to final consumption and beyond.

Growing inter-relatedness of activities of course supports the increasingly intricate division of productive labour frequently referred to in explanations of service employment growth. For Walker (1985), the growth of indirect, as opposed to direct labour in the production process is probably the 'principle locus of industrialism' today. Rather less plausibly he nevertheless seeks to establish that changes in material production play the leading role in driving this process, even while acknowledging the growing complexity and significance of inter-relationships between service functions.

Input–Output data and the social division of labour

At several points, Walker refers to the economic flows underlying changing divisions of labour in terms of input–output relationships. Classification problems of course still bedevil input–output analyses. They only reflect the 'social division of labour', as Walker describes it, between industries, and not the 'detail division of labour' within sectors or between firms or workplaces. They nevertheless measure *inter-relationships* between sectors and Walker's argument suggests that exploration of these offers one significant avenue of enquiry into the complex role of service activities in relation to other economic functions.

This is where the Canadian evidence presented below is so valuable, indicating what might be possible elsewhere if a similar quality of information was more widely available. In the UK, examination through national input–output tables of the output of services to intermediate ('producer') and final ('consumer') demand has been only very sketchy. The poor specification and measurement of service activities and the out-of-date and static nature of the information in the published UK tables have offered only snapshot estimates (see Chapter 3) (Marquand, 1979; Robertson, Briggs and Goodchild, 1982; Wood, 1984). Canadian input–output information allows a much more detailed investigation of national production relationships. It is available in the form of commodity–industry transaction tables, including a number of service 'commodities'. The data have also been available annually since the early 1960s on a comparable basis, the most recent table (in 1985) being for 1980. Quite apart from the inherent value of this series, the consistency of the data for particular sectors or commodities can be verified over a long period. Finally, the information is published on a standard (1971) price basis. Thus services can be identified not only as commodity inputs to various intermediate sectors and to final demand, but changes can be traced in the share of these and other inputs over almost twenty years.

The Canadian data offer a rare opportunity to explore, first, the changing patterns of 'first round', structural interdependence between sectors over a long period. Secondly, by augmenting the data with measures of employment and investment change, work for the Economic Council of Canada by Postner and Wesa (1984) has revealed the indirect, as well as the direct contribution of all sectors to national competitiveness. A 'total factor productivity' approach therefore allows the often neglected significance for labour productivity improvement in each sector of indirect inputs from other sectors, including services. Finally, the Economic Council study also demonstrates the particular significance of different services in such productivity improvements since the 1960s.

Structural relationships in the Canadian economy

The data presented below has been examined in detail elsewhere and compared with other Canadian evidence for economic inter-relationships at the regional and local level (Wood, 1987). Here, three tables will be presented and briefly commented upon to illustrate the changing significance of services for Canadian output since the early 1960s.

Table 9.1 and 9.2 identify three types of *commodity* purchases undertaken in the economy: purchases of, (column 1) 'manual' services (mainly materials handling, utilities, construction, and delivery skills), (column 2) 'information' services (including financial and business services, communications, operating services to business and government, real estate, and travel activities) and, (column 3) materials. The purchasing sectors are divided between intermediate (rows A–C) and final demand (rows D–G). The intermediate sector is assumed to constitute the main element of producer demand, coming from, (A) materials processing enterprises, (B) materials handling enterprises (including utilities and

Table 9.1. Commodity Inputs of Major Intermediate and Final Demand Sectors, Canada, 1980. Percentages of sector purchases (rows)/commodity output (columns).

Purchasing Sectors	Commodities			
	1 Manual[a]	2 Information[b]	3 Materials	Total
Intermediate				
A. Materials processing	12.9	18.7	68.4	100
	9.0	19.3	43.8	
B. Materials handling	36.3	27.6	36.1	100
	13.2	14.9	12.1	
C. Information handling	28.8	28.0	33.2	100
	10.2	19.9	10.7	
Final Demand				
D. Consumers	37.5	27.0	34.6	100
	34.7	38.2	29.2	
E. Government	54.1	35.5	10.3	100
	7.6	7.4	1.3	
F. Business	61.9	4.5	33.5	100
	21.1	2.3	10.5	
G. Trade				
	4.0	−2.0	−7.6	
TOTAL	100	100	100	

[a] *Manual Services*: Construction, Transportation and Storage, Transportation margins, Utilities, Wholesaling, Retailing, Personal/Miscellaneous services.

[b] *Information Services*: Communications, Real estate transactions, Finance, Insurance and real estate, Business services, Office/Laboratory/Food services, Travel/Advertising/Promotion.

Source: Canadian Input–Output Tables.

Table 9.2.   Changes in Commodity Input to Major Intermediate and Final
Demand Sectors, Canada 1962–1980 (at Standard Prices, 1960 = 100)

Purchasing Sectors	Commodities			
	1 Manual services	2 Information services	3 Materials	Total domestic inputs
Intermediate				
A. Materials processing	234	244	217	223
B. Materials handling	237	261	209	231
C. Information handling	219	361	237	265
Final Demand				
D. Consumers	215	236	200	215
E. Government (net)	190	365	64	184
F. Business	259	256	343	282
G. Trade (net)	355 (Exp.)	411 (Imp.)	455 (Imp.)	

Source: Canadian Input–Output Tables.

construction) and, (C) information handling enterprises, In addition, 'business' purchases (by both materials processing and service enterprises) in final demand (F) are interpreted as part of the producer service market. The significance of each transaction is measured in terms of both its share of each sector's spending on commodities (rows) and the pattern of commodity sales to each sector (columns).

The data reveal a complex interdependence of activities and especially how the service sectors themselves generate a large direct market for service commodities. Together, the materials and information handling producer service (B and C) purchased 23% of the gross value of manual service (1) and 25% of information service (2) output. In addition, 21% of manual services (compared with only 2% of information services) were sold to other businesses (F) as 'final demand' mainly by wholesale and construction firms. Thus, including these business services, no less than 45% of the value of manual and 37% of information services were sold to the producer service sectors, compared to 35% and 38% respectively to consumers.

In comparison, direct purchases of services by the extractive and manufacturing industries (A) accounted for only 9% of manual and 19% of information service output. Although these services accounted for 31% of the processing industries' inputs, it therefore appears that the *direct* role of production in driving the service economy is subsidiary to the increasingly specialized and subdivided nature of the service sector itself, including organizations able to serve both producer and consumer markets. This means that the significance of services cannot be examined in isolation from wider shifts in the structure of the economy. Another implication is the valuable and growing market for manufactured goods found in the service sector; more than one third of gross inputs to both types of service activity was in the form of material goods (cf. Table 9.2).

Another way of interpreting the data, however, is to combine producer purchases by materials processing (A) and handling (B) sectors. These 'materials-oriented' enterprises are responsible for 22% of the purchases of manual services (1) and 34% of that for information handling services (2). This compares with only 10% and 20% respectively being purchased by information handling producer services (C). This perhaps puts notions about the growing dominance of the 'information economy' into better perspective, on the basis of output rather than more usual employment measures. In fact, manual services, as here defined, were responsible for 36% of the gross value of commodity inputs to the Canadian economy, compared with about 40% in the form of materials and only 24% from information services.

Over the period 1962–80 (Table 9.2), increases in the real value of inputs to both intermediate and final demand were nevertheless greatest for the information services (2), most markedly to private information handling enterprises themselves and to government (with increases of more than 3.5 times in real terms). There was a similarly high increase in the purchase of finished materials and equipment (3) by business, perhaps reflecting a greater reliance on specialist suppliers for more sophisticated products.

The most striking trend in demand for manual services (1, including utilities) was in the export balance. This reflects a Canadian comparative advantage in these activities, although its exploitation may to some degree have been at the cost of increased deficits in manufactured goods and information services. Domestic growth in demand for manual services was more dependent upon the materials processing, materials handling, and business final demand sectors, rather than the faster-expanding information services.

The processing industries (A) moved towards a greater dependence on outside services in relation to the value of material inputs. They showed a more balanced emphasis on manual as well as information services than did changing inputs to the information handling services or to consumer and government final demand.

Over the eighteen year period, for every extra unit of materials purchased by the processing industries, a further 12% of information and 8% of manual services were also purchased.

Compared with the pattern of final consumer demand (D), the main locus of growth was clearly in intermediate demand and government demand for information services (2). The main expansion of demand for the manual services (1) was in export and domestic business sales. The most buoyant markets for materials (3) were in business purchasing and the information handling industries. The impression is of an economy in which structural changes are increasingly being driven by trends in the information processing services though they remain relatively small in output terms. As a result, patterns of final demand now contain significantly higher service inputs in relation to material commodities than in the early 1960s.

Services and productivity changes

Compared with the UK, these Canadian data allow a much clearer picture to emerge of the growing value and complexity of *demand* for services in the economy at large. A somewhat thornier problem referred to earlier concerns the *efficiency* of their contribution in supporting other activities. This problem underlies any debate on the contribution of services to economic success or failure. Measurement of the productivity of service activities is notoriously difficult, partly because of the problems of evaluating both their inputs and outputs. More significantly still, as has already been argued, their economic contribution, including that to efficiency, can only be evaluated in relation to the improved performance they bestow on the operations of their customers. 'Productivity', as an attribute of a sector in isolation from its wider economic role, is an even less satisfactory concept for services than for manufacturing industries.

Fortunately in Canada this problem has recently been directly addressed, on the basis of the exceptional quality of the input–output data, in a study by Postner and Wesa (1984) for the Economic Council of Canada. This takes a 'total factor productivity' approach to the measurement of productivity growth between 1961 and 1978. In this approach, the productivity of all the indirect inputs from other sectors, as well as a sector's own inputs, are taken into account. In total productivity terms, therefore, the efficiency contribution of 'capital intensive' industries, for example, is shown to be lower when the labour intensiveness of their intermediate inputs and capital replacement needs are allowed for. The general effect is to reduce the real productivity differences between supposedly 'high productivity' sectors such as mining, transport equipment, chemicals, communications, and utilities, and traditionally more labour intensive industries such as textiles, clothing, furniture, construction and, in particular, many of the services. This form of analysis also allows those productivity improvements that might have the most widespread effect throughout the economy at large to be identified.

Postner and Wesa explore the direct and indirect effects of productivity improvements in each sector between 1961 and 1976 (Table 9.3). The 'output effects' of productivity improvements in some sectors upon others were often of greater general significance than their direct impacts (column 5). Total productivity changes in the construction, paper, primary metals, and food and beverages industries, for example, were more dependent on the input effects from other sectors (column 3) than on their own internal productivity improvements (column 2). Between 1961 and 1976, the main contribution to total productivity improvements in Canada were made by the agricultural and transportation and storage sectors, together with important contributions from forestry, construction, and a number of other processing and service sectors ranked in column 4. Conversely, the main slowing effect on total productivity improvement came from the business services and other personal service sectors.

Postner and Wesa pursue the analysis by undertaking several exploratory studies of the possible impacts of various productivity improvements, significantly emphasizing the services. In one of these, an improved measure of output growth in the *finance, insurance, and real estate* sector is employed, mainly to account for high inflation in the 1971–6 period. As the most important supplier of intermediate commodities, it is argued that the measurement of productivity in this sector is especially critical. The postulation of a productivity improvement of 3.3%, instead of the 0.7% loss suggested in earlier studies, results in a widespread effect on total factor productivity, increasing Canadian productivity growth from 2.0% to 2.5%.

A further exercise postulates a 25% productivity improvement from 1976 to 1980 in *five service groups*: transportation and storage, communications, wholesaling, finance, insurance and real estate, and business services. No less than 60% of the resulting total productivity changes would have been felt in other sectors, especially in mineral fuels, petroleum, coal products, trade, primary metals, transport equipment, forestry, paper, and chemicals, and through the indirect effects on the five sectors themselves. Postner and Wesa conclude that this demonstrates the potential for

Table 9.3. Changes in Total Labour Requirements Attributed to 'Own Effects' and 'Input Effects', and Transmitted to Other Industries as a Result of 'Output Effects'. 1961–76, Man-years per 1 million dollars of output. Ranked in order of output effects.

	1. Total change	2. 'Own effect'	3. 'Input effect'	4. 'Output effect'	5. Column 4 % of Column 4 + 2[a]
Agriculture	−136	−109	−27	−264	71
Transport and storage[b]	−58	−39	−18	−108	73
Forestry	−41	−28	−13	−56	66
Construction[b]	−33	−11	−22	−50	82
Paper and allied	−29	−9	−20	−36	79
Textiles	−76	−43	−33	−35	45
Wholesale trade[b]	−40	−25	−15	−34	58
Primary metals	−26	−6	−20	−30	84
Metal mines	−13	−7	−6	−30	81
Wood products	−49	−23	−25	−28	55
Communications[b]	−71	−47	−25	−25	35
Food and beverages	−77	−18	−59	−24	57
Retail trade[b]	−49	−31	−18	−22	41
Electrical products	−53	−29	−23	−22	42
Printing and publishing	−33	−21	−12	−22	51
Business services[b]	−8	−4	−5	+23	120
Other personal services[b]	+40	+49	−9	+15	23
Transportation equipment	−56	−32	−23	+6	−20

[a] Output effect as % of Output + Own effects.

[b] Services.

'Own effect': change in total labour requirements/unit of output of a sector arising from technical change in that sector. Changes include those affecting direct labour inputs and intermediate inputs and capital replacement needs, expressed in terms of their direct labour content.

'Input effect': changes in labour, intermediate, and capital replacement inputs in *other* sectors, as they affect the total labour requirements of a purchasing sector.

'Output effect': effect on total labour requirements in other sectors of productivity changes in a supplying sector.

Total productivity change (labour requirement)/unit of delivered output = Own effect + Input effect.

Source: Postner and Wesa (1984), tables 3.1 and 3.2.

improvement in aggregate productivity through developments in these key services, not directly involved in serving final demand.

In another detailed analysis of the 1973–8 period, during which productivity growth in Canada stagnated, Postner and Wesa examine the trend already noted in Table 9.2 towards the consumption of more intermediate service inputs in production. They found little evidence that productivity shortfalls in these services themselves affected overall productivity trends, as has sometimes been suggested. Rather, it appeared that purchasers failed to complement their greater use of outside services by proportionately reducing their labour forces or inputs of other intermediate commodities. One suggested explanation of this failing was the delay in adjusting production arrangements, following the purchase of outside service expertise, especially during a period of rapid technological change such as the introduction of new communications and computer equipment. Another suggestion is that high inflation at the time led to increased demand for outside service expertise to bring business costs under control.

While emphasizing the growth and significance for modern productive efficiency of bought-in services, therefore, Postner and Wesa suggest that there are productivity inefficiencies, at least in the early stages, if the purchasing sectors are slow to adapt to their use. More generally, they also show the widespread significance of service sector efficiency for the Canadian economy and highlight sectors which have a special status in the study of future national productivity trends. While in the past these have been agriculture and transportation/storage, the roles of communications, finance, insurance and real estate, and business services are regarded as particularly significant for future Canadian competitiveness. The importance of the producer service role in Canada, and its changing form since the 1960s, is strongly confirmed by Postner and Wesa's evidence.

Conclusion

Important questions of course remain unanswered by this form of analysis. At the aggregate level, one concerns the dynamics of self-sustaining growth within the service sector itself. What are the limits to this growth in relation to that of domestic processing industries, trade or consumer or public spending? Also, as has already been suggested, how far do the supply side effects of efficient services actually facilitate import penetration, compared with the assistance they provide to the competitiveness of domestic goods and services? At a local scale the corporate and functional constitution of sectors also obviously require more examination than input–output data can ever provide.

Nevertheless, the type of data presented here illustrates how the performance not only of producer services but of all sectors of the economy can be illuminated by consistent economic monitoring of the inter-relationships between different sectors. The essential nature of service activities implies that their economic worth can be assessed only through the effects they exert on other activities. Thus real progress in service studies, or in understanding the dynamics of 'post-industrial' employment and output trends, can hardly be expected until improvements in economic monitoring reflect the realities of modern economic organization.

9.4. Employment Matters: A Comment
J. Lewis[1]

Anyone who has read this far will appreciate the quantity and quality of the work that has gone into the preparation of the main text. Hopefully, they will also find that some of its contents have been elaborated further—or disputed—by subsequent research, for the greatest possible compliment to a review of this sort is that it should serve as a starting point for the next wave of investigation. In a few years time, it may well be seen as a mark of how little was known about the dynamics of producer services but in 1987 this book represented a significant step forward by bringing together that little in a well organized framework. However, my praise of the achievement is tempered by a number of points of criticism and I wish to raise three that relate to the treatment of employment issues as initial steps towards the deeper theoretical and practical comprehension of producer services.

First, the theoretical context for the argument about the development of producer services should not be the 'post-industrial' versus 'deindustrialization' accounts of structural change (Chapter 3). Far greater insights are to be gained by relating the changing character of producer services to the debates on 'productive decentralization' and 'vertical disintegration' (e.g. Bagnasco, 1977; Brusco and Sabel, 1981; Mingionie, 1981). This approach accounts for well-known empirical trends, such as the declining size of firm, growth of subcontracting and 'flexible specialization' by particular enterprises, by analysing changes in corporate structure, fragmentation of product markets, and new ways of organizing labour. By doing so, the explanations substitute a link to changes in the organization of production for the reliance on a 'structural logic' of post-industrialization and reaffirm the importance of analysing new types of labour process in the face of general claims about 'deindustrialization'. Their relevance is clear from the evidence of Chapters 3 and 5 on the declining importance of administrative, technical, and clerical staff employed in manufacturing, and the growth of jobs in contract physical distribution firms, suggesting that producer service employment within industrial enterprises is being replaced by contracting-in the required services from outside. Although no effort to quantify the effect of such reorganization of industrial firms' labour requirements is made in these chapters,

[1] These comments arise from research undertaken for the Middlesbrough Locality Study, which is part of the initiative on The Changing Urban and Regional System of the UK funded by the Economic and Social Research Council (Grant DO4 250018).

estimates by Rajan and Pearson (1986) attribute some 43% of the employment growth of distribution, financial, and business services in 1979–85 to such 'externalization'. Within this broad category, they stress the importance of this kind of job reorganization to wholesaling (+100,000 jobs) and business services in particular.

Secondly, one aspect of the flexibility that characterizes an increasing proportion of jobs due to these processes of productive decentralization is mentioned in the discussion of the growth of part-time labour. This emphasis is, however, misplaced. While the rise in part-time employment is undoubtedly one of the distinctive trends in UK labour markets in recent years, it is not a key feature of producer services activities. Using the definitions of producer services and mixed producer–consumer services proposed in Table 2.4, the former had 12.8% of its labour force working part-time in both 1981 and 1984, while the latter showed a continued increase in its part-time employment from 14.7% to 16.0% in 1981–4 (Department of Employment, 1983, 1987). These proportions compare with national figures of 21.3% and 22.2% respectively, so both sets of activity are less marked by part-time work than average and fall a long way behind MLHs such as retail distribution (35.7% part-time in 1984), eating places (53.7%), hospitals (36.3%), and even higher education (30.5%). There has been an expansion in part-time work in producer services in the 1980s (as is shown for the 1970s in Chapter 3) but it is concentrated at the consumer service end of the mixed producer–consumer services. As with the general trends in part-time employment growth examined by Townsend (1986), the demand for labour outside the standard working week and to meet short-term fluctuations in consumer contact is a major determinant that should be ranked alongside the development of more routine clerical tasks allocated to part-timers. Thus the provision of lunch-time cover for bank cashiers and the employment of 'evening ladies' by canteens expanding into private catering are as typical as sources of part-time job growth as the expansion of data processing activities in the 'clerical factories' of banks or insurance companies (which deal with large volumes of business precisely because they are catering for numerous 'standard customers'). In those parts of the 'mixed services' such as insurance, where automation and withdrawal from direct contact with customers are occurring simultaneously, part-time work is actually declining more rapidly than total employment (−20.0% compared with −0.9% overall in 1981–4).

Labour flexibility and cost reduction are, however, also requirements of producer services proper. In some instances (e.g. secretarial staff), this can be obtained by using part-time contracts so the

1981–4 growth of part-time employment in producer services was marginally greater—at 13.8%—than the 13.3% growth of total employment (while the comparable figures for the mixed producer–consumer services were +10.5% in part-time work and +1.6% overall). More important, but difficult to quantify, is the provision of flexibility in employment by the use of temporary contracts, agency staff, and the buying-in of a service from the self-employed or another firm in the producer service sector. The demand for numerical flexibility in producer service firms is not simply over the short-period fluctuations of hours and weeks that can be met by part-time work but rather over the months of an audit or management consultancy and years of computer system development. Present methods of collection of employment data fail to consider these kinds of working practice but a survey by Manpower (1986) showed that, in service industries as a whole, 45% of their respondents had increased their temporary labour force between 1982 and 1985 and 38% had increased the volume of subcontracted business (compared with only 26% increasing the number of part-time workers). Although it does not account for a particularly large share of total employment as yet—some 4% in services—and is often related to the need to provide cover for holidays, maternity leave, or sickness, temporary work is seen by employers in the service sector more as a means of coping with variations in their workload than as one for cutting costs. It is a feature of producer service activities that deserves greater attention in future; not least as the limited availability of highly-skilled labour on temporary contracts (or through subcontracting) is likely to reduce the spatial mobility of producer service activities, despite the potential for their spatial deconcentration as shown in Chapter 4.

Finally, the introduction of an international dimension to the analysis of UK producer services (especially in Chapter 5) is most welcome but the study as a whole would have been greatly improved if more international comparisons of processes had been included in the rest of that chapter. This would have helped to identify the extent to which the changes described are specifically British, rather than being widespread amongst producer services elsewhere. Thus the relative weight that should be given to explanations based on the competitive environment, technological innovation, corporate reorganization, or labour market conditions would become clearer. For example, research on the effects of information processing technology in insurance in West Germany (Baethge and Oberbeck, 1986) and banking in Spain (Castells *et al.*, 1986) identify some of the trends, such as centralization of activities and falling branch employment, noted in Chapter 5 but finds that the increased feminization of the labour force is due to an expansion in full-time female employment. Such a comparison picks out the unusual features of British labour markets that part-time workers are cheaper per hour and easier to dismiss than elsewhere and suggests that there is not a direct link between this kind of technological change and the spread of a particular type of work. Similarly, reference to the study of financial service firms in France, West Germany, Japan, Sweden, and the USA by Bertrand and Noyelle (1986) would have shown the importance of competition over distribution channels in explaining variations in the introduction of new technologies (and subsequent changes in the labour force). As producer services themselves become increasingly international, this kind of comparative work will become ever more important.

In short, the arguments advanced in the preceding pages have shown how producer services change in character, and possibly location, in response to new markets, technological innovation, and corporate structures. Employment is presented as responding in volume, type, and location to these changes. However, employment requirements are themselves a cause of new corporate strategies and technological change and so we need to know more about how labour processes in the producer services shape—and are shaped by—the requirements of capital. For as long as producer service firms need workers, employment matters.

Appendix 1 Classifications of Non-Production Employment in Manufacturing Industry

Crum and Gudgin's Classification of Census Occupations (1970)

005	Gardeners and groundsmen
093–98	Construction workers
102	Boiler firemen
115–135	Transport and communications workers
136	Warehousemen, storekeepers, and assistants
138–141	Clerical workers
143–146 148–150	Sales workers
151–168 170–172	Service, sport, and recreation workers
175–180	Administrators and managers
181–206 209–212 214–215 217–220	Professional, technical workers, artists

New Classification of Non-Production Employees using 1980 *Classification of Occupations—Based on Crum and Gudgin's Classification*

0001–006 009	Professional and related management
012–013 015–020 022	Professional and related in education and health
024–033	Professional and related in science, engineering, and technology
034–039 043–044	Managerial
045–057	Clerical and related
060–062	Security and protective services
063–075	Catering, cleaning, hairdressing, and other personal service
078	Horticultural workers, gardeners, groundsmen
139–143 146	Construction, mining, and related
147–153 156–158	Transport operating, materials moving and storing

General Classification of Non-Production Employment used in Section 5.2

Orders

1–3	Professional support staff
4	Professional and scientific
5	Managers
6	Clerical
7	Sales
8–9	Catering, cleaning, personal services, and security
14	Construction
15	Transport and storage

Appendix 2   Sources for the Analysis of Business Service Offices

Accountancy

Accountancy Age, a publication by VNU Business Publications BV, which produces annually a list of the top 50–100 accountancy practices based upon an analysis of the accountancy returns of *The Times* 1000 firms. Institute of Chartered Accountants, a list of all firms and their offices with a practicing accountant who is a member of the Institute. Also a list of management consultancy firms.

Advertising

Advertisers Annual, a list of advertising and marketing firms and their offices in the United Kingdom. The list is compiled by the publisher (Kelly's Directories), there is no charge to firms and the returns are checked by survey procedures.

British Research and Data, a list of advertising firms and their offices in the United Kingdom. The list is compiled by the publishers (Maclean–Hunter Ltd.), there is no charge to firms and the returns are checked by survey procedures.

Campaign, an advertising publication by Haymarket Publishing Ltd which publishes a list of the major advertising agencies and groups in terms of annual billings provided via a postal survey.

Marketing Consultants

Institute of Managment Consultants Year Book, listing all firms and their offices in the United Kingdom where 75% of the principals are members of the Institute.

Management Consultants Association, a list of all firms which are members of the association—which includes all the major firms. See also Institute of Chartered Accountants.

Marketing and Market Research

Market Research Society, all market research companies which have at least one member of the Society. See also *Advertisers Annual*.

Computer Bureau

Computer Services Association Directory, a list of most of the major companies and their ownership and employment characteristics.

Computer Users Year Book, a list of computing bureaux with information on employment size and ownership characteristics. The list is compiled by the publisher (CUY Publications Ltd) from surveys of individual firms. The source was used to identify computer consultancy firms with more than 100 employees for the analysis of major computer firms.

References

Aaronovitch, S., and Sawyer, M. C. (1975), *Big Business: Theoretical and Empirical Aspects of Concentration and Mergers in the UK*, Macmillan, London.

Aaronovitch, S., and Samson, P. (1985), *The Insurance Industry in the Countries of the EEC: Structure, Conduct and Performance*, Commission of the European Communities, Luxemburg.

Accountant, The (1986), 'Touche and Spicers Surge in Boom Year for all Firms', *The Accountant*, 26 Jun., 3.

Ackerman, K. B., and LaLonde, B. J. (1980), 'Making Warehousing more Efficient', *Harvard Business Review*, 58, 4, 2, 94–102.

Alexander, I. (1979) *Office Location and Public Policy*, Longman, London.

Atkinson, J. (1984), '*Flexibility, Uncertainty and Manpower Management*', Report 89, Institute of Manpower Studies, University of Sussex.

Aucott, J. V. (1960), 'Dispersal of Offices from London', *Town Planning Review*, 31, 37–51.

Audit Guide Ltd. (1985), *The Audit Fee Guide*, Vols. 1–13, London.

Baethge, M., and Oberbeck, H. (1986), *Zukunft der Angestellen*, Campus Verlag, Frankfurt.

Bagnasco, A. (1977), *Tre Italie*, Il Mulino, Bologna.

Bailly, A. S., Maillet, D., and Coffey, W. J. (1987), 'Service Activities and Regional Development: Some European Examples', *Environment and Planning*, A, 19, 645–69.

Bailly, A. S., and Maillet, D. (1986), *Le Secteur tertiare en question: Activités de service, developpement économique et spatial*, Éditions Régionales Européennes, Geneva.

Bannon, L., *et al.* (1982), *Information Technology: Impact on the Way of Life*, Tycooly, Dublin.

Bannon, M. J. (1987), 'The Tertiary Sector and National Development: The Case of Ireland', in Ferrer, M., and d'Entremont, A., *The Changing Geography of Urban Places*, University of Navarra, Spain.

—— (1985), 'Service Activities in National and Regional Development: Trends and Prospects', in Bannon, M. J., and Ward, S. (eds.) *Services and the New Economy: Implications for National and Regional Development*, 38–61, Regional Studies Association, Dublin.

—— (1983), 'Urbanisation in Ireland: Growth and Regulation', in Blackwell, J., and Convery, F. (eds.), *Promise and Performance: Irish Environmental Policies Analysed*, 261–85, Resource and Environmental Policy Centre, Dublin.

Bannon, M. J., and Ward, S. (eds.) (1985), *Services and the New Economy: Implications for National and Regional Development*, Regional Studies Association, Dublin.

Barber, N. F. C., and Payne, L. S. (1976), 'The Distribution Company's Role in Retailing'. Paper presented to the Centre for Physical Distribution Management Conference, London.

Barnett, D. (1978), 'Integrating a Major Food Business', *The Grocer*, 29 Apr., 83–6.

Barras, R. (1985), 'Information Technology and the Service Revolution', *Policy Studies*, 5/4, 14–24.

—— (1983) *Growth and Technical Change in the UK Service Sector*, Technical Change Centre, London.

—— and Swann, J. (1984a), *The Adoption and Impact of Information Technology in the UK Accountancy Profession*, Technical Change Centre, London.

—— (1984b), 'Information Technology and the Service Sector: Quality of Service and Quantity of Jobs, in Marstrand, P. (ed.) *New Technology and the Future of Work and Skills*, Frances Pinter, London.

—— (1983), *The Adoption and Impact of Information Technology in the UK Insurance Industry*, Technical Change Centre, London.

Bater, J. H., and Walker, D. F. (1971), *The Linkage Study of Hamilton Metal Industries*, Hamilton Planning Department, Canada.

Bavishi, V., and Wyman H. E. (1983), *Who Audits the World*, University of Connecticut, Storrs.

Bayliss, B. T., and Edwards, S. L. (1970), *Industrial Demand for Transport*, HMSO, London.

BBC (1986), *The Money Programme*, 16 February.

Beattie, D. W. (1973), 'Improving the Structure of a Distribution System', *Operational Research Quarterly*, 24, 353–63.

Bell, D. (1974), *The Coming of Post-Industrial Society*, Heinemann, London.

Bertrand, O., and Noyelle, T. (1986), *Changing Technology, Skills and Skill Formation in French, German, Japanese, Swedish and US Financial Service Firms*, OECD, Paris.

Bienkowski, M., and Allen, K. J. (1985), *Industrial Aids in the UK: 1985—A Businessman's Guide*, Centre for the Study of Public Policy, University of Strathclyde, Glasgow.

Blackaby, F. (ed.) (1978), *De-industrialisation*, Heinemann, London.

Blau, P. M. (1972), 'Interdependence and Hierarchy in Organizations', *Social Science Research*, 1, 1–24.

Bolton Report (1971), *Committee of Inquiry into Small Firms*, Reports 1–18, HMSO, London.

Bowersox, D. J. (1969a), 'Physical Distribution Development: Current Status and Potential', *Journal of Marketing*, 33, 63–70.

—— (1969b), 'Locational analysis', in Schorr, J., Alexander, M., and Franco, R. J. (eds.) *Logistics in Marketing*, Pitman, New York.

Briston, R. J. (1979), 'The UK Accountancy Profession: the Move Towards Monopoly Power', *The Accountants Magazine*, Nov., 458–60.

Briston, R. J., and Kedslie, M. (1984), 'Concentration in the Profession: Danger Signs?, *Accountancy*, Nov., 11–12.

Browning, H. C., and Singelmann, J. (1975), *The Emergence of a Service Economy*, National Technical Information Service, Springfield, Va.

Brusco, S., and Sabel, C. (1981), 'Artisan Production and Economic Growth', in Wilkinson, F. (ed.) *The Dynamics of Labour Market Segmentation*, 99–114, Academic Press, London.

Bullmore, J. D., and Waterson, M. J. (eds.) (1983), *The Advertising Association Handbook*, Holt Rinehart and Winston, London.

Business Statistics Office (1985), 'Retailing', *Business Monitor*, SD 025, HMSO, London.

—— (1979), 'Wholesaling and Dealing 1974', *Business Monitor*, SD 026, HMSO, London.

Buswell, R. J., and Lewis, E. W. (1970), 'The Geographical Distribution of Industrial Research Activity in the UK', *Regional Studies*, 4, 297–306.

Buxton, G. (1975), *Effective Marketing Logistics*, Macmillan, London.

Cairns, D., Lafferty, M., and Mantle, P. (1984), *IAB Survey of Accounts and Accountants 1983–84*, Lafferty Publications, London.

Cambridge Economic Policy Review (1982), *Prospects for the UK in the 1980s*, 8, 1, Gower, Aldershot, Hants.

Castells, M. *et al.* (1986), *Nuevas Tecnologias, Economia y Sociedad en Espana*, ii, Alianza Editorial, Madrid.

Central Statistical Office (various years), *Annual Abstract of Statistics and Regional Statistics*, HMSO, London.

Childerley, A. (1980), 'The Importance of Logistics to the UK Economy', *International Journal of Physical Distribution and Materials Management*, 10/4, 185–92.

Christopher, M. (1986), *The Strategy of Distribution Management*, Heinemann, London.

—— (1981), 'Logistics and the National Economy', *International Journal of Physical Distribution and Materials Management*, 11/4, 1–29.

—— Schary, P. B., and Skjött-Larsen, T. (1979), *Customer Service and Distribution Strategy*, Associated Business Press, London.

Clairmonte, F., and Cavanagh, J. (1984), 'Transnational Corporations and Services: the Final Frontier', *Trade and Development*, 5, 215–73.

Clark, W. M. (1986), *How the City of London Works*, Waterloo, London.

Coakley, J., and Harris, L. (1983), *The City of Capital*, Blackwell, Oxford.

Confederation of Irish Industry (1983), *Grants and Incentives for Irish Industry*, Confederation of Irish Industry, Dublin.

Contini, B. (1984), 'Firm Size and the Division of Labour', *Banca Nazionale del Lavoro Quarterly Review*, 151, 368–80.

Coombes, M. G. *et al.* (1982), 'Functional Regions for the Population Census of Britain', in Herbert, D. T., and Johnson, R. J. *Geography and the Urban Environment* 5, John Wiley, Chichester, Sussex.

Cooper, J. C. (1978), 'Carrying for Others', Discussion Paper 7, Transport Studies Group, Polytechnic of Central London.

Corcoran, P. J., Hitchcock, A. J., and McMahon, C. M. (1980), 'Developments in Freight Transport', *Transport and Road Research Laboratory, Supp. Report*, 580, Crowthorne.

Coulson, A. (1985), 'Local Authority Involvement in Producer Services', Paper presented to the Producer Services Working Party, Institute for Local Government Studies, University of Birmingham.

Cowan, P. (1971), *The Office: A Facet of Urban Growth*, Heinemann, London.

Cranfield School of Management (1984), *Distribution in the Year 2003*, Cranfield Institute of Technology.

Cromton, R., and Jones, G. (1984), *White Collar Proletariat: Deskilling and Gender in Clerical Work*, Macmillan, London.

Crum, R. E., and Gudgin, G. (1977), *Non-Production Activities in UK Manufacturing Industry*, Regional Policy Series 3, Commission of the European Communities, Brussels.

CSPP (1985), 'Regional Policy Issues, an Overview', Centre for the Study of Public Policy, (mimeo), University of Strathclyde.

—— (1986), *AIMS (Assistance to Industry Mainframe System)*, Centre for the Study of Public Policy, University of Strathclyde, Glasgow.

Daniels, P. W. (1986), 'Producer Services in the UK Space Economy', in Martin, R., and Rawthorn, B. (eds.) *The Geography of Deindustrialisation*, Macmillan, London.

—— (1985a), 'Service Industries, Employment and Regional Development in Britain', (mimeo), Department of Geography, University of Liverpool.

—— (1985b), *Service Industries: A Geographical Appraisal*, Methuen, London.

—— (1982), *Service Industries*, Cambridge University Press, Cambridge.

—— (1976), 'Office Employment in New Towns', *Town Planning Review*, 47, 210–24.

—— (1975), *Office Location: An Urban and Regional Study*, Bell, London.

—— (1969), 'Office Decentralisation from London: Policy and Practice', *Regional Studies*, 3, 171–8.

Dawson, J. A. (1979), *The Marketing Environment*, Croom Helm, London.

Delehanty, G. F. (1968), *Non-production Workers in US Manufacturing*, North-Holland, New York.

De Montfort Publishing (1968), *The Square Mile*, De Montfort Publishing, London.

Department of Employment (1987), 1984 Census of Employment, *Employment Gazette*, Jan.

—— (1983), 1981 Census of Employment, *Employment Gazette*, Occasional Supplement, May.

Department of Environment (1976), *The Office Location Review*, Department of the Environment, London.

Department of Trade and Industry (1985), *Value Added Network Services: Ringing the Changes*, Department of Trade and Industry, London.

Department of Transport (various years), *The Transport of Goods by Road in Great Britain*, London (annual publication).

De Smidt, M. (1985), 'Relocation of Government Services in the Netherlands', *Tijd Econ. Soc. Geog.*, 76, 232–6.

Deutscher Bundestag (1985), *Vierehnter Rahmenplan der Gemeinschaft saufgabe Verbesserung der Regionalen Wirtschaftsstruktur*, Drucksache 10/1279.

Dineen, D. (1985), 'The Western Regions and Development of Services', in Bannon, M. J. (ed.), *Services and The New Economy*, 143–74, Regional Studies Association, Dublin.

Dunning, J. H., and Norman, G. (1983), 'The Theory of the Multinational

Enterprise: an Application to Multinational Office Location', *Environment and Planning*, A, 15, 675–92.

Economist, The (1984), 'The Thatcher Government's New Search for Winners', Business Brief, *The Economist*, 18 Aug., 64–5.

ECOTEC Research and Consulting Ltd. (1985). *Producer Services: Regional Variation in Supply and Demand*, Final Report to Department of Trade and Industry, London.

Edwards, L. E. (1982), 'Intra-Urban Office Location: A Decision-Making Approach', Ph.D. thesis, University of Liverpool.

Edwards, R. (1982), 'Developments in the Organisation and Location of Intermediate Distribution in Britain'. Ph.D. thesis, University of Newcastle upon Tyne.

European Conference of Ministers of Transport (1985), *Changes in Transport Users' Motivation for Modal Choice: Freight Transport*, Round Table No. 69, Paris.

Evans, A. W. (1973), 'The Location of the Headquarters of Industrial Companies', *Urban Studies*, 10, 387–96.

—— (1967), 'Myths about Employment in Central London', *Journal of Transport Economics and Policy*, 1, 214–25.

Financial Times (1986), 'Fashioning a Defence Against Cheap Imports', 5 Feb.

Firth, K. (1976), *The Distribution Services Industry: Operator and User Attitudes*, National Materials Handling Centre, Cranfield.

Focus on Physical Distribution Management (1984), 'Survey of Current Practices: UK exporters to Europe', 3/6, 3–5.

Foley, D. L. (1956), 'Factors in the Location of Administrative Offices', *Papers and Proceedings*, Regional Science Association, 2, 318–26.

Fothergill, S., and Gudgin, G. (1982), *Unequal Growth: Urban and Regional Employment Change in the UK*, Heinemann, London.

Foord, J. (1985), 'Women's Service Work: Some Gender and Employment Issues', Paper presented to the Producer Services Working Party, Centre for Urban and Regional Development Studies, University of Newcastle upon Tyne.

Freeman, C., Clarke, J., and Soete, L. (1982), *Employment and Technical Innovation*, Frances Pinter, London.

Fuchs, V. R. (1968), *The Service Economy*, National Bureau for Economic Research, Columbia University Press, New York.

Gad, G. (1975), *Central Toronto Offices: Observations on Location Patterns and Linkages*, City of Toronto Planning Board, Toronto, Canada.

Gaskin, M. (1980), 'Employment in Insurance, Banking and Finance in Scotland', *ESU Research Papers*, No. 2, Scottish Economic Planning Department, Edinburgh.

Gemmell, N. (1982), 'Economic Development and Structural Change: The Role of the Service Sector, *Journal of Development Studies*, 19, 37–66.

Gershuny, J. (1978), *After Industrial Society? The Emerging Self-Service Economy*, Macmillan, London.

—— and Miles, I. (1983), *The New Service Economy*, Frances Pinter, London.

Gillespie, A., *et al.* (1984) *The Effects of New Information Technology on the*

Less-Favoured Regions of the Community, Regional Policy Series 23, Commission of the European Communities, Brussels.

Glyn, A., and Sutcliffe, B. (1972), *British Capitalism, Workers and the Profits Squeeze*, Penguin, Harmondsworth.

Goddard, J. B. *et al.* (1985), 'The Impact of New Information Technology on Urban and Regional Structure in Europe', in Oakey, R., and Thwaites, A. (eds.) *Technological Change and Regional Development*, Frances Pinter, London.

—— (1980), 'Technological Change in a Spatial Context', *Futures*, 12, 90–105.

—— (1979), 'Office Location and Urban and Regional Development', in Daniels, P. W. (ed.) *Spatial Patterns of Office Growth and Location*, Wiley, London.

—— (1975), *Office Location in Urban and Regional Development*, Oxford University Press, Oxford.

—— and Smith, I. J. (1978), 'Changes in Corporate Control in the British Urban System, 1972–77', *Environment and Planning A*, 10, 1073–84.

—— and Pye, R. (1977), R. (1977), 'Telecommunications and Office Location', *Regional Studies*, 11, 19–30.

—— and Morris, D. (1976), 'The Communications Factor in Office Decentralisation', *Progress in Planning*, 6, 1, Pergamon, Oxford.

Gottman, J. (1983), *The Coming of the Transactional City*, Institute for Urban Studies, University of Maryland, College Park, Md.

—— (1961), *Megalopolis: The Urbanised North Eastern Seaboard of the United States*, Twentieth Century Fund, New York.

Greater London Council Economic Policy Group (1985), *The London Industrial Strategy*, GLC, London.

Greater London Council Financial Policy Group (1985), *The London Financial Strategy*, GLC, London.

Green, A. E. (1985), 'Recent Trends in the Service Sector in Tyne and Wear and Berkshire', Discussion Paper 71, Centre for Urban and Regional Development Studies, University of Newcastle upon Tyne.

—— and Owen, D. W. (1984), 'The Spatial Manifestation of the Changing Socio-economic Composition of Employment in Manufacturing, 1971–81', Discussion Paper No 56, Centre for Urban and Regional Development Studies, University of Newcastle upon Tyne.

Green, S. R. (1982), *Location and Mobility of Computer Service Offices*, Department of Trade and Industry, SE Area Office, London.

—— (1981), The Location of the Computer Service Industry in the UK, Department of Trade and Industry, SE Area Office, London.

Greenfield, H. (1966), *Manpower and the Growth of Producer Services*, Columbia University Press, New York.

Grit, S. and Korteweg, P. J. (1976), 'Perspectives on Office Relocation in the Netherlands', *Tidj. Econ. Soc. Geog.* 67, 2–14.

Grocer, The (1986), 'Distribution, more than a lorry', *The Grocer*, 19 July.

Gudgin, G. (1983), 'Job Generation in the Service Sector', Position Paper for the Industry and Employment Committee of the Economic and Social Research Council, London.

—— Crum, R. E., and Bailey, S. (1979), 'White Collar Employment in

UK Manufacturing Industry', in Daniels, P. W. (ed.) *Spatial Patterns of Office Growth and Location*, Wiley, London.

Haig, R. M. (1927), *Major Economic Factors in Metropolitan Growth and Arrangement*, Committee on Regional Plan for New York and its Environs, New York.

Hall, R. K. (1972), 'The Movement of Offices from Central London', *Regional Studies*, 6, 385–92.

Hamilton, A. (1986), *The Financial Revolution*, Viking, London.

Harris, D. F., and Taylor, F. J. (1978), *The Service Sector: Its Changing Role as a Source of Employment*, Research Series 25, Centre for Environmental Studies Ltd., London.

Harris, L. (1985), 'British Capital: Manufacturing, Finance and Multinational Corporations', in Coates, D., Johnston, G., and Bush, R. (eds.) *A Socialist Anatomy of Britain*, Polity Press, Cambridge.

Harrison, R. T. (1986), 'The Standard Capital Grants Scheme in Northern Ireland: a Review and Assessment', *Regional Studies*, 20, 175–91.

—— (1985), 'The Service Sector in Industrial Development Policy: The Northern Ireland Experience', Paper presented at a meeting of the Producer Services Working Party, Department of Business Studies, Queens University, Belfast.

Harvey, J. (1984), 'An Overview of the Changing Chain', paper presented to the Institute of Grocery Distribution Convention, Stratford on Avon.

Hawkins, G. (1976), 'The Case for Contract Warehousing', *Retail and Distribution Management*, 4/1, 45–7.

HMSO (1985), *Industrial Development Act 1982, Annual Report 1984–85*, HMSO, London.

—— (1983), *Regional Industrial Development*, Cmnd 9111, HMSO, London.

—— (1979), *Industry Act 1972, Annual Report 1978–79*, HMSO, London.

—— (1977), *Industry Act 1972, Annual Report 1976–77*, HMSO, London.

—— (1974), *Industry Act 1972, Annual Report 1973–74*, HMSO, London.

Hood, N., and Young, S. (1983), *Industrial Policy and the Scottish Economy*, University Press, Edinburgh.

Howells, J., and Green, A. E. (1985), *Regional Prospects for Service Activities: The UK Experience*, Report to FAST, Centre for Urban and Regional Development Studies, University of Newcastle.

Hubbard, R. K. B., and Nutter, D. S. (1982), 'Service Employment in Merseyside', *Geoforum*, 13, 209–35.

Illeris, S. (1987), 'The Role of Service Activities in Western Europe' in Ferrer, I. M., and d'Entremont, A. (eds.), *The Changing Geography of Urban Places*, University of Navarra, Spain.

—— (ed.) (1986), 'The Present and Future Role of Services in Regional Development', FAST Working paper 74, Commission of the European Communities, Brussels.

—— (1985), 'How to Analyse the Role of Services in Regional Development', in Bannon, M. J., and Ward, S. (eds.) *Services and the New Economy: Implications for Regional Development*, Regional Studies Association, Dublin.

Industrial Development Board (1985), *Encouraging Enterprise: A Medium*

Term Strategy for 1985–1990, Industrial Development Board for Northern Ireland, HMSO, Belfast.

Ingham, G. (1984), *Capitalism Divided? The City and Industry in British Social Development,* Macmillan, London.

Institute of Grocery Distribution (1984), *Specialist Distribution Profiles,* IGD, Letchmore Heath.

Institute of Physical Distribution Management (1986), *Survey of Distribution Costs: A Study into Current Distribution Cost Trends in UK Industry 1985,* IPDM, Corby.

International Accounting Bulletin (1983), 'The World's Top 20 Accounting Groups', *International Accounting Bulletin,* Dec., 13.

—— (1986), 'Arthur Anderson Comes Out on Top Again', *International Accounting Bulletin,* Jan., 6–7.

Investors Chronicle (1985), 'Accountancy: An Investors Chronicle Survey', *Investors Chronicle,* 12 Dec., 115–25.

—— (1984), *The City Directory 1984–85,* Woodhead Faulkner, Cambridge.

James, V. Z. (1978), 'Office Employment in the Northern Region: Its National, Regional and Organisational Context', Discussion Paper 14, Centre for Urban and Regional Development Studies, University of Newcastle upon Tyne.

James, V. Z., Marshall, J. N., and Waters, N. (1979), *Telecommunications and Office Location,* Report to DOE, Centre for Urban and Regional Development Studies, University of Newcastle upon Tyne.

Jenkins, C., and Sherman, B. (1979), *The Collapse of Work,* Methuen, Andover, Hants.

Johnstone, J. (1963), 'The Productivity of Management Consultants', *Journal of the Royal Statistical Society,* Series A, 2, 237–49.

Jones, E. (1981), *Accountancy and the British Economy 1840–1980: The Evolution of Ernst and Whinney,* Batsford, London.

Jones Lang Wootton (1980), *Offices in the City of London,* Jones Lang Wootton, London.

Katouzian, M. A. (1970), 'The Development of the Service Sector: a New Approach', *Oxford Economic Papers,* 22, 362–82.

Keeble, D., Owens, D., and Thompson, C. (1981), *Centrality, Peripherality and EEC Regional Development,* HMSO, London.

Kelly, J. R. (1978), *Own Vehicle Fleet Costs Versus Carriers' Prices,* Post Office, London.

Key, T. S. T. (1985), 'Services in the UK Economy', *Bank of England Quarterly Bulletin,* 25, 404–14.

King, A. D. (forthcoming), 'Capital City: Physical and Social Aspects of London's Role in the World Economy', *Development and Change.*

Kirchener, E., and Hewlett, N. (1983), *The Social Implications of Introducing New Technology in the Banking Sector,* Interim Report, University of Essex, Colchester.

Knight, R. V. (1982), 'City Development in Advanced Industrial Societies', in Gappert, G., and Knight, R. V. (eds.), *Cities in the 21st Century,* Sage, Beverly Hills, Calif.

Kotler, P. (1967), *Marketing Management: Analysis, Planning and Control*, Prentice-Hall, Englewood Cliffs.

Latta, E. (1977), 'Own Account or Third Party', *Commerce International*, March, 21–3.

Leach, S. (1985), 'The Monitoring and Evaluation of Inner City Policy', *Regional Studies*, 19, 59–62.

Leigh, R., and North, D. J. (1978), 'Regional Aspects of Acquisition Activity in British Manufacturing Industry', *Regional Studies*, 12, 227–45.

Lever, H., and Edwards, G. (1981), *Banking on Britain, Reversing Britain's Economic Decline*, (*Sunday Times* reprint of 6 articles), London.

Location of Offices Bureau (1975), *Office Relocation: Facts and Figures*, Location of Offices Bureau, London.

McConkey, R. C. (1979), 'The True Cost of Small Drops', *Retail and Distribution Management*, 7/2, 53–8.

McCrone, G. (1968), *Regional Policy in Britain*, George Allen and Unwin, London.

McKinnon, A. C. (1986a), 'The Physical Distribution Strategies of Multiple Retailers', *International Journal of Retailing*, 1/2, 49–63.

—— (1986b), 'Distributing Imported Goods to British Customers', *Retail and Distribution Management*, 14/5, 86–91.

—— (1985a), 'The Distribution Systems of Supermarket Chains', *Service Industries Journal*, 5, 226–38.

—— (1985b), 'Food Manufacturers' Distribution Systems', *Distribution and Technology Bulletin*, Institute of Grocery Distribution, June.

—— (1985c), 'Distribution Services', paper presented to the Producer Service Working Party, Department of Geography, University of Leicester.

—— (1983a), 'The Causes, Costs and Benefits of Increasing Delivery Distances', in Turton, B. (ed.) *Public Issues in Transport*, Transport Geography Study Group, University of Lancaster.

—— (1983b), 'The Development of Warehousing in England', *Geoforum*, 14, 389–99.

—— (1981), '*The Historical Development of Food Manufacturers' Distribution Systems*', Occasional paper no. 7, Department of Geography, University of Leicester.

—— and Pratt, A. C. (1984). *Jobs in Store: An Examination of the Employment Potential of Warehousing*, Occasional paper no. 11, Department of Geography, University of Leicester.

McRae, H., and Cairncross, F. (1984), *Capital City: London as a Financial Centre*, Methuen, London.

Maister, D. (1976), 'Centralisation of Inventories and the "Square Root Law"', *International Journal of Physical Distribution*, 6/3, 124–34.

Manners, G. (1962), 'Service Industries and Regional Economic Growth', *Town Planning Review*, 33, 293–303.

Manpower (1986), *Flexible Manning in Business*, Manpower, London.

Manser, W. A. P. (1985), *The International Insurance Market: A View from*

London, Economist Intelligence Unit Special Report 193, Economic Publications, London.

Marquand, J. (1983), 'The Changing Distribution of Service Employment', in Goddard, J. B., and Champion, A. G. (eds.), *The Urban and Regional Transformation of Britain,* Methuen, London.

—— (1980), *The Role of the Tertiary Sector in Regional Policy,* Regional Policy Series, 19, EEC, Brussels.

—— (1979), *The Service Sector and Regional Policy in the UK,* Research Series *29,* Centre for Environmental Studies Ltd., London.

Marshall, J. N. (1987), 'Industrial Linkage and Regional Development', in Lever, W. (ed.), *Industrial Change in the UK,* Longman, London.

—— (1985), 'Business Services, the Regions and Regional Policy', *Regional Studies,* 19, 353–63.

—— (1983), 'Business Service Activities in British Provincial Conurbations', *Environment and Planning A,* 25, 1343–60.

—— (1982*a*), 'Linkages between Manufacturing Industry and Business Services', *Environment and Planning A,* 14, 1523–40.

—— (1982*b*), 'Corporate Organisation of the Business Service Sector', Discussion Paper No 43, Centre for Urban and Regional Development Studies, University of Newcastle upon Tyne.

—— (1981), 'Spatial Variations in Manufacturing Industry Demand for Business Services: Some Implications for Government Economic Policies', Discussion Paper 35, Centre for Urban and Regional Development Studies, University of Newcastle upon Tyne.

—— (1979), 'Ownership, Organisation and Industrial Linkage: A Case Study in the Northern Region of England', *Regional Studies,* 13, 531–57.

—— Damesick P., and Wood, P. (1987), 'Understanding the Location and Role of Producer Services in the UK', *Environment and Planning A,* 19, 575–95.

—— —— —— (1985), 'Understanding the Location and Role of Producer Services', paper presented at the Regional Science Conference, Manchester, Sept.

Massey, D., and Meegan, R. (1982), *The Anatomy of Job Loss,* Methuen, London.

Masuda, Y. (1980), *The Information Society as Post Industrial Society,* Institute for the Information Society, Tokyo.

Mawson, J., and Miller, D. (1983), *Agencies in Regional and Local Development,* Occasional Paper No 6, Centre for Urban and Regional Studies, University of Birmingham.

Miles, I. (1985), 'The Service Economy and Socioeconomic Development', paper prepared for UNCTAD, Science Policy Research Unit, University of Sussex, Brighton.

Mingionie, E. (1981), *Social Conflict and the City,* Blackwell, Oxford.

Ministry of Transport (1970), *The Allocation of Freight Traffic,* HMSO, London.

Moir, C. B. (1984), 'Wholesaling in GB', unpublished working paper, National Economic Development Office, London.

Montangnon, P. (1986), 'Eurobonds: Pragmatic Approach to City Rules', *Financial Times* (*City Revolution Survey*), 27 Oct., 52.

Morris, D. (1984), *An Inquiry into Changes in the Insurance, Banking and Finance Sector and their Influence on the Location of its Activities*, Report to the Department of Trade and Industry, London.

NEDO (1985), 'Factors Affecting the Cost of Physical Distribution to the Retail Trade', unpublished paper, London.

—— (1982), *Technology: the Issues for the Distributive Trades*, Distributive Trades EDC, London.

Neilsen Researcher (1974), Annual Grocery Review, London.

Newson, P. L. (1978), *The Future Role of Depots in a Distribution Network*, Post Office, London.

Newton, W. H. (1985), *Trends in Road Goods Transport 1973–1983*, Research Report 43, Transport and Road Research Laboratory, Crowthorne.

Northern Ireland Economic Council (1982), *Private Services in Economic Development*, Report No. 30, NIEC, Belfast.

Northern Region Strategy Team (1976), *Office Activity in the Northern Region*, Technical Report 8, HMSO, London.

Noyelle, T. J. (1986), 'The International Services Economy', paper presented at Localities in An International Economy Workshop, University of Wales Institute of Science and Technology, Cardiff, 11–12 Sept.

Noyelle, T. J., and Stanback, T. M. (1984), *The Economic Transformation of American Cities*, Rowman and Allanheld, Osman, Totowa, NJ.

Oakey, R. P., Thwaites, A. T., and Nash, P. A. (1982), 'Technological Change and Regional Development: Some Evidence on Regional Variations in Product and Process Innovation', *Environment and Planning A*, 14, 995–1138.

—— (1980), 'The Regional Distribution of Innovative Manufacturing Establishments in Britain', *Regional Studies*, 14, 235–54.

OECD (1984), 'The Contribution of Services to Employment', *Employment Outlook*, Sep., 39–54.

—— (1983), *Industrial Services*, Industry Committee, Directorate for Science Technology and Industry, Paris.

—— (1981), *Information Acitivities, Electronics and Telecommunications Policy: Impact on Employment Growth and Trade*, i, Paris.

O'Hara, D. J. (1977), 'Location of firms within a Square Central Business District', *Journal of Political Economy*, 85, 1189–1207.

Pactel (1980), *Automation in European Banking*, PA Management Consultants, London.

Palmer, L. S. (1980), 'Technical Change and Employment in Banking', M.Sc. thesis, University of Sussex, Brighton.

Parsons, G. (1972), 'The Giant Manufacturing Corporations and Balanced Regional Growth in Britain', *Area*, 4, 99–103.

Pedersen, P. O. (1986), 'Business Service Strategies: The Case of the Provincial Centre of Esbjerg', FAST Programme, Working Paper 19, EEC, Brussels.

Petit, P. (1986), *Slow Growth and the Service Economy*, Frances Pinter, London.

Pike, J. (1982), *Major Factors Influencing Modal Choice in the UK Freight Market*, Research Report No. 52, Transport Operations Research Group, University of Newcastle upon Tyne.

Plender, J., and Wallace, P. (1985), *The Square Mile*, Century Hutchinson, London.

Polese, M. (1982), 'Regional Demand for Business Services and Inter-regional Service Flows in a Small Canadian Region', *Papers of the Regional Science Association*, 50, 151–63.

Porat, M. (1977), *The Information Economy*: *Definition and Measurement*, Office of Telecoms, Washington, DC.

Postner, H. H., and Wesa, L. (1984), *Canadian Productivity Growth*: *An Alternative (Input–Output) Analysis*, Economic Council of Canada, Ottawa.

Price, K. (1986), *The Global Financial Village*, Banking World, London.

Quarmby, D. A. (1985), 'Distribution, the Next Ten Years: The Market Place', *Focus on Physical Distribution Management*, 4/6, 3–6.

Rabey, G. F. (1977), 'Contraction Poles: An Exploratory Study of Traditional Industry Decline within a Regional Industrial Complex', Discussion Paper 3, Centre for Urban and Regional Development Studies, University of Newcastle upon Tyne.

Rabiega, W. A., and Lamoureux, L. F. (1973), 'Wholesaling Hierarchies, a Florida Case Study', *Tidj. Econ. Soc. Geog*, 64/4, 226–36.

Racine, J. B., and Cunha, A. (1986), 'Service Agencies in Swiss Regional Dynamics: From Cumulative Growth to Poly-centres Decentralisation', in Borchert, J. *et al.* (eds.) *Urban Systems in Transition*, Geografische Studies 19, 99–110, Netherlands.

Rajan, A. (1987), *Services—The Second Industrial Revolution?* Butterworth, London.

—— (1985), Office Technology and Clerical Skills', *Futures*, Aug., 411–13.

—— (1984), *New Technology and Employment in Insurance, Banking and Building Societies*: *Recent Experience and Future Impact*, Gower, Aldershot, Hants.

—— and Pearson, R. (1986), *UK Occupation and Employment Trends to 1990*, Butterworth, London.

Ray, D. L. (1981), 'Assessing UK Manufacturing Industry's Inventory Management Performance', *Focus on Physical Distribution Management*, 27, 5–11.

Reed, H. C. (1983), 'World City Formation', in Audretsch, D. (ed.) *The Multinational Corporation in the 1980s*, MIT Press, Cambridge, Mass.

Regional Studies Association (1983), *Report of an Inquiry into Regional Problems in the United Kingdom*, Regional Studies Association, Geo Books, Norwich.

Revell, J. R. S. (1983), *Banking and Electronic Fund Transfers*, OECD, Paris.

—— (1980), *Costs and Margins in Banking*: *An International Survey*, OECD, Paris.

Rhodes, J., and Kan, A. (1972), *Office Dispersal and Regional Policy*, Cambridge University Press, London.

Riddle, D. (1986), *Service Led Growth*, Praeger, New York.

Robertson, J. A. S., Biggs, J. M., and Goodchild, A. (1982), *Structure and Employment Prospects of the Service Industries*, Research Paper No 3, Department of Employment, London.

Robinson, O., and Wallace, J. (1984*a*), 'Growth and Utilisation of Part-time Labour in Great Britain, *Employment Gazette*, 92, 391–7.

—— (1984*b*) *Part-time Employment and Sex Discrimination, Legislation in Great Britain*, Research Paper 43, Department of Employment.

Robson, A. (1985), 'Retail Grocery Distribution', *Focus on Physical Distribution Management*, 4, 8–13.

Rothwell, R., and Zegweld, W. (1979), *Technical Change and Employment*, Frances Pinter, London.

Rura, J. (1986), 'Supply and Demand of Services and Regional Development', FAST Programme, Working Paper 93, EEC, Brussels.

Rushton, A. (1984), 'Future Trends in Distribution', *Logistics Today*, 3, 10–13.

Rybczynski, T. M. (1982), 'Structural Changes in the Financing of British Industry and their Implications', *National Westminster Bank Quarterly Review* May, 25–36.

Sabolo, Y. (1975), *The Service Industries*, International Labour Office, Geneva.

Schary, P. B. (1983), 'The Market Place View of Customer Service', in Gattorna, J. (ed.) *Handbook of Physical Distribution Management*, Gower, Aldershot, Hants.

Schwamm, H., and Mericia, P. (1985), *Multinationals in the Service Sector*, Wiley, Chichester.

Scott, C., and Cooper, J. C. (1985), 'Hub Operations in UK Parcels Distribution', *Logistics Today*, 4/4, 4–10.

Scottish Development Agency (1985), *Annual Report 1984–5*, Scottish Development Agency, Glasgow.

—— (1984), *The Scottish Service Sector in Context*, Scottish Development Agency, Glasgow.

Sema Metra (1986), *Services to the Manufacturing Sector*, Phase 2 Preliminary Report to FAST, Paris.

Shaw, E. R., and Coulbeck, N. S. (1983), *UK Retail Banking Prospects in the Competitive 1980s*, Staniland Hall, London.

Simmons, M., and Gordon, L. (1980), 'Pattern of Market Research in the 1980s, *Market Research Society, 23rd Annual Conference Papers*, 11–27.

Singh, A. (1977), 'UK Industry and the World Economy: A Case of Deindustrialisation', *Cambridge Journal of Economics*, 2, 113–36.

Sleigh, J., Boatwright, B., Irwin, P., and Stanyon, R. (1979), *The Manpower Implications of Microelectronic Technology*, HMSO, London.

Stanback, T. M., and Noyelle, T. J. (1982), *Cities in Transition: Changing Job Structure in Atlanta, Denver, Buffalo, Phoenix, Columbus (Ohio), Nashville and Charlotte*, Rowman and Allanheld, Osmun, Totowa, NJ.

—— et al. (1981), *Services: The New Economy*, Allanheld, Osmun, Totowa, NJ.

Stationery Office (1984), *White Paper on Industrial Policy*, The Stationery Office, Dublin.

Stevens, M. (1985), *The Accounting Wars*, Macmillan, New York.

—— (1982), *The Big Eight*, Macmillan, New York.

Stigler, G. J. (1956), *Trends in Employment in Service Industries*, National Bureau for Economic Research, Princetown University Press, New York.

Stoker, R. B. (1978), 'Incorporating Market Characteristics into Physical Distribution Models', *European Journal of Operational Research*, 2, 232–45.

Stoneman, P. (1976), *Technological Diffusion and the Computer Revolution*, Cambridge University Press, London.

Stonier, T. (1983), *The Wealth of Information*: *A Profile of the Post-Industrial Economy*, Methuen, London.

Sussams, J. E. (1969), *Industrial Logistics*, Gower, Aldershot, Hants.

Sutherland, P. (1986), 'Europe and the Principle of Convergence', *Regional Studies*, 20, 371–7.

Tauchen, H., and Witte, A. D. (1983), 'An Equilibrium Model of Office Location and Contact Patterns', *Environment and Planning A*, 15, 1311–26.

Taylor, M., and Thrift, N. J. (1983), 'Business Organisation, Segmentation and Location, *Regional Studies*, 17, 445–66.

Thirwell, A. D. (1982), 'De-industrialisation in the UK', *Lloyds Bank Review*, Apr., 22–37.

Thorngren, B. (1970), 'How do Contact Systems Affect Regional Development?', *Environment and Planning A*, 2, 409–27.

Thrift, N. J. (1986*a*), 'The "Fixers": The Urban Geography of International Commercial Capital', (mimeo) Department of Geography, University of Wales, Lampeter.

—— (1986*b*), 'The Internationalisation of Producer Services and the Integration of the Pacific Basin Property Market', in Taylor, M. J., and Thrift, N. J. (eds.) *Multinationals and the Restructuring of the World Economy*, Croom Helm, London.

—— (1985), 'Taking the Rest of the World Seriously? The State of British Urban and Regional Research in a Time of Economic Crisis', *Environment and Planning A*, 17, 7–24.

Thwaites, A. T. (1982), 'Some Evidence of Regional Variations in the Introduction and Diffusion of Industrial Products and Processes within British Manufacturing Industry', *Regional Studies*, 16, 371–82.

Tinker, T. (1984), *Paper Prophets*: *A Social Critique of Accounting*, Holt, Rinehart and Winston, Eastbourne.

Tornquist, G. (1973), 'Contact Requirements and Travel Facilities: Contact Models of Sweden and Regional Development Alternatives in the Future', in Pred, A., and Tornquist, G. (eds.) *Systems of Cities and Information Flows*, Lund Studies in Geography, Series B, Department of Geography, University of Lund.

Townsend, A. R. (1986), 'Spatial Aspects of the Growth of Part-time Employment in Britain', *Regional Studies*, 20, 313–30.

Transport Development Group (1985), *Annual Report and Accounts 1985*, London.

UK Accounting Bulletin (1985), 'UK Firms: Best Year on Record', *UK Accounting Bulletin*, May, 4–5.

Urry, J. (1986), 'Services: Some Issues of Analysis', Working Paper 17, Lancaster Regionalism Group, University of Lancaster.

Walker, D. F., and Bater, J. H. (1976), *A Study of the Linkages of Metal-working Plants in Midwestern Ontario*, Report to Regional Development Branch, Ontario Department of Treasury and Economics, Toronto, Canada.

Walker, R. (1985), 'Is there a Service Economy? The Changing Capitalist Division of Labour', *Science and Society*, 49, 42–83.

Waller, A. G. (1983), 'Use and Location of Depots', in Gattorna, J. (ed.) *Handbook of Physical Distribution Management*, Gower, Aldershot, Hants.

Warner, B. (1986), 'The Future Impact of Economic Trends in Physical Distribution', *Focus on Physical Distribution Management*, 5, 30–40.

Warneryd, O. (1984), 'The Swedish National Settlement System', in Bourne, L. S. *et al.* (eds.) *Urbanisation and Settlement Systems*, 92–112, Oxford University Press, Oxford.

Warwick University (1985), *Review of the Economy and Employment*, Institute for Employment Research, University of Warwick.

Waters, C. D. J. (1984), 'Is UK Manufacturing Industry Really Overstocked?', *International Journal of Physical Distribution and Materials Management*, 14/5, 5–10.

Werneke, D. (1983), *Microelectronics and Office Jobs: The Impact of the Chip on Women's Employment*, International Labour Office, Geneva.

Westaway, E. J. (1974), The Spatial Hierarchy of Business Organisations and its Implications for the British Urban System', *Regional Studies*, 8, 145–55.

Westwood, J. B. (1981), *Integrated Distribution Management: The Formula for the Eighties*, Transfleet lecture, Transfleet Ltd., Stirling.

Wettmann, G., and Nicol, B. (1977), *Deglomeration Policy in Great Britain*, ii: *Non-financial Office Location Policies*, International Institute of Management Studies, Berlin.

Whiteman, J. (1981), 'The Service Sector—a Poor Relation? A Review of its Role, Performance and Prospects in the UK', Discussion Paper 8, National Economic Development Office, London.

Williams, J. (1982), 'Automated Storage and Retrieval Systems', *Logistics Today*, 1/2, 4–6.

Williamson, O. E. (1978), *Markets and Hierarchies: Analysis and Antitrust Implications*, Collier Macmillan, West Drayton, Middlesex.

Wilson Committee (1980), *Committee to Review the Functioning of the Financial Institutions, Report and Appendices*, Cmnd. 7937, HMSO, London.

Wood, P. A. (1987), 'Producer Services and Economic Change: UK Reflections on Canadian Evidence', in Chapman, K., and Humphry, G. (eds.) *Technological Change and Industrial Policy*, Blackwell, London.

—— (1985), 'Producer Services and Economic Change: Some Canadian Evidence', paper presented at the joint IAASG/CAG Conference, University of Swansea, Aug.

—— (1984), 'The Regional Significance of Manufacturing–Service Sector Links: Some Thoughts on the Revival of London's Docklands', in Barr, B. M., and Waters, N. M. (eds.), *Regional Diversification and Structural Change*, BC Geographical Series, Tantalus Research, Vancouver.

Woolcock, S. (1984), 'Information Technology: The Challenge to Europe', *Journal of Common Market Studies*, 22, 315–31.

Wright, M. (1967), 'Provincial Office Development', *Urban Studies*, 4, 218–57.

Yuill, D., and Allen, K. J. (eds.) (1985), *European Regional Incentives*, Centre for the Study of Public Policy, University of Strathclyde, Glasgow.

Index